THE
BHAGAVAD
GITA

THE
BHAGAVAD
GITA

A Life-changing Conversation

VANDANA R SINGH

NIYOGI
BOOKS

Published by
NIYOGI BOOKS
Block D, Building No. 77,
Okhla Industrial Area, Phase-I,
New Delhi-110 020, INDIA
Tel: 91-11-26816301, 26818960
Email: niyogibooks@gmail.com
Website: www.niyogibooksindia.com

Text © Vandana R Singh

Editor: Shalini Arun/Arkaprabha Biswas
Design: Shashi Bhushan Prasad

ISBN: 978-93-91125-08-0
Publication: 2022

Printed at: Niyogi Offset Pvt. Ltd., New Delhi, India

In memory of
Rakesh

who quietly reaffirms through this work that
when one journey ends…
a new one begins…

Speaking on a rather mysterious and fantastical note, Krishna talks of an upside-down tree. It is said that there is an eternal, imperishable tree, he says, with its roots above and branches below—it is called the *ashvatth* tree.

(Verse 15.01)

Contents

Prologue

Making the Bhagavad Gita your own…a beginning

I. THE WAR WITHIN

a. Dilemmas

I have spent a large part of my life without knowing much about the *Bhagavad Gita*. Brought up in a non-ritualistic home by 'work is worship' kind of parents, in my growing up years what I saw happening around me all the time was work, rarely any elaborate worship per se. I knew as much of the *Gita* as almost everyone brought up in this country does—as a nice book that teaches one good things.

For most of us the *Gita* evokes an image of Krishna addressing Arjuna who is dutifully kneeling before him with folded hands, with a chariot and the battlefield as a backdrop. We have seen versions of this image on wall calendars, diaries, amateur paintings, and walls of religious spaces. Year after year, our exposure to the *Gita* remains limited to these fleeting visual engagements as they become part of our muscle memory as we go about our chores.

It is fascinating though, how no one in this part of the world needs to be told of what is depicted in this image beyond the familiar scene of a battlefield. We seem to know the context instinctively, and are quite content to accept it for what it is—a pictorial depiction of something sublime.

This image and several artistic versions of it, are an inextricable part of our consciousness and yet very few—including the most questioning of minds—ever experience the curiosity to know more. At the cost of being repetitive, I would say again that I have lived a long part of my life with minimal knowledge of this text—but I will also add that it has also meant living with innumerable unanswered questions.

The eternal questions regarding why things happen the way they do, all the 'why me' questions, good things happening to not so good people, innocent lives being cut short, charlatans being rewarded while good Samaritans find themselves in the dock... kept popping up every now and then in my head, and these were routinely swept under the carpet as one reconciled to the idea that there simply are no answers to many questions. Friends and well-wishers heartily and reassuringly concurred with this strategy as an aid in moving on, as most of them were playing ostrich themselves.

b. In Quest

If one were to take a step back here and briefly think of how to approach the *Bhagavad Gita* I would humbly suggest two possibilities.

Option 1

Have no faith in what the *Gita* suggests. Take the line that each one of us is just another organism comprising living cells—one out of thousands of species on earth. Like all of them, we are born, we live, and then one day we die. In this case there is no room for further discussion. However, the above-mentioned questions remain unresolved. Doubts emanating from existential dilemma continue to thrive, and for all the 'why me' and other questions this provides no answers beyond attributing all the ups and downs of life to 'chance or luck'...or as some might shrug their shoulders and say...'whatever...'

Option 2

Read the *Gita*, understand and apply its teachings in letter and spirit, internalise it and make it your own. I doubt if there will be any questions that you may still not find answers to.

Why do some of us live longer than others? Why are different people driven by different pursuits? Why are some good to the point of being simple, while others appear to be inherent trouble-makers? Is there life after life? Or is death simply a biological event, the grand finale?

What is that little voice inside us that instinctively knows good from bad? Why are there so many choices in this world, and why do we not always make the right one? Why is life a long painful trudge for some, and a cakewalk for others?

Yes, there are answers to each of these questions and many more. The precondition, of course, is an open mind and a desire to discover and accept. I found myself reading the *Gita* at a time when I was ready for it. I didn't realize how ready I was till each verse started to permeate into my consciousness like water seeping through the parched roots of a long-neglected plant. As the verses made inroads into my being they addressed questions that had been festering for long. Questions and dilemmas, big and small, lying unanswered not because there are none, but because I never seriously looked for them.

The verses flowed inwards in what felt like a natural movement, and gradually pieces of the puzzle started falling into place. Bit by bit, as a new comprehensive picture took shape, simultaneously, it also started to become a significant part of me.

Having found emotional solace and cerebral nourishment, I am at peace, and now feel compelled to share my interpretation of the *Bhagavad Gita,* a text that has the potential to change lives.

c. Conflict Resolution

The *Bhagavad Gita* comprises 18 chapters and 700 verses…

To call it a storehouse of knowledge would be to undervalue it.

To equate it with any other text in the world would be a futile exercise.

To consider it to be a text that belongs to a particular religion or culture would be to de-universalise it.

The *Gita* is a guide to be befriended, a text to be comprehended, and a way of life to be adopted. Simply put, it is a text which, among other more exalted descriptions, must be seen as a handbook on life skills containing detailed lessons on self-improvement.

The Bhagavad Gita: A Life-changing Conversation is an interpretation of the *Gita* put together in a language we speak, and contextualized with situations we confront on a day-to-day basis. In a conscious effort made at simplifying the reading of this multi-layered discourse, cross-referencing with other preceding Vedic texts and scriptures has been consciously avoided. This has also been done in support of the conviction that the *Gita* is a stand-alone study of the human mind and behaviour that does not require a database of existing knowledge, or further acquisition of it, to understand what it has to say.

The Bhagavad Gita is a world unto itself that needs no props to roll it out and be understood. Read it, internalise it, apply it to your day-to-day existence and be ready to savour the satisfaction that is bound to follow. Believe me, it is possible.

II. THE BHAGAVAD GITA

a. Structure and Context

The *Bhagavad Gita* literally means 'Song of God', and is believed to have been compiled anywhere between 5th century and 2nd century BCE. Its authorship is usually attributed to Ved Vyas, though some theories of the present day suggesting it a compilation of several scriptures from different sources, are a subject of continued interest and discussion.

The *Gita*, an accepted shorter title of the text, as we know it today, is a subset of the epic *Mahabharata*, and is basically a conversation between a distraught Arjuna and his mentor Krishna. It is this conversation that is the text of the *Bhagavad Gita*. This consists of 18 chapters, divided into 3 segments.

- Chapters 1–6 describe karma yoga—attaining deliverance through actions performed without a desire for reward.
- Chapters 7–12 describe bhakti yoga—attaining deliverance through sincere devotion.
- Chapters 13–18 describe *jñāna* yoga—attaining deliverance through knowledge and pursuit of knowledge.

The *Gita* revolves around the soul's journey from birth to rebirth, and explores different paths leading to deliverance from this endless cycle, which is moksha.

Albert Einstein had said, 'When I read the *Bhagavad Gita* and reflect about how God created this universe, everything else seems so superfluous'. The veracity of this description is well established as one progresses with a perusal of this analytical commentary on life on earth and what lies beyond.

The stress on good deeds and selfless service is well understood by most. So is the belief that when evil starts to overtake the good in the world, the Almighty descends in human form to set right the skewed balance, by annihilating evil. These beliefs have parallels in other cultures and faiths too.

The role of popular culture must be acknowledged here in ensuring that the themes of selfless service, duty before self (karma and dharma) have received sufficient footage. The storyline featuring the appearance of a powerful hero to save the world from the clutches of the anti-hero has also been well entrenched into our collective consciousness through varied sources.

While on one plane, the *Gita* is multi-layered and granular, on another, it is simple, direct and pragmatic. The entire set of teachings is based on the realistic premise that each individual is born with a particular temperament, and so laying down a single spiritual path for all to walk on, is simply not possible.

This sets the tone for the underlying message of acceptance of individuality as well as plurality. Multiplicity of ideas, thought processes, and subsequent individual actions, are concepts that lie at the heart of this understanding and acceptance.

The fascinating conversation between Arjuna and Krishna therefore, touches upon, and synthesises several paths to spiritual realisation, without overtly declaring one to be superior to another. It will not be inappropriate to conclude that the *Gita* is an unequivocal supporter of free will, and actively encourages human beings to make their own choices in life.

As we proceed from verse to verse, and then chapter to chapter, we are told of the different patterns of life we can opt for while on earth. We can choose between goodness, passion or ignorance to be the driving engines of our actions. Gradually, the ultimate destination of the path we choose to walk on becomes clear to the reader and the outcome of each of our actions is explained in no uncertain terms.

As the reading progresses we can feel—sometimes with a gnawing sense of foreboding—our hitherto innocently made life choices, slowly but surely, turning into well-informed choices.

As we read the *Gita*, it becomes amply clear that every step we take is the initiating link in the eternal chain of cause and effect, and of action and reaction. No thought or action remains unaccounted for, and is eventually paid for, in the balance sheet of life. Or indeed of life after life.

Being privy to the inevitable outcomes of actions, it eventually becomes easier to define our ultimate objectives and identify our destination. Be mindful of how you use the luxury of free will which is at your disposal, and optimise on your individual capabilities for your own good as well as that of the world—these are some of the many things that the *Gita* tells us.

b. Yoga and the Gita

The word yoga is by now universally associated with an ancient Indian system of physical postures and meditation. This, however, is just one of the aspects of the multi-faceted science of yoga which has innumerable applications in practical life. These lie way beyond mere stretching and bending exercises carefully choreographed to soothing but invigorating music. It is possible that yoga initially developed at the time of the Indus Valley Civilization, around 3000 BCE. The manner and frequency with which yoga finds a mention in the *Gita* makes it obvious that by the time the epic battle was fought at the historic site of Kurukshetra, it was a well-developed, tried and tested way of life.

What makes yoga a unique science is that applying it to oneself in real life, is nothing short of an art!

The Sanskrit word 'yoga' comes from the verb root '*yuj*', which means to link or to connect. The word 'link' immediately brings to mind the question—link to what? In the case of yoga this implies linking or connecting individual consciousness with the Supreme consciousness. It is important to remember here that linking does not mean merging.

While being alive in the world yoga teaches an individual to feel one with the Supreme Soul through focus and concentration, and thus prepare for ultimately merging with it when its designated time on this earth is over.

A quick look at the table of contents will reveal that every chapter carries the word yoga as its title. Thus clearly, each of the following is perceived as a form of yoga—knowledge, philosophy, action, renunciation, meditation, judgement, divine manifestation, divine vision, matter and spirit, human nature, the Supreme Self, the divine, the demoniac, faith, liberation, and deliverance.

To the extent that as reflected in the very first chapter even overcoming distress, dilemma, dejection, and inner conflict are a form of yoga.

What could this mean then? What is yoga?

To arrive at a simple definition it can be said that yoga is a disciplined method of attaining a goal by making use of practised techniques for controlling both, the body and the mind. Outwardly it may not appear to be so, but to control the mind is a far tougher challenge than keeping the body in check.

Here the *Gita* is clearly suggesting that successful rejection of distress and dilemma is also yoga. A yogi may disallow a war within from erupting, and if it does, can easily overcome the crisis and salvage his or her equanimity.

Reverting to the issue of the origin of the word, according to a school of thought, this may have evolved from *yujir* yoga which means to yoke, or yoga *samadhau* which means, to concentrate. This then translates to mean, controlling one's energies and thoughts through intense concentration.

A person who practises yoga or follows the philosophy of yoga with complete and unwavering commitment, is said to be a yogi (for a man) and yogini (for a woman).

In the *Bhagavad Gita,* the practice of yoga is used to
- come to terms with inner conflict
- decipher the complexities of the human mind
- understand the supreme significance of duty
- understand and accept that everything we see around us is part of a grand plan
- accept the mortality of the human body and the immortality of the soul

- learn of different paths to salvation
- accept the futility of material pursuits
- appreciate the significance of knowledge, action and renunciation
- prepare for an after life commensurate with the pattern in which the present life is lived
- adopt techniques of self-improvement
- acquire better mental and physical health, and a sense of overall well-being
- find and maintain peace of mind and live a disciplined, balanced life

III. THE BHAGAVAD GITA: A LIFE-CHANGING CONVERSATION

a. Another book on the *Gita*...but why?

Swami Vivekananda, Mahatma Gandhi, Bal Gangadhar Tilak, C. Rajagopalachari, S. Radhakrishnan, and countless other luminaries, philosophers and thinkers have written or spoken about the *Bhagavad Gita*. The text has been analysed, researched, and taught over and over again, presumably from the time that it was compiled.

The *Gita* continues to offer itself as an infinite source for sermons, quotes, thought-of-the-day and read-one-verse-a-day kind of guidelines. The ultimate refuge in situations both favourable and unfavourable, it has provided the basic concept and storyline for innumerable self-help books for better living, and handbooks designed as a ready reckoner to refer to in a moment of crisis.

Whether we may have read the *Gita* or not, we in the subcontinent—or may be everyone the world over—know that this is one text whose name is to be taken with respect and care. This despite the fact, that very few are inclined to actually read it, or if they do, then to really understand it.

An ironic case of a book being judged entirely by its cover!

Given its universal appeal, its unshakeable status in the spiritual canon, its own immortality, and the reams of material already available on it, one may well ask, another book on the *Gita,* but why? And that too by a novice with barely any grounding in the study of Vedic scriptures.

It is a valid question that must be asked, and that must be answered.

Let me begin by citing George Mallory, a well-known mountaineer who climbed the Mount Everest. On being asked the question, 'Why did you want to climb the Mount Everest?'

He replied simply, 'Because it's there.'

That, in a nutshell, is my answer too. I have put together an interpretation of the *Gita*—the mother (yes, I do believe it is the mother and not necessarily the father) of all spiritual, philosophical texts—simply because it is an exceptionally enriching text, meant to be read and interpreted.

The *Gita* was compiled thousands of years ago to be read, understood, interpreted, internalised and applied in real life. After all, what does anyone write a book for? Clearly for all of the reasons · cited above.

Besides, each interpretation of this fascinating text is unique and personal. Interestingly, this personal interpretation does not remain static with the passage of time. Unlike a mathematical formula, each time anyone reads the *Gita* a new meaning invariably emerges. Because the *Bhagavad Gita* is an unparalleled mix of the physical and the metaphysical, the natural and the supernatural, the human and the superhuman.

This multi-layered text is also a curious mix of the dynamic and the static—very much in the spirit of the adage that the more things change, the more they remain the same. The meanings might keep changing with each reading, but the text remains the same. There are the same 18 chapters, same 700 verses, the same speakers and the same battlefield. But like a kaleidoscope, where the hues change each time it is rotated, the meaning/s of the verses keep evolving, not necessarily replacing the earlier one, but certainly enhancing it.

b. A Contemporary Interpretation

This compilation comprises 251 verses of the original 700. The shortlisting was labour-intensive and time-consuming. Mercifully neither of these was an issue, as this project is purely a labour of love, and time has been in abundance during the inward-looking existence during the pandemic.

The year 2020 was when time stood still as at the historic battlefield of Kurukshetra.

The basis of selecting the verses, however, was a real challenge and remained one literally till going to press. How do you decide which rose to pick from a rose bush? How do you make up your mind about which puppy to take home from the litter cuddled up with its mother? How and which one do you make your own? And which one do you let go? Dilemma and inner conflict, indeed.

The only factor that made the selection even possible, and perhaps feasible, was the tendency for repetition of concepts and postulations throughout the text. This could be by design—divine or otherwise— presented thus with the purpose of reiteration and reaffirmation of complex ideas. Or this could be the outcome of several versions of the text being compiled into one to constitute what we today know as the *Bhagavad Gita*. There is a robust school of thought that believes this to be a fact.

c. The Discourse

Care has been taken to keep the progression of the discourse linear and connected—avoiding repetition but also not missing out a link inadvertently. Each of the 251 verses has been dealt within three parts.

- Verse in original Sanskrit
- Translation
- Interpretation

Each of the 18 chapters has been presented with a brief introduction. This is a sneak peek into the chapter and has been written along the lines of what-to-expect kind of reviews. It also highlights the central theme of the forthcoming chapter.

A concerted effort has been made to

- Understand the text in its own social and historical context. To refrain from judging it on the basis of principles of critical appraisal at play five thousand years after its writing.
- Establish connects with our lives today. This proved to be surprisingly simple as it is not for nothing that the *Gita* has stood a considerable test of time, and continues to be as relevant today as it was when Krishna emphatically declared—'I am Time itself'.
- Alas, the trials and tribulations of human existence remain unchanged despite the thousands of calendar years in between then and now.
- Keep the language simple and direct. A conscious attempt has been made to do away with verbosity and spiritual jargon so as to avoid a convoluted manner of presentation.
- Avoid looking at this valuable text through the prism of any contemporary -isms. This is significant as preferably the text must be assessed not merely as a piece of writing, but as a set of teachings that have the potential to change the world view of its readers.

So let us not miss out the ethereal woods of paradise for a forest of '-isms'!

d. Who is this interpretation for?

The answer to this question too is simple. This interpretation is for anyone and everyone.

- It would, of course, be gratifying if the young and the uninitiated choose to pick this up to read.
- If those who don't 'have time for all this', find time for it.
- If those who feel 'there'll always be time to read this later in life', find the time now.
- If those who have so far perceived it as mumbo jumbo, find contemporary value in it.
- If readers of all ages feel it was worth the time and effort of going through this.

This interpretation of the *Gita* is reader-segment-agnostic, and should appeal to readers from varied walks of life, different geographies, individual or collective life-goals, and diverse cultures and socio-economic groups. It will be a source of satisfaction if it succeeds in making its readers agree that the conversation between a distressed warrior and his super composed charioteer has indeed the potential of changing lives.

I shall now humbly step aside and allow you to initiate your journey into the illuminating world of the *Bhagavad Gita*.

Welcome to the battlefield—both within and without. But do not let the prospect of a battle worry you beyond a point. We have a master counsellor and sharp strategist at hand to help you manoeuvre through the complex maze that is the human mind.

So give in to some empathetic hand-holding and prepare yourself to be made privy to the Supreme Secret. In all likelihood, you will emerge on the other side calm, composed and in control...of your own self.

Mahabharata
the story

The *Mahabharata* is an ancient Indian epic where the main story revolves around two branches of a family, the Pandavas and the Kauravas. Composed by the sage Ved Vyas, it is the longest epic poem ever written comprising 100,000 verses. Believed to have been composed in the 4th century BCE or earlier, it is said that Vyas dictated the verses, and Lord Ganesha wrote them down.

The narrative is situated in northern India, and the story is a well-established part of Indian folklore. The name *Mahabharata* is derived from King Bharata as the story revolves around his descendants. Included within the *Mahabharata* is the *Bhagavad Gita*, a storehouse of knowledge and instructions delivered by Krishna to Arjuna on how to live an exemplary life.

***

Dhritarashtra and Pandu were brothers born in the Kuru dynasty. As Dhritarashtra was born blind, at the time of ascension to the throne he was bypassed as the next ruler, and his younger brother Pandu was anointed as king. Pandu, however died early leaving behind five sons, Yudhishtira, Bheema, Arjuna, Nakula and Sahadeva, collectively known as the Pandavas. They were brought up under the guardianship of Dhritarashtra, who was made king as an interim arrangement till the boys grew up. Dhritarashtra himself fathered a hundred sons, who came to be known as the Kauravas.

The 105 princes grew up together and were trained by Dronacharya, an expert in the art of warfare. Bhishma, the revered senior-most member of the Bharata clan who had taken a vow never to be king, to remain celibate, and to always remain loyal to the throne irrespective of who sat on it, imparted to the princes, what might today be known as, value education.

However, seeds of animosity between the two sets of brothers were sown early, as the Kauravas always viewed their five cousins with suspicion, quite certain in their devious minds that the Pandavas were usurpers at heart.

Duryodhana, the eldest Kaurava, who in any case despised the Pandavas, felt further encouraged as he sensed his father Dhritarashtra's desire to see his own eldest son on the throne of Hastinapur and not its rightful heir Yudhishtira, Pandu's eldest son. Duryodhana and his brothers made several attempts at killing the Pandavas by deceit, but with support of their clever uncle Vidura, who could see through these plans and blessings of their other cousin Krishna, they repeatedly survived.

In the early part of the *Mahabharata*, Krishna is seen as a cousin of the Pandavas who they are related to from the maternal side. Krishna and the Pandavas are also good friends, though the former always seemed to be more accomplished than the others, and was someone who could manage situations well, without ruffling any feathers. Right through Krishna is favourably inclined toward his first cousins, the Pandavas, rather than his second cousins, the hundred Kauravas.

After several failed attempts at taking the lives of the Pandavas, a frustrated Duryodhana and his conniving uncle Shakuni, hatch a plan to invite the five for a gambling session. This is done keeping in mind that Shakuni, brother of Duroydhana's mother Gandhaari, was a gambler par excellence and had never lost a game of dice.

The Pandavas walked into the trap and lost all their possessions, including their wife Draupadi. Having succeeded in their plan, the winners tried to molest Draupadi in the presence of the entire court, but Krishna intervened and saved Draupadi from public humiliation.

However, the Pandavas were forced to go into exile for thirteen years, of which the last year was to be spent incognito.

On their return from exile, in the fourteenth year, the Pandavas faced more adversities, as they were refused their share of the kingdom by the Kauravas. The five brothers then requested for just five villages, but this too was denied by Duryodhana who saw this as an opportunity of completely ruining his cousins.

Pushed against the wall, the Pandavas now realized that war was the only option for them to win back what was rightfully theirs. As a final effort at peace, Krishna himself went to Dhritarashtra to arrive at a mutual settlement between the two sides. The short-sighted Kauravas however refused to yield from their position of strength, and Krishna returned empty-handed.

Soon the armies of the two sides met at the historic battlefield of Kurukshetra ready to fight a battle of epic proportions. So as not to appear partial, Krishna offers that one side could make use of his large army, while another could have Krishna himself as advisor and strategist. The Kauravas, unable to see value in Krishna as mentor opted for the use of his substantial army. Consequently, Krishna joins the Pandavas, offering to be Arjuna's charioteer.

Just as the battle is poised to begin Arjuna sees before him his relatives: his great-grandfather Bhishma who had practically brought him up, his teachers Kripa and Drona, his brothers, the Kauravas. The thought of fighting or eventually even killing them leaves him numb. Confused and agitated, Arjuna asks Krishna to turn the chariot back, to abandon the battle. 'I can't kill these people. They're my brothers, my uncles, my teachers. What good is a kingdom that's gained at the cost of the lives of one's own people?'

It is at this point that Krishna delivers a philosophical discourse known as the *Bhagavad Gita*. Krishna explains to Arjuna the immortality of the soul and the temporary nature of the body. Revealing himself as the

Supreme Power, he stresses upon the importance of doing one's duty, and of adopting the right path, with no desire for the fruits of one's actions.

Time stands still for the two armies as Krishna and Arjuna are in conversation. Arjuna is temporarily granted divine vision to enable him to see Krishna in his *viraat roop*, i.e., the magnificent manifestation of the Lord, where his physical form encompasses the entire universe and all that lies in it.

This discourse is known as the *Bhagavad Gita*, and lies within the epic *Mahabharata*. On completing the conversation with Arjuna, Krishna breaks the spell he had cast, thus activating the armies.

Enlightened and rejuvenated Arjuna picks up his bow again, and soon enough after a bloody battle lasting eighteen days the Kauravas are vanquished. The Pandavas come out as winners but they lose everyone on the other side whom they hold dear: Bhishma, the revered senior of the Kuru dynasty, guru Dronacharya, the teacher, and Karna, the sixth brother of the Pandavas, who by an accident of birth and subsequent events, found himself on the side of the Kauravas.

After the war, Yudhishtira becomes king of Hastinapur and Indraprastha. The Pandavas ruled for thirty-six years, after which they abdicated in favour of Arjuna's grandson, Parikshit. The Pandavas and their wife Draupadi proceed on foot to the Himalayas with the idea of living out their last days there.

***

The comple yet fascinating story of the *Mahabharata* has been retold countless times over centuries, and remains popular to this day in India. It has several versions and is sometimes narrated differently in different regions and languages.

Even today children are named after characters in the epic and most Indians pick up bits and pieces of the story as they grow up, without necessarily sitting down for a single comprehensive narration of the saga, which has all the elements of a contemporary thriller.

The *Mahabharata* is routinely enacted out on stage, and has been made into several documentaries and films. The story continues to inspire and entertain, but it is unclear if any real lessons have been learnt from the bloody end of hostilities between the two sides.

Despite the passage of time since the epic was compiled, human nature continues to be just as contentious and avaricious. Battles for possession of property continue to be fought—maybe no longer on an elaborate battlefield—but now within domestic confines, boardrooms and courtrooms. Therein lies the undiminished popularity and relevance of the story of the *Mahabharata*.

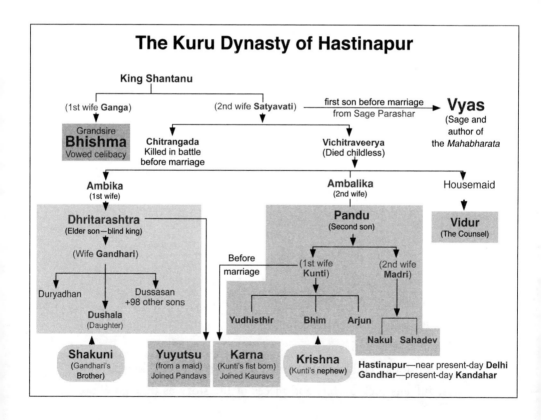

Ī

Distress, Dilemma and
Inner Conflict

The *Bhagavad Gita* is primarily a conversation between Krishna and Arjuna. The armies of the Kauravas and the Pandavas stand poised to fight at the battlefield of Kurukshetra. This is set to be a decisive battle as relations between the two sides have reached a point of no return, and a war seems to be the only way forward.

The first chapter opens with Dhritarashtra anxious to hear an account of the events taking place far away from Hastinapur where he himself is confined on account of his blindness. Miles away, on the battlefield, we see Arjuna, distressed and agitated, at the thought of having to raise arms against his own flesh and blood.

As he seeks his cousin and now charioteer Krishna's counsel, his dilemma leads to a lengthy discourse after which, regaining lost composure, he gets ready to fight.

The first chapter is also the beginning of the first of the three segments of the *Gita*, and describes karma yoga or devotion in action. The table of contents will reveal that the title of every chapter is suffixed with the word yoga. The meaning of yoga has unfortunately shrunk today and has become synonymous with a physical fitness regime, which practised over a period of time eventually leads to both good physical health and mental wellbeing. While this might be an accurate description in a particular context, it is actually an extremely limiting one.

Exploring the meaning of yoga and examining its usage in several Vedic scriptures makes it amply clear that any activity performed with devotion, determination and firm discipline is yoga. Focus and single-mindedness are the keys to attaining an acceptable level of expertise in any, and every form of yoga.

... simple everyday tasks can also come under the vast umbrella of yoga so long as these are carried out with honesty of purpose, undiluted sincerity, and with the clear goal of attaining ultimate perfection.

Thus, simple everyday tasks can also come under the vast umbrella of yoga so long as these are carried out with honesty of purpose, undiluted sincerity and with the clear goal of attaining ultimate perfection.

Chapter titles of the *Gita* reveal the varied use of the word yoga, and its liberal but focussed application in various aspects of life. Some of these are listed below.

- action
- detachment
- devotion
- duty
- faith
- judgement
- knowledge
- liberation
- meditation
- renunciation
- self-control
- self-realisation
- self-restraint
- selfless service

A cursory glance at the list could make it appear to be nothing more than a compilation of abstractions arranged in alphabetic order. Interestingly, each of these 'abstractions'—and many more—is presented as a form of yoga in the *Bhagavad Gita*.

And now a word about the title of Chapter One: *Arjuna Vishaad Yoga*. How can distress and dilemma be yoga, one may legitimately ask. A close look at Arjuna's agitation makes it obvious that it stems from a deep inner conflict. Unable to reconcile himself to the idea of fighting— to kill—members of his own extended family, mentors and teachers, Arjuna loses heart and questions the very purpose of the war that is about to begin.

In other words, the war raging within Arjuna makes him incapable of fighting the war without. Ironically, the legendary ambidextrous archer, Arjuna, is unable to handle the ambiguity of the situation, and is frozen with fear of fighting. Eventually, he comes out of this defeatist state of mind, emerging victorious in the war.

But what is the process by which this happens? The first stage here is Arjuna focussing on himself and his reluctance. Recognising his own inner conflict he goes on to articulate it. He unhesitatingly seeks counsel and is offered solutions. Acceptance of the solution finally results in resolution of conflict.

Thus, delving into one's own consciousness with the intention of self-improvement is also yoga. Honest introspection and self-realisation are key to locating life-changing solutions.

> *...delving into one's own consciousness with the intention of self-improvement is also* yoga. *Honest introspection and self-realisation are key to locating life-changing solutions.*

The depth of despair to which Arjuna had fallen is apparent in the following verse. This has to be read in the context of an exemplary warrior entertaining such despondent thoughts on the battlefield. The war within and its damaging consequences on our actions, are well reflected in these words.

It will be better for me if, with weapons in hand, the sons of Dhritarashtra kill me, unarmed and unresisting on the battlefield.

–Verse 1.46

chapter 1

Arjuna Vishaad Yoga
Yoga as the War Within

1.01

धृतराष्ट्र उवाच |

धर्मक्षेत्रे कुरुक्षेत्रे समवेता युयुत्सवः |
मामकाः पाण्डवाश्चैव किमकुर्वत सञ्जय || 1||

1.01: Dhritarashtra said: O Sanjaya, after assembling on the field of Kurukshetra, and desirous to fight, what did my sons and the sons of Pandu do?

In this opening verse of the *Bhagavad Gita,* King Dhritarashtra and Sanjaya are in Hastinapur, the capital city of the kingdom, while the armies of Kauravas and Pandavas have gathered on the battlefield of Kurukshetra. Dhritarashtra is blind and thus unable to fight.

Sanjaya, his charioteer, had earlier been blessed by his guru Ved Vyas with the gift of clairvoyance, by which he can envision the battlefield miles away. Thus now he can narrate an 'eye witness account' of fateful events taking shape far away from the palace.

While mentioning the location of the battlefield Dhritarashtra seems to make a distinction between *dharma-kshetre,* the land of dharma and *kuru-kshetre,* Kurukshetra, the land of Kurus. It is unclear, perhaps even to himself, whether he sees these two as descriptions of the same place or does he make a distinction between duty and ownership?

In an ideal world the two should be synonymous, but in the warped world of Dhritarashtra and his sons, the two seem independent of one another. It is possible that while the Pandavas see the battlefield as the land of their duty, the Kauravas view it simply as land that they own.

Both sides are in a state of readiness to fight as there is no hope of a settlement. Knowing all this well, King Dhritarashtra still asks Sanjaya what his sons and his brother Pandu's sons were doing on the battlefield? It was obvious that the battle was about to begin, then why did he make this enquiry? Is it a rhetorical question to which he is not really expecting a reply or is it a manifestation of his own anxieties?

Blinded by his love for his sons, Dhritarashtra's judgement is clouded and he fails to see the reality. Conscious in his heart of hearts that injustice has been done towards his brother's sons—by himself and his sons—he feels occasional pangs of guilt. Clearly, by referring to them as Pandu's sons and not his nephews, Dhritarashtra draws a line and distances himself from them. Knowing that the Pandavas are able warriors Dhritarashtra is apprehensive of the outcome of this battle.

Significantly, this is the only occasion when Dhritarashtra speaks in the entire *Gita*. This is in keeping with his character so far, of remaining silent when he should speak. As this juncture, it is also indicative of the reality that, being largely responsible for the unfortunate turn of events nothing is in his hands any more. The saga by now has gained a life of its own as it moves forward organically.

In asking Sanjaya why the armies had gathered, it appears he is almost in a hurry to hear that the battle has ensued, and soon his sons would emerge victorious. Ironically in his eagerness for the battle to begin, he seems to be hastening his own and his sons' end.

Dhritarashtra's life and actions, or lack of them, is a critical commentary on how an error of judgement, blind love for one's children and a subjective view of their character and capabilities can have disastrous, even fatal, consequences.

This opening verse also sets the pace for the recurring theme of attachment in the *Gita*. The events so far in the *Mahabharat* have shown that Dhritarashtra and his sons come across as personifications of material attachment. They are unable to rise above ambition and avarice, and their way of life is a continuing example of all that an intelligent and discerning human being should strive to stay away from.

1.28

अर्जुन उवाच |
दृष्ट्वेमं स्वजनं कृष्ण युयुत्सुं समुपस्थितम् |
सीदन्ति मम गात्राणि मुखं च परिशुष्यति || 28||

1.28: Arjuna said: O Krishna, seeing my own kinsmen ready for battle here and intent on killing each other, my limbs are quivering and my mouth is drying up.

This verse marks the beginning of Arjuna's distress and dilemma as he realizes with finality that all the warriors on both sides of the battlefield are none other than his relatives, friends, and family. Understandably, this fills him with horror as the moment of reckoning is upon him.

Widely accepted as an archer and warrior par excellence, at this moment Arjuna simply comes across as a vulnerable human being, and a good one at that, with his heart in the right place, so to speak. Arjuna's reaction here makes us easily identify with him, as these are the thoughts ordinary mortals would have in a similar situation.

Imagine, for a moment someone initiating a battle, where the enemy is one's own flesh and blood, and doing it without batting an eyelid. That would certainly be unusual, and unsavoury.

Arjuna's limbs are trembling, and his mouth is parched when he speaks aloud and shares his angst with his cousin, and presently his charioteer, Krishna.

1.32–33

न काङ्क्षे विजयं कृष्ण न च राज्यं सुखानि च |
किं नो राज्येन गोविन्द किं भोगैर्जीवितेन वा || 32||
येषामर्थे काङ्क्षितं नो राज्यं भोगाः सुखानि च |
त इमेऽवस्थिता युद्धे प्राणांस्त्यक्त्वा धनानि च || 33||

1.32–33: O Govinda, of what use are a kingdom, all pleasures, or even life itself, when the very persons for whom we may desire them, are standing across us for battle? I have no desire for such victory and kingdom, or the happiness that may come from it.

Continuing to speak, Arjuna poses a rhetorical question to Krishna wondering what use would a victory be in this situation, and what would be achieved by decimating his own near and dear ones.

In the Indian context, the concept of a nuclear family is a fairly recent one. Traditionally, extended families lived together with several generations under one roof. Earnings went into a common kitty, and family members ate their meals together. It was not unusual to grow up with cousins, and not quite be able to discern between them and one's siblings, till much later in life.

Having grown up in close proximity with his cousins, Arjuna is unable to reconcile to the idea of having to fight them over rights to a kingdom. In his view, no kingdom could compensate for what he stands to lose in the process, and no gain can be worth its while if it is at the cost of shedding blood of his own people.

1.34–35

आचार्याः पितरः पुत्रास्तथैव च पितामहाः |
मातुलाः श्वशुराः पौत्राः श्यालाः सम्बन्धिनस्तथा || 34||
एतान्न हन्तुमिच्छामि घ्रतोऽपि मधुसूदन |
अपि त्रैलोक्यराज्यस्य हेतोः किं नु महीकृते || 35||

1.34–35: O Madhusudana, teachers, fathers, sons, grandfathers, maternal uncles, grandsons, fathers-in-law, grand-nephews, brothers-in-law, and other kinsmen are all present here, putting at stake their lives and properties. I do not wish to kill them, even if they attack me. I am not prepared to fight with them even in exchange for power over the three worlds, let alone this earth.

Seeing his teachers, Dronacharya and Kripacharaya, grand uncle Bhishma, uncle Dhritarashra's hundred sons, their sons, grandsons, and several other relatives, Arjuna loses the will to fight. Addressing Krishna as Madhusudana, the killer of the demon Madhu, he voices his unwillingness.

Speaking metaphorically he says, leave alone a mere kingdom, he would not want to raise arms against his own family, even if he were to gain the entire universe by killing them.

1.36–37

निहत्य धार्तराष्ट्रान्नः का प्रीतिः स्याज्जनार्दन |
पापमेवाश्रयेदस्मान्हत्वैतानाततायिनः || 36 ||
तस्मान्नार्हा वयं हन्तुं धार्तराष्ट्रान्स्वबान्धवान् |
स्वजनं हि कथं हत्वा सुखिनः स्याम माधव || 37||

1.36–37: O Janardana, what pleasure will we derive from killing the sons of Dhritarashtra? Even though they may be the aggressors, it would be sinful to kill them. It is not right to kill our own cousins, the sons of Dhritarashtra, and their allies. O Madhava, how can we hope to be happy by killing our own kinsmen?

Addressing Krishna as Madhava, husband of the goddess of wealth, Arjuna wonders what pleasure and satisfaction could possibly be derived from killing one's own kin. Not only would any kingdom not be worth it, Arjuna also wonders how they could be happy ever again in the future after killing their own kinsmen over property.

It is interesting to note how Arjuna addresses Krishna by different names, almost as if trying to appeal to different manifestations of his multi-talented cousin's personality. When he speaks for the first time Arjuna calls him Govinda, referring to Krishna's family occupation of taking care of cows. He then goes on to calling him Madhusudana, the slayer of the demon Madhu; followed by Madhava, husband of the goddess of wealth; and Janardana, one who looks after his people.

This might also be a sign of Arjuna's desperation and frustration at not getting any response from Krishna. Perhaps he is trying a fresh approach with each name, appealing to different sides of Krishna in the desperate hope of an endorsement of his own distress at this difficult time.

1.45–46

अहो बत महत्पापं कर्तुं व्यवसिता वयम् |
यद्राज्यसुखलोभेन हन्तुं स्वजनमुद्यताः || 45||
यदि मामप्रतीकारमशस्त्रं शस्त्रपाणयः |
धार्तराष्ट्रा रणे हन्युस्तन्मे क्षेमतरं भवेत् || 46||

**1.45–46: Alas! How strange it is that we have set our mind to carry out
this sinful act. Driven by the desire for royal pleasures, we are intent
on killing our own kinsmen. It will be better for me if, with weapons
in hand, the sons of Dhritarashtra kill me, unarmed and unresisting
on the battlefield.**

The absence of any reaction from Krishna throws Arjuna further into
an abyss as he now begins to slip into dangerous territory. What we
have seen him experiencing up to this point is distress, remorse and
confusion, and his dilemma is understandable.

But what is happening now is a reflection, and a clear admission,
of cowardice. For a warrior like Arjuna to say on the battlefield that
he would choose to die unarmed, and that too without any resistance,
is an unambiguous declaration of shirking from his duty as a warrior.
Once on the battlefield, be it a general or a foot soldier, the duty of a
person in uniform is to fight. It is also the primary, and perhaps the
only duty, at that point of time.

It is important here to delve deeper into Arjuna's 'act of
cowardice' as it is not one borne of any physical inadequacies or
lack of courage to fight otherwise. On the contrary, he feels unable
to pick up the Gandiv, his famous bow, because of his emotional

ties with those who, by a quirk of fate, happen to be his enemy on the battlefield.

It is a peculiar situation where Arjuna's duty as a warrior gets overshadowed by his love for his family on the other side. A clear case of allowing one's heart to rule over one's head at a critical juncture, where the obvious call of the hour is forceful action and delivery.

Needless to reiterate here, that on the battlefield, a soldier's first duty is to fight and vanquish the enemy, irrespective of who it may be.

Only two relationships must determine a warrior's action while on the battlefield—friend and foe.

2

Self Realisation,
Seeking Solutions

The second chapter is perhaps the most important, for more reasons than one. It is here that Krishna initiates his discourse. The chapter encompasses the essence of all the teachings that are to follow in the remaining sixteen chapters.

Having shared his distress and dilemma in the previous chapter, Arjuna is now composed, and ready to listen to what Krishna has to say. Arjuna has submitted himself as the shishya or student to Krishna, his guru.

Krishna patiently listens to Arjuna when he spoke of his reluctance to fight, as it meant killing his dear ones. However, Krishna does not sympathise with Arjuna's emotions as he feels his angst is misplaced. Krishna reminds a distressed Arjuna that it is his duty to fight, and advises him to overcome his anxiety.

The conversation starts with Krishna impressing upon Arjuna the futility of grieving over the death of a living being. Stressing upon the transcient nature of physical life on earth, he draws upon real-life illustrations to drive the point home.

Speaking as his spiritual guru, Krishna talks of the

- distinction between the mortal nature of the physical body and the immortality of the soul; while one is characterised by the transactional nature of life, the other is essentially eternal.

- process of transmigration of the soul
- significance of selfless service
- importance of positive use of intellect
- characteristics of a self-realised individual
- three kinds of human nature
- material and physical attachment—excessive attachment of any kind is the root cause of most problems
- significance of performing activities purely out of a sense of duty, and not in the hope of returns or reward
- self-control and single-mindedness
- time management and resource utilisation

Krishna assures Arjuna that no effort made towards walking on the spiritual path is ever wasted. It is critical to remain purposeful in one's endeavours and not be deflected from the path of duty or shirk from performing good deeds.

Masterfully crafted, Chapter Two provides an evenly spaced glimpse of the various themes and aspects of life that are elaborated upon in the chapters that follow. Touching upon all that is to come, it seems as though Krishna is gently preparing a tormented Arjuna by giving him a brief sense of the multi-layered discourse that he is about to listen to.

Mindful of the different temperaments of human beings, Krishna briefly talks of the individual nature of each person. We may feel helpless in the face of our pre-dominant qualities of being egoistical, quick-tempered, impulsive or gullible, but with the required conviction and perseverance, self-improvement is always a real possibility.

Selfless service, an oft-repeated maxim throughout the *Gita*, is briefly introduced here. The significance of remaining detached from the fruits of one's labour is of essence at every stage of life.

Self-control is the key to a wholesome and balanced life—an aphorism we are taught right from our early years. Despite the timely introduction of this basic truth, gaining control over our senses continues to be a lifelong challenge for ordinary

Self-control is the key to a wholesome and balanced life

mortals. While on the one hand our five senses greatly enrich our lives, by mindlessly succumbing to them we are likely to be reduced to a state of spiritual penury.

Like a good teacher who immerses his student gradually into complex learning sessions, here Arjuna is given an opportunity to dip his feet in the deep waters of the ever-flowing river of knowledge. Little does the unwilling archer realise that he is on the verge of being exposed to the greatest lesson ever delivered by any teacher to his student.

He is also unaware of the fact that in turning to his charioteer for advice he has actually asked God himself to speak to him. Spiritual serendipity indeed!

Perhaps the best-known verse of the *Gita* lies in Chapter Two. Capturing the very essence of Krishna's discourse, the verse says:

You have a right to perform your assigned duties,
but you are not entitled to the fruits of your actions.
Never think of yourself to be the cause of the results of your efforts,
nor should you be attached to inaction.

–Verse 2.47

chapter 2

Saankhya Yoga
Yoga as Knowledge and Philosophy

2.07

कार्पण्यदोषोपहतस्वभाव:
पृच्छामि त्वां धर्मसम्मूढचेता: |
यच्छ्रेय: स्यान्निश्चितं ब्रूहि तन्मे
शिष्यस्तेऽहं शाधि मां त्वां प्रपन्नम् || 7||

2.07: I am confused about my duty, and am enveloped in anxiety. I have lost my composure. I am your disciple, and my soul is surrendered to you. Please guide me and show me the way.

It is at this juncture in the *Bhagavad Gita*, when for the first time Arjuna requests Krishna to be his guru that he realises that he was afraid, anxious and hesitant and had lost the will to fight. The thought of having to take aim at his own relatives and mentors distresses Arjuna, and he finds himself unable to resolve his new-found dilemmas on his own. Krishna, who up till then has been just his cousin and friend, first becomes his charioteer, and now takes on the role of his guide.

Arjuna requests Krishna to show him the correct path. This marks an abiding change in their relationship, as from being Arjuna's charioteer on the battlefield, Krishna now becomes his guru in the most sublime sense possible.

Arjuna's request encourages us to self-introspect and understand our strengths and weaknesses. It also establishes that when one is in an anxious, uncertain state of mind it is advisable to seek help. Choosing one's guru carefully, and seeking help at a critical time can help us find the right path, and take correct decisions.

Not only is it important to assess oneself and the given situation, and weigh the available options, it is equally important to find a genuine, guru to redeem oneself and be saved from disaster.

2.11

श्रीभगवानुवाच |
अशोच्यानन्वशोचस्त्वं प्रज्ञावादांश्च भाषसे |
गतासूनगतासूंश्च नानुशोचन्ति पण्डिताः || 11||

2.11: The Supreme Lord said: You speak words of wisdom, but you are mourning for that which is not worthy of grief. Those who are wise lament neither for the living nor for the dead.

Krishna initiates his discourse with this advice to Arjuna. While Arjuna feels his doubts and anxiety are well founded, Krishna does not concur with him. He tells Arjuna that though what he is saying sounds wise, there is no reason for him to feel that way. Because those who are truly wise, the pundits*, never lament, either for the living or for the dead. The grief that Arjuna is experiencing at the thought of

---

* There is a differentiation between the caste Brahmin (also referred to as pundit), and the Brahman—the wise one, the one whose mind expands to become one with the universe—as the *atma* (soul) strives to merge with the *paramatma* (the Supreme Soul). The word pundit used in the verse, similarly, means 'the wise one' and is not be confused with the caste.

killing his cousins is illusory, and shows that he has not yet attained complete wisdom.

Why does Krishna say that the wise never grieve either the living or the dead? The *Gita* tells us that all life is borne of God and returns to God. Later, Krishna reveals his true divine form to Arjuna.

When this verse is considered in the context of what follows, one understands that the body, was, is and always will be transient, the *atma*, or the soul, on the other hand is neither created, nor destroyed.

2.12

न त्वेवाहं जातु नासं न त्वं नेमे जनाधिपा |
न चैव न भविष्याम: सर्वे वयमत: परम् || 12||

2.12: Never was there a time when I did not exist, nor you, nor all these kings; nor in the future shall any of us cease to be.

Touching upon the knowledge of the self, Krishna says that the soul is eternal. The soul always was, always is and always will be. What we mortals see as death and grieve over, is merely the dissipation of the body. The soul lives forever and can never be destroyed. Our real self is our soul, and the soul is imperishable.

The soul has no linear past, present or future as its journey is cyclical (more on this later). For the soul, there is no birth or death at any time. The body is born, lives and dies, forever growing, ageing and changing till it finally ceases to exist. But as the soul is never born in the manner that living beings are, so it never dies. It merely takes on a body which ordinary mortals mistakenly believe to be the self. And hence they grieve when the body becomes inactive, and finally dies.

2.13

देहिनोऽस्मिन्यथा देहे कौमारं यौवनं जरा |
तथा देहान्तरप्राप्तिर्धीरस्तत्र न मुह्यति || 13||

2.13: Just as the embodied soul continuously passes from childhood to youth to old age, similarly, at the time of death, the soul passes into another body. Those who are wise are not mystified by this transition.

Continuing to speak about the eternal quality of the soul, Krishna lays down the principle of the transmigration of the soul from one body to another. The body undergoes several transformations in one lifetime. It takes shape in the womb of the mother, is born, lives and grows, constantly changing, it reaches its peak, and gradually starts to weaken. The body is continuously ageing and moving towards death. Having lived through its cycle of life, it can no longer function, and finally dies.

The soul which is indestructible, cannot be destroyed or diluted, and cannot be burned or buried, continues to live and enters another body. All souls exist forever in eternally separated bodies. Those who are wise and recognise this eternal truth are not surprised by this transition of the soul from one body to another.

2.14

मात्रास्पर्शास्तु कौन्तेय शीतोष्णसुखदुः खदाः |
आगमापायिनोऽनित्यास्तांस्तितिक्षस्व भारत || 14||

2.14: O son of Kunti, the transactional presence of happiness and distress, and their absence at another time, is like the appearance and disappearance of winter and summer seasons. These perceptions are transient, and arise from an interaction between the senses and the world around us. O descendent of Bharata, one must learn to tolerate them without feeling disturbed.

The five senses, sight, smell, taste, touch and hearing, play a critical role in determining one's mental state of being. The mind experiences happiness and sorrow based on the perceptions the senses convey.

These perceived sensations are transient and do not last forever. Thus, happiness, anxiety, sorrow, and distress, all come and go. The state of mind changes constantly like the seasons, and if we allow ourselves to be deeply affected by them we will always be in a state of flux, or uncertainty. A person blessed with equanimity lives through these experiences without being perturbed by them.

In other words, do not allow moments of happiness and success to make you complacent, nor should experiences of unhappiness and sorrow overwhelm you or break your spirit. None of these is permanent, and like changing seasons, shall sooner or later give way to another experience.

The thought here is reminiscent of the frequently used axiom— 'This too shall pass'.

2.20

न जायते म्रियते वा कदाचि
नायं भूत्वा भविता वा न भूय: |
अजो नित्य: शाश्वतोऽयं पुराणो
न हन्यते हन्यमाने शरीरे || 20||

2.20: The soul is neither born, nor does it ever die; nor having once existed, does it ever cease to be. The soul is unborn, eternal, immortal, and primeval. It is not destroyed when the body ceases to exist.

That which ceases to exist, or is annihilated, after coming into being is said to die. All life forms go through the six stages of existence; they first take form in the womb, are born, grow, then procreate, age, and finally die. This cycle is inevitable for all living beings but since the soul is never born, it never dies. The soul is ageless—it never diminishes and it never decays. What we call death is the destruction of a body. The soul that resides within, moves on to take another form, and is neither destroyed nor ever dies.

The eternal nature of the soul is stressed upon here, accentuating the fact that the existence of the soul is beyond the cycle of life and death. The soul is immortal, and thus lives forever.

Thus, while it is important for earthly success to nourish the body and keep it healthy, it is equally important, indeed if not more, to nurture the soul if one wishes to attain eternal peace and satisfaction.

2.22

वासांसि जीर्णानि यथा विहाय
नवानि गृह्णाति नरोऽपराणि |
तथा शरीराणि विहाय जीर्णा
न्यन्यानि संयाति नवानि देही || 22||

2.22: Just as a person gives up old, worn-out garments and puts on new ones, similarly, at the time of death, the soul sheds off its worn-out, useless body and enters a new one.

Krishna here establishes the concept of rebirth. He uses the analogy of a person getting out of old, and tattered clothes, and putting on new clothes. When we change our garments we ourselves remain the same, unchanged and unaltered, it is only the old clothes that are rejected and new ones are accepted. Similarly, when the body ages and finally dies, the soul leaves it, intact and immortal, and enters a new body somewhere else.

By accepting the theory of rebirth, a plausible explanation can be found for a lot of misery and disease in the world. What seems like a punishment in this life, for no apparent wrong doings, is actually an outcome of misdeeds committed in a past life. This is explained in greater detail as the discourse progresses.

2.23

नैनं छिन्दन्ति शस्त्राणि नैनं दहति पावक: |
न चैनं क्लेदयन्त्यापो न शोषयति मारुत: || 23||

2.23: The soul can neither be destroyed by any weapon, nor can fire burn it. Water cannot make it moist, nor can the wind make it dry.

The five basic elements are fire, earth, water, metal, and wood. These elements are understood as different types of energy in a state of constant interaction and flux. Though these five elements influence and impact every living being, the soul is not affected by them. The soul is all-pervading, hence weapons, fire, water and air are incapable of cleaving, burning, wetting or drying it. It is indestructible and is more subtle, stable, and primeval than the elements. In other words, the soul is ever present and immortal, and can never be destroyed.

Krishna explains the concept of the immortality of the soul and the mortality of the body repeatedly, and in many different ways. He realises that this is one the harshest realities of life. It is also the most challenging phenomenon for human beings to come to terms with, and to accept with any degree of equanimity. Making use of analogies and drawing instances from the physical world, he makes sure the concept is well understood by his visibly perturbed pupil.

2.27

जातस्य हि ध्रुवो मृत्युर्ध्रुवं जन्म मृतस्य च |
तस्मादपरिहार्येऽर्थे न त्वं शोचितुमर्हसि || 27||

2.27: Death is certain for one who has been born, and the one who has died will certainly be reborn. Therefore, you should not lament over what is bound to happen.

As certainly and inevitably as day turns into night, and then night turns into day, those who live will die, and will eventually be born again. Everything in life is uncertain, except death, and we all know that. And yet, we live in mortal fear of it, and our worst anxieties are always to do with losing a loved one.

While consoling a grieving friend or relative, we stress upon the inevitability of death, and the certainty of each one of us facing it one day. But we fail to apply this bitter truth to ourselves, and are unable to reconcile to the finality of death. We live in a fool's paradise imagining that death is something that happens only to others.

To accept our own mortality, and of those around us, is to face the Ultimate Truth. Krishna explains in this verse that life will always end with death, and so a wise person does not grieve over the inevitable.

2.30

देही नित्यमवध्योऽयं देहे सर्वस्य भारत ।
तस्मात्सर्वाणि भूतानि न त्वं शोचितुमर्हसि ॥ 30॥

2.30: O Arjuna, descendant of Bharata, the soul that dwells within the body is immortal and eternal; therefore, you need not mourn for any living being.

During his discourse, the immortality of the soul is a concept Krishna explains in great detail, spanning many verses. This is a summary of explanations of immortality of the soul, and reiterates its distinction from the body, which is mortal and exists only for a finite length of time.

Touching upon the knowledge of self, Krishna has earlier said (verse 2.12) that the soul is eternal. The soul always was, always is and always will be. What we mortals see as death and grieve over is merely the dissipation of the body. The soul lives forever and can never be destroyed. Our real self is our soul, and the soul is eternal.

2.40

नेहाभिक्रमनाशोऽस्ति प्रत्यवायो न विद्यते ।
स्वल्पमप्यस्य धर्मस्य त्रायते महतो भयात् ॥ 40॥

2.40: While persevering in this endeavour, there is no loss or adverse outcome, and even a small effort saves one from great danger.

One of the fears that is real in the cycle of rebirth is that of being reborn as a lowly creature in the next life. This is also the motivation for following one's dharma (duty), and doing good karma (deeds) to earn a satisfactory afterlife. If we fail in any of these, there is the possibility of not being reborn as a human being but as some lower species of life, such as insects, birds, animals, fish, etc. Being blessed with this life in no way ensures another life cycle as a human. That will be determined solely by how we live this life.

According to Hindu philosophy, there are 84 lakh species of life forms, of which human beings are the most evolved and exalted as they are blessed with intellect. A human being who does not move beyond performing the basic acts of eating, sleeping and reproducing thus fritters away opportunities, and reduces his chances of being born a human again. On the other hand, someone who makes good use of his intellect to evolve further is likely to be rewarded with rebirth as a human.

Therefore, it is important to start our journey of following one's dharma and performing good karma. Even if our tasks are left unfinished, whatever has been achieved will remain with us even after death. However, all material things we may have accumulated in a lifetime will certainly be left behind when we die.

Thus our *abhikrama,* or the efforts we make in this life, are never wasted and no good deed performed, however, big or small, shall ever have any *pratyavyah* or adverse effect. Any endeavour to walk on the path of spirituality will bear fruit in the next life. We might even be fortunate enough to be reborn as human beings as the Maker may bless us with another opportunity to complete the unfinished tasks of our past life.

2.41

व्यवसायात्मिका बुद्धिरेकेह कुरुनन्दन |
बहुशाखा ह्यनन्ताश्च बुद्धयोऽव्यवसायिनाम् || 41||

2.41: O scion of the Kuru dynasty, the intellect of those who are on this path is resolute, and they are single-minded in their purpose. But the intellect of those who are irresolute has innumerable branches.

Addressing Arjuna as the descendant of the great Kuru dynasty, Krishna further elaborates on the finer qualities of those who tread the right path. This path is found by performing one's duty and doing good karma in one's life.

Describing those who head in the right direction, Krishna says that they are single-minded and purposeful in everything they do, and in every step they take. The goal is clear and they move towards it with steady resolve, never losing focus of their destination. Such people can control their thoughts and thought processes, and not allow themselves to get distracted from the chosen path. Their progress is sharp and linear, driven by sheer grit and determination. They optimise on the good fortune of being born a human being, a species blessed with intellect, and consistently use their faculties to improve every aspect of their lives and of those around them. These individuals are on the right spiritual path.

On the other hand, there are those who are irresolute and whose attention is diffused. Krishna compares them to a tree with numerous branches, none of them bearing any fruit. These people are easily distracted, are of weak resolve and unclear about which journey to embark upon. They have no control over their thoughts and desires, and confused and vague in their endeavours, trying to walk on several different paths simultaneously. Thus, their progress is minimal and their journey of an entire lifetime fails to cover much ground. In other words, they fritter away wonderful opportunities that befall them. Failing to take steps towards self-improvement, they have little or no sense of direction. Such people reduce their own chances of attaining salvation.

2.44

भोगैश्वर्यप्रसक्तानां तयापहृतचेतसाम् |
व्यवसायात्मिका बुद्धिः समाधौ न विधीयते || 44||

2.44: Deeply attached to worldly pleasures and their intellect thus disoriented, they fail to be resolute. Their inner being lacks the determination to find success in the path to the Supreme Lord.

Elaborating further on individuals having distinct traits of character, Krishna now talks of those who are deeply attached to worldly pleasures and material possessions. They use all their energy and resources in augmenting their wealth, and indulging in the physical pleasures that life has to offer. Such individuals are engrossed in deriving satisfaction from sensual gratification (*bhog*), and immerse themselves in enjoying all possible luxuries of life (*aishwarya*).

Easily distracted by anything or anyone who promises pleasure, these kind of people are usually the ones with weak resolve and lack of vision. Preoccupied with material and physical pursuits, they are unable to make good use of their intellect and fail to move in the direction of finding the path to salvation.

Without categorically condemning this way of life, Krishna seems to suggest that drifting from one day to the next, remaining devoted to worldly pursuits and pleasures, is in effect a wasted life. Choosing to fritter away the precious gift of being born as a human being, by choosing to live this way, one is in no way working towards rising above the endless cycle of birth and rebirth.

2.45

त्रैगुण्यविषया वेदा निस्त्रैगुण्यो भवार्जुन |
निर्द्वन्द्वो नित्यसत्त्वस्थो निर्योगक्षेम आत्मवान् || 45||

2.45: The *Vedas* lay down three modes of material nature. O Arjuna! Transcend to a spiritual state of pure consciousness and rise above these. Free yourself of all dualities and the anxiety of material gain and safety, and allow yourself to be the core of your being.

The *Vedas* lay down three modes of material (human) nature—*sattva, rajas* and *tamas*. *Sattva* is the mode of goodness, *rajas* is the mode of passion, and *tamas* is the mode of ignorance. While the word *traigunya* means three modes, here it describes persons in whom *sattva, rajas* and *tamas* are in abundance.

Based on how they have lived their past lives, the three modes exist in different proportions in different individuals. The *Vedas* accept this as a human trait, and so have spelt out suitable instructions for all kinds of people. Specific rituals are recommended for those who have a material bent of mind, and so can only appreciate material rewards. On the other hand, those who are spiritually inclined are constantly making efforts at moving towards divine knowledge. In this way, with the right approach those in whom ignorance dominates can move towards passion, and those whose nature is ruled by passion can aspire to reach goodness.

Thus the *Vedas* show the path to self-improvement to all, taking into account their individual personality traits. Without this support for making oneself better, most ordinary mortals would slip further down and reach abysmal levels of ignorance and damnation. The *Vedas* contain both kinds of knowledge, ritualistic ceremonies for the materially attached, and divine knowledge for spiritual aspirants.

Here, Krishna asking Arjuna to rise above the *Vedas*, is to be understood at a more sublime level, and its essence is to be seen in continuation of the preceding verse and flowing into the next. He is asking Arjuna to not concern himself with the rules, rituals and ceremonies prescribed for those who are embroiled in material pursuits in the hope of receiving tangible returns. Krishna is encouraging Arjuna to rise above these and focus on those teachings of the *Vedas* that help one understanding the Absolute and Ultimate Truth.

By exercising self-control and by entertaining no desire for any material outcome Arjuna must elevate himself to a higher plane, and concentrate on acquiring Ultimate Knowledge.

2.46

यावानर्थ उदपाने सर्वतः सम्प्लुतोदके |
तावान्सर्वेषु वेदेषु ब्राह्मणस्य विजानतः || 46||

2.46: Whatever purpose is served by a small water body is naturally served in every possible way by a large reservoir as well. Similarly, one who realises the Absolute Truth naturally fulfils all the purposes of the *Vedas*.

The teachings of the *Vedas* are to help the soul reach the Supreme Lord through prayers, rituals, practices, duties and the pursuit of knowledge. Different paths are suitable for different people. The *Vedas* are rich with thousands of mantras that show the way to every individual.

For those who are inclined towards material possessions the *Vedas* offer material outcomes as this could be the only way to keep them moving in the right direction. It is suggested that while on that path they may be gradually weaned away from these attractions. The idea is to ultimately get detached from worldly attachments, and focus on higher goals.

But if someone already detached from worldly pleasures and material possessions, is face to face with the Absolute Truth, and is in possession of Ultimate Knowledge, she or he is already fulfilling the purpose of the *Vedas*.

Therefore, that person has already risen above the *Vedas*. This completes the thread of thought running through the last two verses (verses 2.44 & 2.45) where Krishna asks Arjuna to rise above the *Vedas* and elevate his Self to a higher plane of consciousness.

2.47

कर्मण्येवाधिकारस्ते मा फलेषु कदाचन |
मा कर्मफलहेतुर्भूर्मा ते सङ्गोऽस्त्वकर्मणि || 47 ||

2.47: You have a right to perform your assigned duties, but you are not entitled to the fruits of your actions. Never think of yourself to be the cause of the results of your efforts, nor should you be attached to inaction.

This is one of the most well-known verses of the *Bhagavad Gita*, and has even made way into popular Indian culture. This verse is inspiring and motivational, offering a rare insight into work, and how and in what spirit work should be done.

The verse talks about work in several ways underscoring the philosophy of karma yoga, which resonates positively with the concept of work is worship.

a. Do your duty but do not concern yourself with the outcomes.
   Krishna advises Arjuna to perform his duty in a selfless manner and focus on the work itself, and not on its results. The reasons for this are more than one.
   Firstly, work done for the sake of doing is the highest kind of effort. Secondly, it is important to remember that the nature of the outcome is not entirely dependent on the effort put in, as a lot of extraneous factors determine outward success. Therefore, quantitative result might not always be an indicator of the qualitative work done.

b. The result of your actions are not for you alone.
   Krishna tells Arjuna that performing one's duty does not imply that we enjoy its fruits ourselves. The effort might be of one individual but the result should be there for all to savour. Just as one person may sow the seed of a tree but everyone enjoys the fruits it bears. In fact, seeing others benefit from your work should be the real source of joy, not claiming ownership of the effort.

c. Do not become egoistical in seeing yourself as the performer.
   While performing one's duty one must not lose sight of the fact that we are merely the means through whom the end is achieved. Our performance is what it is because of divine will. We are the resource, making a contribution to a larger plan, and left to ourselves, we may not be able to achieve our goals. If we are chosen by the Lord to perform certain duties, then the ability to deliver

is also bestowed upon us by Him. Without the gift of ability we are unable to do anything, and so humility is the key, no matter how mammoth a task we have performed. Ego is an enemy to be shunned and avoided at all cost.

d. Do not allow yourself to become inactive.

No matter how challenging a situation, one must strive to perform one's duty and not withdraw and become inactive. Doors of opportunity will open to only those who knock on them, and solutions will present themselves only to those who try to solve the problem. Nothing changes in the lives of people who choose to be static and inert. If anything, inertia will only lead to dissipation, dilution and eventual destruction of everything around us.

2.48

योगस्थ: कुरु कर्माणि सङ्गं त्यक्त्वा धनञ्जय |
सिद्ध्यसिद्ध्यो: समो भूत्वा समत्वं योग उच्यते || 48||

2.48: Be consistent in the performance of your duty, O Arjuna, and abandon attachment to success and failure. Such equanimity is called yoga.

In this verse Krishna defines yoga as the balance, composure and equanimity to accept success and failure with equal grace. Anyone who can achieve this state of mind is a yogi, or a master of yoga.

Only when one understands the meaning of the previous verse (2.47) and the philosophy that only the effort is in our hands not its result, only then can one calmly accept the outcome, whether it is success or failure, pleasure or pain, ascent or descent, even life and death. Therefore, we should concern ourselves only with doing our duty to the best of our ability without focussing on the outcome, and allowing it to disturb us, just as a tree accepts the changing seasons as an inevitable reality. When it is autumn it effortlessly sheds its leaves and stands bare, exposed to the elements. But this does not prevent it from continuing to perform its duty, which is to spread its roots, grow, provide shade and bear fruit.

And so without being upset or disheartened by the drying of its old leaves, it uses all its natural resources to do what it is there to do. Soon it bears fresh leaves and fruits, and derives pleasure and satisfaction from giving shade and fruit to all.

To draw another lesson from this analogy it is humbling to remember that a tree uses neither its shade nor its fruit for itself. All the efforts it makes at performing its duty are entirely for the benefit of others.

2.58

यदा संहरते चायं कूर्मोऽङ्गानीव सर्वशः |
इन्द्रियाणीन्द्रियार्थेभ्यस्तस्य प्रज्ञा प्रतिष्ठिता || 58||

2.58: One who is able to withdraw the senses from their objects, just as a tortoise withdraws its limbs within its shell, is well established in divine consciousness.

Being in control of the senses is the litmus test that separates a yogi from others. A self-realised soul masters the senses and rules over them rather than allowing them to determine any course of action.

Most people are driven by the senses, and this results in their deflection from the true path.

To achieve divine consciousness one has to be strong and single-minded, without losing the capacity to utilise the senses as tools for self-improvement. For instance, using our eyes for reading good books, or using our ears to listen to the problems of others so we can be of help.

Krishna here draws an analogy of the tortoise that has the fascinating trait of being able to withdraw its head and limbs into its hard shell, and bringing these out for use whenever required. The tortoise retracts and recoils in reaction to danger, and once the moment passes it activates its head and limbs and moves on. Similarly humans should also detach themselves from the material world which could pose a threat, be in control of their senses and focus on awakening the inner self.

The hard shell of the tortoise teaches a lesson of its own. Though the turtle's body is soft and vulnerable inside, its outer shell is tough and impermeable, not letting any outside elements to make way and pollute the inner body. Mastering the ability to retract and extract at will is a remarkable step towards attaining divine consciousness.

2.59

विषया विनिवर्तन्ते निराहारस्य देहिन: |
रसवर्जं रसोऽप्यस्य परं दृष्ट्वा निवर्तते || 59||

2.59: Even when one practises self-restraint the taste for enjoyment of the senses remains. This taste ceases to be when one experiences a more sublime satisfaction, and feels the Supreme Lord, who then becomes central to one's consciousness.

Self-restraint and discipline are important components contributing to character-building. Putting these to practice results in challenging the senses and encourages individuals to overcome earthly and sensual desires. The attempt must be to be in control of all the five senses, and not be driven by what these may desire. The concept of fasting, and abstaining from certain foods and activities on certain days, is an exercise in self-control leading us to instil discipline in our lives.

But fasting and abstinence may lead to only temporary or transactional restraint. The desire to pander to the senses, and the penchant for the emanating pleasures lingers, and so we might quickly revert to the earlier pattern once the designated period of self-control is over.

It is only when one experiences the joy and satisfaction of being one with the Supreme Lord, that these desires abate as one sees the futility of these as compared to what the Ultimate Knowledge has to offer. Once one is truly with the Lord these flames of earthly desires will naturally extinguish, never to return, as the soul merges with the Supreme Power. This is the state of ultimate bliss, and one that is not even remotely comparable to any earthly, materialistic pleasure.

What Krishna suggests here is to practise self-restraint and discipline, but not just for short-term goals and their outcomes. He asks Arjuna to aim for and work towards long-term, indeed eternal, satisfaction and gratification, by letting the soul merge with the Lord.

2.62

ध्यायतो विषयान्पुंसः सङ्गस्तेषूपजायते |
सङ्गात्सञ्जायते कामः कामात्क्रोधोऽभिजायते || 62||

2.62: While focussing on the objects that are of interest to the senses, one develops an attachment to them. This attachment leads to desire, and from desire arises anger.

Desire, lust, greed and anger are considered to be the baser instincts of human beings. Just as a disease can make the body unhealthy and sick, pre-dominance of these qualities, desire, greed and anger, can make the mind diseased. Since we do not realise how these are making our mind unhealthy, we continue to pander to them and fail to rid ourselves of these ailments.

In this verse and the next, Krishna explains the functioning of the mind, saying that when we find satisfaction from an object of desire we become greedy for more. Gradually we become attached to it and depend on it for gratification. So long as we continue to pamper these baser instincts we are happy, not realising that in the process our moral fibre is being steadily destroyed.

On the other hand, if we are denied these pleasures we become angry and lose our balance. In this way, desire makes us greedy for more, and any obstruction in the path of these pleasures makes us frustrated and angry.

In this way, desire, greed and anger, form a vicious cycle that weakens our character. When we give way to these, allowing desire to determine our actions, we are likely to be living an unsteady, precarious life, where we often find ourselves feeling dissatisfied, irritable, resentful and unfulfilled.

2.63

क्रोधाद्भवति सम्मोह: सम्मोहात्स्मृतिविभ्रम: |
स्मृतिभ्रंशाद् बुद्धिनाशो बुद्धिनाशात्प्रणश्यति || 63||

2.63: Anger leads to clouding of judgment, which in turn results in confusion in the mind. When the mind is confused the intellect is destroyed; and when the intellect is destroyed, one is ruined.

Anger is an undesirable emotion for innumerable reasons. One of the most important is the loss of one's mental balance when seized with anger. An angry person's judgement is clouded, and he loses that sense of propriety that would normally help him discern between right and wrong, proper and improper, and acceptable and unacceptable social and professional conduct and behaviour.

This loss of balance leads to a loss of face and affects relationships and reputations. Having frequent anger management issues can seriously affect life, both at home and at the workplace. As one descends further into this abyss of inappropriate behaviour, followed by undesirable actions, one's intellect is adversely affected. One starts to lose equilibrium, and thus begins the journey of falling into a dark bottomless pit.

Thus the vicious cycle of anger leading to unclear thinking, further results in loss of sublime thought and evolved thought processes. This moving away from the trajectory of intelligence and knowledge spells doom for an individual, eventually leading to the complete destruction of one's life and aspirations.

2.64

रागद्वेषवियुक्तैस्तु विषयानिन्द्रियैश्चरन् ।
आत्मवश्यैर्विधेयात्मा प्रसादमधिगच्छति ॥ 64॥

2.64: One who can control the mind, even while using the objects of the senses, and can be free of attachment and aversion, attains the blessings of the Lord.

Everyone aspires for happiness, and it is natural for human beings to be constantly in search of this. Perhaps no one in their right minds would ever feel or say that she or he does not wish to be happy.

But the issue here is not of being desirous of happiness, but of what one derives happiness from. If the only source of happiness is pandering to the senses then we shall remain embroiled in these pleasures alone, and our mind will be constantly thinking of these and hankering after earthly gratification. Eventually one will develop a strong unshakeable attachment to these, becoming their slaves.

Attachment and aversion, emanate from the same mind. It is a question of how we train our mind and thoughts. If one can rise above excessive attachment and extreme aversion, and find balance, then it is a positive evolution of thought. An evolved person continues to use the senses for functional purposes like tasting, touching, smelling, hearing, and seeing, without being obsessively attached to the satisfaction these provide. Nor is such a person completely averse to these. He simply accepts them as an essential requirement, and relies on them and their uses for practical purposes.

Having reached this level of evolution, if one can condition one's mind to find happiness in the pursuit of God, then one is moving in the right direction. If we can develop an attachment to the Supreme Being, and look for and find happiness there, then the mind will become pure. This attachment is not regressive and decadent, it is progressive and pure. Progressive because one is moving in the right direction, and pure because it is to do with the divine.

Thus, once one has experienced the joy of divine bliss, the pleasures derived from earthly pursuits lose their attraction and eventually become meaningless.

2.67

इन्द्रियाणां हि चरतां यन्मनोऽनुविधीयते |
तदस्य हरति प्रज्ञां वायुर्नावमिवाम्भसि || 67||

2.67: Just as a strong wind sweeps a boat off its charted course on water, even one of the roaming senses on which the mind focuses can carry away a person's intelligence.

The five senses that humans are blessed with are naturally drawn to their objects in the material world. Individuals gravitate naturally towards delicious food, fragrances, sensual pleasures etc. An excessive indulgence in any of these can be detrimental to our spiritual progression.

Krishna draws an analogy of a boat sailing in still waters. A single gust of wind can cause the boat to deviate, sometimes permanently, from its charted path.

The boat might have been making good progress with an able boatman rowing towards its destination, with adequate provisions and the required wherewithal, but a single mishap can ruin the journey. The boat might come back to its original course but there is a possibility that being once deflected it might find it impossible to regain what it has lost.

Therefore, to attain divine consciousness it is important to have all senses equally in control. Even if one of them indulges itself unduly or excessively—or sometimes a single act of indiscretion—can lead one to disaster, losing one's way forever.

2.69

या निशा सर्वभूतानां तस्यां जागर्ति संयमी |
यस्यां जाग्रति भूतानि सा निशा पश्यतो मुने: || 69||

2.69: What is night for all, is the time of awakening for those who have self-control. And what all other beings consider to be day is night for the ones who are in control of their senses.

Here the reference to day and night is metaphorical, not to be taken literally. Ordinary mortals with no higher purpose in life look upon material pursuits as the driving force of life. They also measure their success by acquisition of these material possessions, and so this for them is 'day'. The time when they are unable to luxuriate in these pleasures is 'night' which is equivalent to darkness, or a time when no progress is made.

On the other hand, for those walking on a path leading to divine knowledge, these worldly pleasures have no meaning and amount to 'night' or nothingness. The moments they devote to self-improvement are their 'day'.

This difference in priorities, and perception of success, is what defines day and night for different people. In other words, people living in the same place, having a lot of other commonalities in their lives, could be pursuing completely different goals. Despite their physical proximity, in their minds they could be living in two different worlds, and walking on different paths leading to entirely different destinations.

To each his own.

3

Virtue in Action and
Selfless Service

Moving on from saankhya yoga, Krishna now talks of karma yoga, the yoga of action in the third chapter. Each one of us must engage in some activity for as long as one is in this material world. The stress on activity is so intense here that it may not be inappropriate to deduce that life and action are synonymous terms.

As a natural corollary of this, inaction becomes synonymous with death. Viewed in a larger perspective, here activity also implies change. As the cliché goes change is the only constant, and it is only the dead or ignorant who never change.

Though naturally driven by individual personality traits, our voluntary actions must be chosen carefully. These should not be such that further bind us to this life on earth. Ideally, our actions should be of the kind that encourage selfless service and detachment, leading to eventual liberation from life itself.

Condemning outward manifestation of renunciation, Krishna stresses that this can fool ordinary mortals but does not result in any advancement on the path of spirituality. True renunciation must come from within, and must satisfy a need in one's own self. This must not be motivated by any vested social interest in gaining brownie points for being a spiritually exalted person.

For as long as we are alive, basic activities like eating, sleeping, etc., are essential. Familial and professional responsibilities must all be fulfilled, especially by those who are in responsible positions, so as to lead by example. Even while in a state of renunciation these basic activities must be performed, but with no desire for any return in terms of monetary gains, or to fulfill expectations of a particular peer group.

Chapter Three clarifies in no uncertain terms that any task performed with sincerity and honesty is equivalent to the most elaborate of religious rituals. This declaration of the *Gita* might come as a rude shock for those who believe that the size of the donation is directly proportionate to the credits earned. This is possible but only if the act of charity is performed with a genuine desire to do so, and not for social or any other recognition.

Here Krishna delves into details of

- action and reaction
- the inevitability of action
- the impossibility of inaction
- being alive and being active are synonymous
- social need for an inspirational leader
- exemplary leadership qualities
- desire as an inherent human failing
- conquering the mind with intellect
- overcoming lust by exercising self-control

Desire and lust are the worst enemies of human beings, and more often than not cloud better judgement, resulting in serious impairment of the discerning power in individuals. These twin evils can sometimes make even right-minded people act 'out of character'.

Carefully built lives and reputations acquired through years of hard work and exemplary conduct, can be razed to the ground when people perform rash acts blinded by desire and lust. These adversaries

...any task performed with sincerity and honesty is equivalent to the most elaborate of religious rituals

of a balanced human mind should be overcome with judicious use of the intellect and by mastering the art of self-control.

The primary focus of this chapter remains action and its paramount importance in our daily lives. In a nutshell, Krishna is telling Arjuna—to act is to be, and to be is to act.

Equally important is the 'what, why, when and how' that propels our actions. The ethos of human action and why we do what we do is best articulated in the following verse.

There is no one who can remain without doing something even for a moment. All beings are compelled to act by the qualities born of their individual material nature:
The three gunas—knowledge, passion or ignorance.

—Verse 3.05

chapter 3

Karma Yoga
Yoga as Action

3.03

श्रीभगवानुवाच |
लोकेऽस्मिन्द्विविधा निष्ठा पुरा प्रोक्ता मयानघ |
ज्ञानयोगेन साङ्ख्यानां कर्मयोगेन योगिनाम् ॥ 3॥

3.03: The Supreme Lord said: O sinless Arjuna, I have already explained the two paths leading to enlightenment: the path of knowledge, for those inclined toward contemplation, and the path of work for those inclined toward action.

Earlier on, Krishna had explained the two paths leading to spiritual perfection, namely saankhya yoga and karma yoga. This is explained here in greater detail.

Saankhya yoga is the acquisition of knowledge through analytical study of the nature of the soul, and its distinction from the body. Those with a philosophic bent of mind are inclined towards this path of knowing the self through intellectual discourse and analysis.

Karma yoga is the spirit of devotion to God through constructive work. Krishna also calls this Buddhi yoga. Work done in this manner purifies the mind, enabling acquisition of knowledge which in turn leads to enlightenment.

Of all the people interested in walking the spiritual path, there are those who are inclined towards philosophy and contemplation, and on the other hand, there are those inclined to action and a work-oriented lifestyle. Both these paths have coexisted since the beginning of time. Krishna upholds both of them since his message of enlightenment is meant for people of all dispositions and individual mental makeup.

3.04

न कर्मणामनारम्भान्नैष्कर्म्यं पुरुषोऽश्रुते |
न च संन्यसनादेव सिद्धिं समधिगच्छति || 4||

3.04: One cannot achieve freedom from karmic reactions by merely not performing work, nor can one attain perfection of knowledge by mere physical renunciation.

The first line of this verse refers to the karma yogi (one who subscribes to the discipline of work), and the second line refers to the *saankhya* yogi (one who subscribes to the discipline of knowledge).

Though the two paths to salvation may appear to be well defined and quite distinct from one another, there are certain aspects that may have commonalities. One who believes in focussing on his work or duties is a karma yogi. But physical performance of duties and completion of assigned tasks in not enough even for a karma yogi. His thoughts also have to be pure, and even when he is not engaged in any fruitful activity his mind must remain pristine, and not entertain any unacceptable thoughts and ideas.

The *saankhya* yogi is one who adheres to strict discipline in life and renounces the world and all the material pleasures that it has to offer.

He might also don saffron clothes and live away from people. But just renunciation is not enough. He must have control over his thoughts also, and not allow any impure ideas or desires to pollute his mind.

Therefore, whether one chooses either the path of work or of renunciation, purity of the mind and control over one's thoughts, are important. In other words, outward manifestations of one's convictions are good but unless the mind and body are in complete sync with each other it's a job half done.

Salvation can be achieved only when our thoughts and actions are in perfect harmony, and our words, deeds, actions, appearance, thoughts and philosophy of life are subsets of the same narrative. The propensity or inclination for one or another of these may vary from person to person, but ultimately both action and knowledge are essential for both karma yoga and saankhya yoga. It is only their proportion that is at variance and creates an impression of the two paths being completely different from one another.

3.05

न हि कश्चित्क्षणमपि जातु तिष्ठत्यकर्मकृत् ।
कार्यते ह्यवश: कर्म सर्व: प्रकृतिजैर्गुणै: || 5||

3.05: There is no one who can remain without doing something even for a moment. All beings are compelled to act by the qualities born of material nature, the three *gunas*.

Each of us acts by our individual mode of nature (*gunas*) which could be driven by knowledge, passion or ignorance (*sattva, rajas,* and *tamas*).

It is the nature of the physical body to be always active and engaged. We mistakenly believe that activity implies only visible acts such as reading, eating, drinking, sleeping, walking, etc. We also tend to feel that our professional work is the only work we perform. These are only partial realities.

The truth is that nobody can remain inactive for even a moment. When Krishna talks of activity in this verse he refers to something much larger than these tangible physical acts. Since the mind is as much a part of us as any other limb, everything that the mind thinks, voluntarily or involuntarily, also constitutes activity.

And so complete inactivity is never possible. When we are asleep our body may be immobile but continues to work on the inside. The heart beats, food is digested and blood runs through our veins. The mind seems to be at rest but it makes us dream while the body is in slumber.

Till such time as we are alive we are always at work. Thus Krishna declares that for human beings inactivity is an impossible state to be in, since the triangle of the body, mind and intellect is constantly propelled by its own individual inclination towards the three modes of nature to perform work in the world.

3.21

यद्यदाचरति श्रेष्ठस्तत्तदेवेतरो जन: |
स यत्प्रमाणं कुरुते लोकस्तदनुवर्तते || 21||

3.21: Whatever actions a great person performs, the common man follows. Whatever standards they set by performing exemplary acts, the world follows in those footsteps.

Most people feel the need to have a role model. This can be a political leader, a spiritual guru, a mentor, a teacher, a senior, a parent, a celebrity or a historical figure. Human beings are inspired by the ideals that they see in people they admire, and try to emulate these in real life. Role models play an important part in character development and sometimes even in the day-to-day actions of the masses. It is possible that they may also emerge as popular leaders, and eventually wield a lot of power over the minds, and indeed lives, of the masses.

Leaders therefore carry a huge responsibility on their shoulders, and have a moral responsibility to live an impeccable life and inspire others by their words, deeds, and character. When leaders are exemplary in their conduct society naturally looks up to them for setting standards of morality, selfless service, moral courage, and spiritual strength.

If there is a vacuum in the presence of inspirational leadership, then society may experience waywardness, moral bankruptcy, and deflection from the spiritual path. Therefore, leaders are an important cog in the wheel that keeps the moral fibre of social groups or individuals intact on the path of positive growth.

Leaders and change-makers may have personally risen above having to perform mundane tasks, but doing these every now and then helps people identify with them. For instance, when a district magistrate cycles to office, she does it not because she lacks other means of transport, but to set an example to others. This act of actually cycling as compared to delivering a speech on the merits of cycling, is a far more effective way of getting the message across.

In another scenario, when the commander of a military unit leads from the front, he is giving a message to the soldiers to fight fearlessly. On the other hand, if he were to issue the instructions sitting in a safe place, the men may not feel motivated to do their best.

3.25

सक्ता: कर्मण्यविद्वांसो यथा कुर्वन्ति भारत |
कुर्याद्विद्वांस्तथासक्तश्चिकीर्षुर्लोकसंग्रहम् || 25||

3.25: As ignorant people perform their duties with attachment to the results, O scion of Bharata, the wise must similarly act without attachment, for the sake of leading people on the right path.

Krishna says that one of the duties of those who are wise and learned should be to always act for the benefit of humankind, and to set an inspirational example.

People who are ignorant and have not yet started their spiritual journey tend to perform their duties with an eye on the result. Their service is not selfless, even their charity is not to help someone but to gain a reputation as a philanthropist. They do not perform good deeds for the sake of doing something good, but for what the deed will translate into in material terms. For instance, feeding the poor but making sure your picture, while distributing food, is splashed on social media. Or, lending money to a person in need, not out of compassion but for eventually earning interest on the principle amount.

Krishna explains to Arjuna, that to correct this unfortunate tendency amongst the less evolved people, the learned and wise ones must lead by example. They must perform acts of kindness but not for personal gain. They must be visibly empathetic, compassionate and trustworthy so others can emulate these qualities. The learned must remain constantly engaged with working for humanity, and for humanitarian causes, with no thought of any returns and no attachment or desire to gain name or fame from the deed performed.

Helping those who can return the favour also reeks of ulterior motives, and is not acceptable as a pure deed. The wise and the learned extend unconditional support to anyone in need, including those who are too poor or underprivileged to do anything as quid pro quo.

This is reminiscent of Mahatma Gandhi's words when he said that, when in dilemma while taking decisions, one of must think of how this decision is going to benefit the last man in the queue.

3.38

धूमेनाव्रियते वह्निर्यथादर्शो मलेन च |
यथोल्बेनावृतो गर्भस्तथा तेनेदमावृतम् || 38||

3.38: Just as a fire is covered by smoke, as a mirror is covered by dust, and an embryo is covered by the womb, a living being is similarly covered by desire.

Of all the challenges that human beings face, the ability to overcome desire, or desires, is the toughest. It could be a desire to earn more money no matter how, to gain power to rule over others, or to succumb to lust. Most forms of desire broadly fall under these three driving forces—money, power and lust.

While these distinguish humans from other species and make them superior to other life forms, they are not the only qualities that set them apart. The ability to recognise right and wrong, fair and unfair, just and unjust is also a unique gift humans are blessed with. Unfortunately, this innate ability to discern good from bad is not always put to proper use, and certainly not often enough. So we frequently fail to see what may lie behind an attractive façade, and succumb to inappropriate desire and perform unacceptable deeds.

Krishna illustrates this with three examples.

- Fire, which is the source of light, gets covered by smoke, and we may misjudge its intensity and harm ourselves by venturing too close.
- A mirror which can show us what we really are gets covered by dust, and so we fail to see the reality though we may be face to face with it.
- An embryo is concealed in the womb, and till the child is born we find it difficult to think of it as a human being. Heart-wrenching incidents of foeticide are a case in point.

Similarly, though we know in our heart what is right, we choose not to face it, and instead go by the outward appearance of what is visible to us, and what we want the reality to be. To see through the smoke or dust requires the conviction that we may not have, and the effort which we are not always willing to make.

To justify our disagreeable acts, and to conveniently succumb to avoidable desire, we alter the reality that may prick our conscience, into a version that suits us and helps us legitimise the path we take.

A classic example of this is of an obstinate patient abandoning the doctor whose prescription of drastic change in lifestyle for his well-being doesn't suit him.

3.43

एवं बुद्धेः परं बुद्ध्वा संस्तभ्यात्मानमात्मना |
जहि शत्रुं महाबाहो कामरूपं दुरासदम् || 43||

3.43: Thus knowing the soul to be superior to the material senses, O mighty armed Arjuna, make the mind steady by using intellect, and thus by spiritual strength conquer this formidable, insatiable enemy that is lust.

In this last verse of this chapter which is devoted to karma yoga, Krishna emphasises that we should gain control over this enemy called lust through knowledge of the self.

No matter how much gratification we experience from material acquisitions it shall never be enough, as a material outlook and lust are insatiable—very reminiscent of the legendary monster who needs to be fed constantly. No amount of offerings are enough for this creature whose belly is a dark, bottomless pit, and so his hunger knows no end.

Real, long lasting peace and satisfaction can only be derived from spiritual gains. The longing of the soul and its eternal search for tranquillity, can only be met through attainment of divine bliss.

We must discipline and train the intellect to control the mind and the senses, and focus on the pursuit of the divine.

By exercising self-control, by entertaining no desire for any material outcome, and by overcoming lust and desire, Arjuna must elevate himself to a higher plane, and concentrate on acquiring Ultimate Knowledge.

4

Wisdom in Action and
Transcendental Knowledge

In Chapter Four, Krishna talks of the origin of transcendental knowledge itself and spiritual understanding of the soul. The soul's relationship with God is both purifying and liberating, and is an eternal science that has been passed on through the ages from the origin of Time, and is a continuous tradition.

Krishna now reveals the supreme science of yoga to Arjuna. Unlike ordinary mortals God is unborn and eternal. Yet by the power of yogamaya, the mystic power of yoga that provides material energy, he descends on earth from time to time. The 'Divine Power' appears in a human form with a three-fold purpose which is to

- annihilate the wicked
- protect the pious
- establish dharma

However, his birth and actions while on earth remain above the usual material pursuits that humans are engaged in. Those who truly understand the nature and purpose behind the Supreme Soul taking on a human body are rewarded spiritually,

Those who truly understand the nature and purpose behind the Supreme Soul taking on a human body are rewarded spiritually and thus relieved from the cycle of rebirth.

and thus relieved from the cycle of rebirth. Such people are genuinely detached from the material world and are completely focused on a spiritual existence.

Verse 4.13 touches upon an important aspect of social structure. In the context of active engagement and for the purpose of leading a fulfilling life, Krishna talks of occupation or profession, and the manner in which this must be taken up on the basis of one's capability, interest and aptitude. His articulation of this becomes especially significant, in the light of the fact that he does not mention birth or class as being the criterion, either for selection of occupation or for being assigned a job.

Sadly, as we know the class and caste structure that emerged over the years, was and is, at considerable variance with this logical and thoroughly pragmatic recommendation.

It is disheartening to see how, over the years, aptitude and capability have taken a back seat and, in some sections of society even today, social position is assumed based purely on birth.

The atrocities perpetrated in the name of caste, and the discrimination certain communities have had to live with for centuries, can hardly be justified when viewed from the prism of ability, determining one's occupation in life.

Moving from profession to health, Krishna talks of the ancient practice of *pranayama*. The art and science of yoga gained international recognition and acceptance largely in the twentieth century. We frequently hear the word *pranayama*, especially when health benefits of exercise are being discussed. In this chapter of the *Gita*, Krishna elaborates on *pranayama*, which broadly translated, means control of one's breathing pattern.

Pranayama is a specialised technique in which the breathing process is regulated. Scientifically proven to have positive effects on the overall well being of the human body, *pranayama* is well defined as having many stages of breathing, particular techniques and resultant benefits.

Krishna reiterates that when practised regularly and to perfection, the act of *pranayama* itself is an offering to God and is equivalent to any other sacrifice undertaken to please him. While we all may be aware of the obvious benefits of *pranayama*, for it to be declared an offering to the Almighty indeed sheds new light on this specialised breathing technique.

To achieve perfection and mastery in yoga the following attributes are extremely important. These are:

- accurate knowledge
- purity of thought
- honesty of purpose
- self-control

Chapter Four has the distinction of featuring two consecutive verses that define the purpose of God's appearance on earth in human form.

Whenever there is a decline in righteousness and an increase in unrighteousness, O Arjuna, at that time I manifest myself on earth.

–Verse 4.07

In order to protect the righteous, to annihilate the wicked, and to re-establish the principles of dharma I appear on this earth, era after era.

–Verse 4.08

chapter 4

Jnana Karma Sanyasa Yoga
Yoga as Renunciation of
Action through Knowledge

4.03

स एवायं मया तेऽद्य योग: प्रोक्त: पुरातन: |
भक्तोऽसि मे सखा चेति रहस्यं ह्येतदुत्तमम् || ३||

4.03: The same ancient knowledge of yoga, which is a mystery, I am today revealing unto you, because you are my friend as well as my devotee, who can understand the transcendental wisdom of this science.

Krishna tells Arjuna that he is going to reveal to him that which is a mystery to most. He is doing this, he says, because Arjuna is his friend as well as devotee, but more importantly because he feels that Arjuna will be able to comprehend it.

What Krishna is about to share with him is the ultimate transcendental wisdom that most ordinary mortals are unable to grasp. This wisdom, or yoga, remains little known because most lack the devotion to persevere and understand.

There are several layers to what Krishna is saying and is the basis for acquiring true knowledge. This verse could also be read as a guru–shishya exchange. It is a given that unless the student has the will, perseverance and commitment to learn, he cannot make optimum use of what is being taught to him, no matter how distinguished the teacher.

What is also on display here is the teacher's understanding of the student's capabilities. An able teacher will first gauge the aptitude of her student, and then deliver the lesson at an appropriate level, time and stage. The teachings, or any lesson, whether from a book or in life, can be fully internalised only when the student is ready to learn in a holistic manner, and the desire to augment knowledge is genuine, sincere and comes from deep within.

Also, if the student is a sceptic and does not have faith in the teacher learning remains incomplete. In other words, those who do not have complete faith in the supreme force cannot understand the importance of devotion, and hence their understanding and interpretation of the supreme reality continues to be patchy and vague.

Just as teaching and learning are interdependent and complimentary to each other, so too are devotion and salvation. He who is devoted and focussed will attain salvation, and salvation will come only to those who are ready for it, and are sincere and genuine in their efforts.

4.05

श्रीभगवानुवाच |
बहूनि मे व्यतीतानि जन्मानि तव चार्जुन |
तान्यहं वेद सर्वाणि न त्वं वेत्थ परन्तप || 5||

4.05: The Supreme Lord said: Both you and I have had many births, O Arjuna. You have forgotten them, while I remember them all, O Arjuna, destroyer of the enemy.

Krishna's message is to a larger audience, including the sceptics and non-believers. Addressing Arjuna, Krishna says that both of them have had many births and rebirths, but because Arjuna's soul is ordinary, each birth and its events, get wiped out of its memory when it is reborn and takes on a new body.

Though most of us may have lived through many lives, we have no memory of it. However, the curiosity to know what or who we were in our past lives remains unabated. There exists an entire school of thought, the world over, that believes in, and indeed facilitates, past life regression. There are others who claim to have memory of events of some past life.

Krishna, on the other hand, is Divine, and so in his case the meaning and purpose of many births on earth is different. Whereas Arjuna's soul may have lived through the cycle of many life forms based on his karma in the previous life, the birth of the Divine in human form takes place for a different reason. This is done for a particular purpose—either to deliver some teachings, set an example of an exemplary life by actually living in a human form, or to destroy evil. Several instances of gods and spiritual leaders come to mind here, and each one of us is free to make these connections for ourselves.

To establish a rapport with people and to gain their confidence, it is important to be empathetic and to live life in a manner an ordinary person can identify with. Herein lies the reasoning behind the Divine taking a human form.

To look at an example closer home, Gandhi abandoned the practice of wearing upper class apparel, and took to wearing a simple dhoti not because he could not afford to cover his body with more expensive and elaborate clothes. He did it to express solidarity with the common people of India, and to underline his empathy and understanding of the trials and tribulations of the poor. This put ordinary people at ease as they viewed the Mahatma as one of them.

Thus what Krishna is conveying here is to not take things at face value. What appears in front of our eyes may be simple, but its meaning, implication and purpose may be much deeper, and multi-layered. Two people who may outwardly appear to be leading similar lives may actually be negotiating an inward journey, completely different from one another.

4.06

अजोऽपि सन्नव्ययात्मा भूतानामीश्वरोऽपि सन् ।
प्रकृतिं स्वामधिष्ठाय सम्भवाम्यात्ममायया ॥ 6॥

4.06: Although I am unborn, am the Lord of all living entities, and have an imperishable nature, yet I appear in this world by virtue of yogamaya, my Divine Power.

Krishna divulges to Arjuna that though he is eternal and is the lord, master and creator of all living entities, yet he appears in this world from time to time. This verse sets in motion Krishna's explanation—spilling over to several following verses—of how, when and why he chooses to, or deems it fit to, take human form and live alongside ordinary mortals.

The question, should or does God manifest Himself in a palpable form has many answers. These answers are obviously based on our personal faith, belief, fears and perhaps apprehensions. For some the answer could lie in experiencing the sheer joy of living, and the feeling of being fortunate and blessed.

So why does the Supreme Being appear among ordinary mortals?

Perhaps, because human beings with their limited understanding of the universe and the life forces that might exist, can identify only with those who look like themselves. For instance, in science fiction films, the aliens always have some human-like features—arms, legs, eyes, etc. Though they are made to look quite different because they are supposedly from another planet, interestingly, they are also made to look like us or we as audience will lose interest in the story.

Similarly, to create an understanding of the Divine, it might be important for the Supreme Being to take on a human form to establish a connect with people at large.

Also, most people find it difficult to concentrate on a mere idea or an invisible presence, and need something more tangible to focus on. Many of us may need a role model to show us the way.

And so when Krishna appears as a man he is spreading the message of love, affection and friendship by mingling with ordinary people. He is also living an exemplary life and establishing himself as a role model to be admired and emulated. By finding extraordinary solutions for challenging situations, he is suggesting that there is always a way out and a better way to living life. All one needs is strength of character scaffolded by courage, conviction and commitment.

4.07

यदा यदा हि धर्मस्य ग्लानिर्भवति भारत |
अभ्युत्थानमधर्मस्य तदात्मानं सृजाम्यहम् || 7||

4.07: Whenever there is a decline in righteousness and an increase in unrighteousness, O Arjuna, at that time I manifest myself on earth.

Taking forward the discourse he started in the earlier verse, Krishna contextualises his appearance in the world. The Supreme Being is normally invisible and only the devoted and enlightened can sense His presence, being in possession of refined sensibilities. For the less evolved, in the absence of any palpable symbol, the reality of this sublime and invisible presence is debatable, and so starts to gradually become diluted.

With the passage of time and with degenerate mindsets of an ignorant populace gaining ground, the moral fabric of society begins to decay. Based on a misguided value system, social norms take on decadent dimensions as more and more people become incapable of seeing the larger picture, too preoccupied with wallowing in transactional pleasures.

As the saying goes, a lie can travel halfway round the world while the truth is still putting on its shoes, and so this moral decadence starts to grow exponentially as material pleasures and the lure of money, power and desire attract more into its fold. The downhill journey into abject moral dissolution can only end in disaster, and at this critical juncture corrective action becomes imperative.

It is when humankind is thus precariously placed and hurtling headlong into a bottomless pit of ignominy and infamy, that the

Supreme Power has to descend to salvage the situation. Since Krishna loves all creatures equally, he feels compelled to save the souls of both saints and sinners. Taking human form and mingling with ordinary mortals, living an exemplary life and teaching by example is a more effective way of bringing about a change, as compared to pontificating or remaining an invisible force.

Just as an effective administrator knows when to exercise discipline from behind the scenes, and when to step out and personally restore calm and peace in a disorderly situation, similarly Krishna says that when unrighteousness starts to eclipse righteousness, and evil starts to overtake good, it is time for him to manifest himself and take the required corrective action.

4.08

परित्राणाय साधूनां विनाशाय च दुष्कृताम् |
धर्मसंस्थापनार्थाय सम्भवामि युगे युगे || 8||

4.08: In order to protect the righteous, to annihilate the wicked, and to re-establish the principles of dharma I appear on this earth, era after era.

Krishna tells Arjuna that when unrighteousness starts to eclipse righteousness, and evil starts to overtake good, he manifests himself to take the required corrective action. He now elaborates on the purpose behind this grand manifestation.

The 'Divine Power' appears with a three-fold purpose. These are to

- annihilate the wicked
- protect the pious
- establish dharma

The analogy of an administrator taking steps to maintain law and order, or a teacher ensuring discipline in the classroom make these strategies easy to understand. In a situation where a teacher enters a noisy class where students are shouting, being abusive and the bullies are ridiculing and even physically tormenting the docile ones in the classroom, what will one do?

The first step would be to make one's presence felt, drawing attention to oneself, diffuse any situation where someone is likely to get hurt, and single out the trouble makers and ask them to quieten down or step aside. The teacher will then restore normalcy in the classroom by asking everyone to sit in their designated places, and once there is peace and quiet, will start teaching the lesson for that day.

The above is an extremely simplistic analogy of what Krishna is saying, but is not entirely inappropriate. Taking it forward, it is not hard to imagine what would have happened had the teacher not arrived on time. In all likelihood the ruckus would have increased, the bullies would have brought their victims to their knees, and soon indiscipline would have escalated, possibly spilling over to other classrooms, and eventually turning the entire school into a tumultuous centre for aggression, belligerence and unacceptable behaviour.

Perhaps the worst aspect of not taking corrective action on time would be the bullies establishing themselves as objects of adulation. The docile, on the other hand, would become servile and reduced to thinking that the only way to survive in the pandemonium is to become a part of it. Willingly or unwillingly, abandoning their own better sense and judgement, they would eventually accept the brutal authority of the miscreants.

Similarly, when evil is on the verge of destroying the good, Krishna says he thinks it appropriate to appear in the world to first punish and annihilate the unrighteous, to protect the righteous, and once this is accomplished, to restore and establish the principles of dharma, or order.

4.09 & 4.10

जन्म कर्म च मे दिव्यमेवं यो वेत्ति तत्त्वत: |
त्यक्त्वा देहं पुनर्जन्म नैति मामेति सोऽर्जुन || 9||
वीतरागभयक्रोधा मन्मया मामुपाश्रिता: |
बहवो ज्ञानतपसा पूता मद्भावमागता: || 10||

4.09: Those who understand the divine nature of my appearance and activities, O Arjuna, upon leaving the body, do not have to take birth again, but come to my eternal abode.

4.10: Being freed from attachment, fear, and anger, being fully absorbed in me, and taking refuge in me, many persons in the past have become purified by knowledge of me, and thus they have attained my transcendental love.

Krishna's thoughts are in a flow here. Earlier, he divulges to Arjuna that though he is eternal and is the Lord, Master and Creator of all living entities yet he appears in this world from time to time (verse 4.06). Taking forward the discourse he started in the previous verse he contextualises his appearance in the world (verse 4.07).

Continuing from the previous verse where Krishna tells Arjuna that when unrighteousness starts to eclipse righteousness, and evil starts to overtake good, he manifests himself to take the required corrective action (verse 4.08). He appears in this world to annihilate the wicked, protect the pious, and establish dharma.

Now Krishna goes on to explain to Arjuna what happens to those who are seeped in pure devotion of the Lord. They comprehend the divine nature of his appearances in the world when he takes on new avatars and also understand and identify with the purpose behind these manifestations. Such individuals who have a holistic understanding of these actions and activities of the Supreme Being find the doors of his eternal abode open to them. When it is time to leave their mortal bodies, they seamlessly go through these elusive doors to be with the Lord for eternity, and are relieved from the rigorous cycle of rebirth, and thus spared the trials and tribulations of living on this earth.

The enlightened ones who have freed themselves of the clutches of attachment, fear and anger, having turned their focus on the Lord, have become purified in this life itself. Thus, owing to their well-directed daily actions, and by consistently walking on the spiritual path they attain the transcendental love and affection of the Lord.

In a nutshell, first and foremost, it is important to be in control of ourselves and live an exemplary life. Attachment to worldly pleasures and possessions and allowing desire, anger, fear, etc. to rule our minds and actions must be abandoned. Attachment leads to both fear and anger—apprehension of not getting what we are attached to leads to fear, and finding any obstruction in the way of reaching the desired object makes us angry. Thus attachment is at the root cause of an undesirable state of mind and actions, and contributes to making us lose our discerning power.

In addition to the reasons that Krishna cites here for his appearance there is another one (verse 3.21) Most people feel the need to have a role model. This can be a political leader, a spiritual guru, a mentor, a teacher, a senior, a parent, a celebrity or a historical figure. Human beings are inspired by the ideals that they see in the people they admire, and try to emulate these in real life.

By appearing in human form Krishna is providing human beings with a live role model they can emulate. Those who do this and optimise on the opportunity of being shown the path to salvation, eventually reach the eternal abode, and are no longer part of the tedious cycle of rebirth.

4.13

चातुर्वर्ण्यं मया सृष्टं गुणकर्मविभागशः |
तस्य कर्तारमपि मां विद्ध्यकर्तारमव्ययम् || 13||

4.13: According to the qualities and activities of people, the four categories of occupations were created by me. Although I am the creator of this system, you should know that being unchangeable, I am still the non-doer.

In the earlier verses, Krishna stresses on the need for controlling one's desires to attain salvation. Talking about the human species and its need to discipline itself, Krishna now touches upon other human qualities, aptitude and engagements that should keep people occupied through their lifetimes. Each one of us is born with a set of qualities that determines the course of our lives. While the Lord has put this system in place for human beings, he Himself is above it. The term 'non-doer' used here does not imply a passive state of inactivity but rather a chosen exclusion from the framework designed for human beings.

Every society, country, and even city is a balanced mix of people pursuing different occupations. It is impossible to even imagine a set up where everyone is a doctor, or a town full of only engineers, or a country comprising only poets and writers. Having said that, people of similar professions tend to socialise more with one another, and might even end up living in close proximity of each other. This is a natural societal progression, and these close associations may at some point of time result in marriages among the offspring. In due course, this group that originally started out as like-minded professionals may come to view themselves as an exclusive community.

Be that as it may, every society necessarily requires its people to engage themselves differently in order to make up a composite social and economic unit. Which brings one to the question of who does what? And who will decide this?

Let's take the example of a school. In a utopian situation, how are children selected for say, sports, dramatics, elocution or debate? Clearly, on the basis of each one's talent and aptitude. No right-minded principal would select a basketball champion to play a theatrical character on stage. Or pick a child good at recitation to score a goal in hockey. When and if a selection is made based on any extraneous considerations other than talent—as in a child's parentage or her family's social position, etc.—outcomes of the activities in question are going to be adversely affected.

It is well known that in olden times, prior to the evolution of the monarchical system where the eldest son became the accepted successor, heads of kingdoms were chosen on the basis of merit and capability, and not family lineage. Over time, as personal ambition gained ground merit was eventually compromised. Each ruler's desire to see his own son succeed him on the throne, made capability a non-essential requirement for royal succession. This tendency gradually became the trend down the social ladder. When talking of occupation, Krishna's focus is entirely on personal qualities. Nowhere are the words class or birth mentioned. There is no ambiguity here in Krishna's discourse when he says that each person is blessed with different qualities or capabilities, and must remain engaged in an occupation that is commensurate with these. Every society has an inherent need for its people to follow different professions. This is essential to keep the system running, and to provide a balance in various professional arena. It appears that in Vedic times selection for a particular role may have been made based on aptitude, but the system eventually gave way under the weight of personal ambition.

Love for one's flesh and blood, considerations of economic positioning, the desire to create and maintain a superior identity, ultimately gave way to the evolution of a class and caste structure. The learned became possessive of their knowledge, the physically strong took pride in owning land and did not believe in sharing, while the ones blessed with sharp business sense filled their coffers with wealth. Those who worked with their hands and performed essential tasks to keep life going came to be held with misplaced contempt.

This arrangement suited the upper classes well, and they ensured that the manual workers made no progress at all and remained where they were, at the end of the food chain. As they say, one way of appearing superior yourself is to make someone else look inferior.

The abhorred caste system, as we know it today, divides society into four broad classes solely on the basis of birth. Clearly, this social curse that continues to destroy the fabric of our society even in the twenty first century is a later manmade construct.

It is also abundantly clear from the context of *Mahabharata* that by the time this saga played out, the heirarchy of caste had become well established. The idea of four broad categories of occupation which were to be adhered to on the basis of aptitude had long given way to considerations of birth and parentage.

So then knowing all this, can it be that Krishna is here reminding us of the original purpose of the four categorisations and the manner in which occupation was to be selected?

Could this also be one of the reasons for which he has taken birth in human form? To articulate a reminder of the original purpose at a critical juncture?

Could this be the reason why Krishna—using divine will— chooses to be brought up by foster parents who are themselves not upper caste?

Could there be an underlying message in the fact that the one who can cast a spell on two mighty armies and make time stand still, was brought up in humble, rustic surroundings, and had not received exclusive schooling from learned gurus?

4.29 & 4.30

अपाने जुह्वति प्राणं प्राणेऽपानं तथापरे |
प्राणापानगती रुद्ध्वा प्राणायामपरायणा: || 29||
अपरे नियताहारा: प्राणान्प्राणेषु जुह्वति |
सर्वेऽप्येते यज्ञविदो यज्ञक्षपितकल्मषा: || 30||

4.29 & 4.30: Still others offer as sacrifice the exhaled breath in the inhaled breath, while some merge the inhaled breath into the exhaled breath. Some arduously practise *pranayama* and restrain the inhaled and exhaled breaths, and remain purely absorbed in the regulation of the life-giving breaths. Yet others curtail their food intake and offer the breath into the life-energy as sacrifice. All those knowledgeable of the purpose of performing sacrifice are cleansed of their impurities as a result of such performances.

Talking of various ways in which individuals can discipline their lifestyles and exercise self-control, in the previous verse (4.28) Krishna mentions detachment from earthly possessions, practising yoga and studying the *Vedas*. These three contribute to finding the correct path to ultimate transcendental knowledge.

He now elaborates on *pranayama*, which translated broadly means control of one's breathing. *Pranayama* is a specialised technique in which the breathing process is regulated and is well defined as having many stages.

- the process of drawing breath into the lungs.
- the process of emptying the lungs of accumulated breath.
- holding the breath in the lungs after inhalation. The breath to be exhaled remains suspended during this period.
- keeping the lungs empty after exhalation. The act of inhalation remains postponed during this period.

The duration between inhalation and exhalation and vice versa is a test of our ability to remain without breathing for a certain length of time. As breathing is directly linked to the body being alive, in this intermittent period we condition our body to this technique. Simultaneously we also make an offering of this specific period of sacrifice to the Lord as a form of yoga.

Those who are inclined toward the practice of *pranayama* utilise this process of breath control to master the senses, training the mind to focus. As they gain mastery over the senses and the mind sharpens with practise, they find it easier to meditate for long periods of time, and subsequently walk on a spiritual path.

Another way of exercising self-control is by fasting. Diet has an effect on our behaviour and can motivate people to indulge in otherwise avoidable activities, for instance, gluttony, obsession with food, making eating the sole purpose of living etc.

It is important to understand and remind ourselves that while food is essential for us to remain alive, healthy and active, it cannot be the only driving force of life. Food and eating are merely a means to, and not an end, and looking at these in the right perspective is what sets us apart from other life forms.

As humans we must be able to discern between eating to live and living to eat, and set ourselves some higher goals in life. Thus fasting is an exercise in self-control, where unlike animals, we let our mind decide our behaviour vis-à-vis food, and not allow our senses to drive us to gluttony, and mindless calorie consumption.

4.37 & 4.38

यथैधांसि समिद्धोऽग्निर्भस्मसात्कुरुतेऽर्जुन |
ज्ञानाग्निः सर्वकर्माणि भस्मसात्कुरुते तथा || 37||
न हि ज्ञानेन सदृशं पवित्रमिह विद्यते |
तत्स्वयं योगसंसिद्धः कालेनात्मनि विन्दति || 38||

4.37: As a blazing fire reduces wood to ashes, O Arjuna, so does the fire of knowledge burn to ashes all reactions to material activities.

4.38: In this world, there is nothing as sublime and pure as transcendental knowledge. One who has attained purity of the mind through prolonged practise of yoga, in due course of time receives such knowledge within oneself.

Just as a blazing fire reduces to ashes everything that comes in its way, similarly *gyan agni*, the fire of knowledge, burns all desires and attachment to material activities and possessions. The stronger the fire the quicker and final will be the dispensation.

There is nothing stronger, or more pure and unflinching, than knowledge. Just as we light a fire on a cold dark night to give us light and warmth, and keep the fire going by feeding it firewood till the day breaks, similarly we must make efforts to keep enhancing our knowledge and continue learning till we are finally enlightened. Ultimately, knowledge will help us live a life free of attachments, and lead us to salvation.

It is interesting and heartening to note, how in the *Bhagavad Gita,* the quest for knowledge is seen as being a way of life. Simply by remaining on the path of learning we are constantly reducing the distance between ourselves and the Eternal Abode. Pursuit of gyan or knowledge is recommended as being at par, or indeed superior, to rituals and renunciation.

Krishna goes on to say that there is nothing as pure and sublime as knowledge. However, just acquiring knowledge is insufficient. All that is learned in theory, must also be applied in practice. It is only when knowledge is shared and applied that it becomes pristine and sublime. Divine knowledge will ultimately be attained by keeping the mind pure, living a disciplined life, practising yoga, and seeking gyan.

As knowledge has no boundaries, applying oneself to learning new skills or improving upon existing skills, creating something new, keeping oneself updated, all fall under the ambit of knowledge. Learning can be in any field, at any level and for any length of time. There are no full stops in the path of learning, as gyan is infinite and all-pervading. No pursuit of knowledge is ever wasted, and sooner or later the time and effort spent on it, stands us in good stead.

5

Rejuvenation in Renunciation

Now that Arjuna is beginning to come out of his distress he is becoming increasingly engaged in the knowledge being shared by Krishna. Indeed, his desire to know more and to understand fully what is being said, now seems insatiable.

Well immersed in Krishna's discourse and successfully going with its flow Arjuna has by now been exposed to several aspects of life and afterlife, as well as the possibility of adopting different spiritual paths while on this earth.

In the fourth chapter, the principle of karma sanyas, was introduced. This means renouncing ritualistic duties and social obligations, and remaining engaged in devotional work.

While performing one's duty is essential as it takes the mind to an exalted level, for a karma sanyasi who is already in an exalted state, however, there is no compulsion to perform social duties.

The fifth chapter opens with Arjuna seeking

... there are two ways of attaining nirvana. One is to continue doing work but with no desire for any personal gain in return, i.e., karma yoga. The other is indicative of those who are wise, have acquired transcendental bliss and have risen above looking for peace and contentment in mere material pursuits. Such persons are said to be practising karma sanyas as they eventually abandon day-to-day duties

a clarification. Krishna has at one point suggested renunciation of work. Simultaneously, he also endorses doing work with devotion. As this sounds like a contradiction in terms, Arjuna requests his mentor to explain his words in greater detail.

Once understood clearly, this supposed ambiguity simply means there are two ways of attaining nirvana. One is to continue doing work but with no desire for any personal gain in return, i.e., karma yoga. The other is indicative of those who are wise, have acquired transcendental bliss and have risen above looking for peace and contentment in mere material pursuits. Such persons are said to be practising karma sanyas as they eventually abandon day-to-day duties.

While clarifying Arjuna's doubts Krishna once again elaborates on the following.

- Karma yoga—work in devotion
- Karma sanyas—renunciation of actions
- Power of meditation
- Social obligations
- Familial duties
- Pitfalls of ignorance
- Finding the right path through knowledge
- *Pranayama*—controlled breathing

Krishna clearly states that working with complete devotion i.e. karma yoga is superior to karma sanyas yoga. Discharging one's duties selflessly, and with utmost sincerity is the most noble way of living one's life.

The lotus flower is a frequently used example—both in poetry and philosophy—of how one can preserve one's character and purity despite being surrounded by filth. The lotus plant is native to Asia and flourishes in a wide range of climates. It is an aquatic perennial that has its roots firmly in the mud, and is known to grow in stagnant, dirty water, and seems to thrive on algae and weeds.

Magically, the plant produces exotic flowers that are in complete contrast to the place where they bloom. Not only are the flowers of exceptional beauty, the leaves are unique too. Characterised by their smooth texture, the leaves always remain afloat. Constantly drawing sustenance from putrid ponds the leaves keep themselves clean and immaculate.

Interestingly, even if drops of water settle on lotus foliage the large round plate-like leaves are clean and dry always. By sheer willpower the leaves seem to ensure that the water slides off their smooth exterior sooner rather than later, leaving behind a pristine, unsullied surface.

Asian scriptures make abundant use of the lotus imagery. Based on its exceptional beauty, purity, and inherent individuality, the lotus has acquired a revered position amongst the flora and fauna in spiritual texts.

Here Krishna uses the lotus leaf as an illustration of his ideas. The leaf is a case in point of how those who engaged in selfless work remain pure, and untouched by the glamour of material returns.

The spirit of karma yoga is beautifully captured in the verse below:
One who performs his duty without attachment, dedicating his actions to God, remains untouched by sin, just as a lotus leaf remains unaffected by water.

—Verse 5.10

chapter 5

Karma-Sanyasa Yoga
Yoga as Renunciation

5.02

श्रीभगवानुवाच |
संन्यास: कर्मयोगश्च नि:श्रेयसकरावुभौ |
तयोस्तु कर्मसंन्यासात्कर्मयोगो विशिष्यते || 2||

5.02: The Supreme Lord said: Both, renunciation of actions, and working with devotion, lead to the path of liberation. But working with devotion is better than renunciation of actions.

Counselling a visibly agitated Arjuna, Krishna pulls him out of the well of despair gently bringing him back to his normal, composed state. Patience is one of the many remarkable qualities that Krishna manifests. Like a good teacher, genuinely invested in his student, Krishna is a picture of patience and understanding, and takes pains to answer each one of Arjuna's queries.

Earlier, explaining to him the futility of grieving for the dead as the soul is immortal, Krishna reminds Arjuna to do his karma, or duty, which in his case was to fight and decimate the enemy. He also encourages Arjuna to dedicate the outcome of his actions to God, as this would make him a true karma yogi.

A person engaged in karma yoga—a karma yogi—performs both spiritual and social duties. While the body is involved in fulfilling social and familial obligations, the mind remains engaged with the higher reality.

On the other hand, once an exalted spiritual platform has been reached, an individual earns the status of a karma sanyasi. Such a person lets go of all social expectations and remains completely devoted in the service of God. Karma sanyasis do not perceive themselves as a physical body, and only pander to the elevation of their soul to the next level, relieving themselves of all social duties.

Krishna's simultaneous praise of both karma sanyas (renunciation of all work) and karma yoga (work performed in devotion) sounds paradoxical to Arjuna. Is it possible to perform both? Is one expected to do both? If yes, then how?

Arjuna now seeks a clarification on what he views as an ambiguity and requests Krishna to specify which of the two is superior.

Contrary to expectation, Krishna here declares categorically that karma yoga is recommended over karma sanyas. Both paths lead to the same destination but persons who continue to fulfil social obligations with no desire for reward or recognition, and also move forward on a spiritual journey, are actually adopting the tougher option.

Managing a balancing act between the social and the spiritual can be a constant challenge. But then the higher one climbs a mountian, the more exhilarating is the view.

Those who don the appearance of a sadhu or a godman are not necessarily superior individuals. They could be charlatans at heart and may have chosen this life as an easy way out of responsibilities. Escapism should never be mistaken for spiritualism.

It only makes a mockery of a commitment that should come out of true devotion. Fake or half-baked spiritualism also puts the genuine karma sanyasis in a poor light, doing a great disservice to a way of life that could actually lead to salvation.

5.04

साङ्ख्ययोगौ पृथग्बाला: प्रवदन्ति न पण्डिता: |
एकमप्यास्थित: सम्यगुभयोर्विन्दते फलम् || 4||

5.04: Only the ignorant speak of renunciation of actions, and work in devotion as different. Those who are truly learned say that by applying oneself to any of these paths, one can achieve the results of both.

Krishna elaborates on a significant aspect of devotion here, one that is especially relevant today for each one of us engaged in busy professional lives, and feel that there is no time to get involved with more spiritual activities.

It is generally believed that those who have renounced worldly attachments, moved away from family, given up all wealth, and maybe even taken on the appearance of a hermit, are the people close to God, and the ones who will attain moksha. These are *saankhya* yogis who choose to remain involved in meditation etc., and have adopted karma sanyas, i.e., a decision to live in seclusion and not perform any duties expected of them in a given social order.

The karma yogis on the other hand, perform every duty assigned to them, or is expected of them with complete devotion. These duties can be those of a professional at the workplace, a parent, a friend, or any other. Each role that one plays comes with a set of principles and duties, and a karma yogi performs each of them with sincerity, honesty and devotion expecting nothing in return. To do your work for the sake of doing it, and to do it to the best of your ability, expecting no gratification in return, is the hallmark of a karma yogi.

Explaining what takes us closer to the Supreme Power, Krishna says that it is only ignorant people who think of saankhya yoga and karma yoga as distinct from one another. The wise know that though outwardly they may appear to be different, these are actually closely intertwined. The one who only prays and meditates must do it as selfless duty or karma, while the one who performs worldly duties must do it as *saankhya*, or with complete devotion. If work sincerely done can substitute worship, then worship must also be done as diligently and honestly as work. Innumerable charlatans who dupe sincere believers in the garb of being holy men and women come to mind here.

Thus neither of the two is superior to another, these are simply two different routes taking us to the same destination. A strong sense of duty, devotion and selfless living are the essential ingredients of both as they are two sides of the same coin. By following either sincerely, one gains the advantages of both. Just like when you hold a coin in your palm, no matter which side of the coin you are facing, when you close your fist the coin is yours.

5.10

ब्रह्मण्याधाय कर्माणि सङ्गं त्यक्त्वा करोति यः |
लिप्यते न स पापेन पद्मपत्रमिवाम्भसा || 10||

5.10: One who performs his duty without attachment, dedicating his actions to God, remains untouched by sin, just as a lotus leaf remains unaffected by water.

Karma yoga, or performing one's duty without any desire for the fruits, is a recurring theme right through the conversation between Arjuna and Krishna. Right from Chapter Two till the last chapter the merits of karma yoga are reiterated.

The one obvious reason for doing this is to reinforce this form of yoga as being dear to the Supreme Power. And the other could be based on the common understanding that most people, no matter how devout they are at heart, must work to make a living. This is also instrumental in keeping the world going, and essential for society to build on gains made over generations, and evolve to the next level.

Economic activity at all levels is the key to survival of any community. A society where everyone were to renounce the world and retire to the mountains to meditate, would be an extremely skewed one indeed, and cannot be self-sustaining.

Like a good, realistic and practical spiritual leader who realises that meditation on an empty belly cannot last long Krishna, repeatedly talks of karma yoga. Using a beautiful analogy here he says that those who are involved in performing duty minus any agenda, a quid pro quo arrangement, or any expectation, are like the leaf of a lotus plant that always remains above the water it lives in and continues to thrive.

The lotus performs to perfection its natural duty to grow and produce exotic flowers, but never allows the imperfections around it to deflect from its path of duty. Despite all odds, it bears flowers season after season, while remaining in a world brimming with impurities, without allowing itself to be affected by its unclean surroundings.

Similarly, karma yogis, perform their duty without getting unduly attracted to what the world could offer in return for their work. While living in the midst of material activity, immersed in the ongoings of a world driven by ideas of profit making, a karma yogi effortlessly does what has to be done with no digressions, regrets or diversions.

5.27 & 5.28

स्पर्शान्कृत्वा बहिर्बाह्यांश्चक्षुश्चैवान्तरे भ्रुवोः |
प्राणापानौ समौ कृत्वा नासाभ्यन्तरचारिणौ || 27||
यतेन्द्रियमनोबुद्धिर्मुनिर्मोक्षपरायणः |
विगतेच्छाभयक्रोधो यः सदा मुक्त एव सः || 28||

5.27-5.28: Shutting out all thoughts of external satisfaction, with the gaze fixed between the eyebrows, suspending the flow of the inhaled and exhaled breath in the nostrils, and thus controlling the senses, mind, and intellect, the one who becomes free from desire and fear, is certainly liberated.

Krishna initiates a discourse on yoga and its various forms. As yoga is the art (or science, depending on how one chooses to look at it) of controlling the mind and disciplining the body, this discourse has much detailing, spanning several verses that follow.

In this verse, there is a preliminary explanation followed by more detail in the next chapter. Here, Krishna starts with describing how, by moderating the breathing pattern, one can control the mind, and therefore one's thoughts. As a first step it is imperative to cease being vulnerable to sound, touch, form, taste and smell.

Having collected one's thoughts, the next step is to focus between the two eyebrows and concentrate on the tip of the nose with half-closed eyes. Closing the eyes completely may make one drift into sleep, while keeping eyes open will lead to distractions. Therefore a semi-shut state is recommended.

Following this the inhalation of breath must be in harmony with exhalation, until both are done with equal concentration. It is important to allow the breath to remain suspended between inhaling and exhaling, to train the body to live without breathing, and put its resilience to test.

Those who can practise this yoga to perfection enter into a state of yogic trance. Detached from sensory gratification, they simultaneously master their breathing. Moving away from having material energy as the only focus, they evolve to an exalted spiritual level. Such people attain liberation from the humdrum of a mundane life, which routinely revolves around mediocre goals and average achievements.

ত

Self-restraint and Meditation

Continuing the comparison between karma yoga, which is practising spirituality while continuing to perform worldly duties, and karma sanyas yoga, which is practising spirituality while living a life of renunciation, Krishna clearly recommends karma yoga.

Meditation need not always mean isolating oneself in a quiet corner and chanting mantras. Any task performed with sincere devotion in a selfless manner is also meditation.

Those who remain engaged in their work, while also experiencing complete detachment are in a state of complete meditation. Meditation need not always mean isolating oneself in a quiet corner and chanting mantras. Any task performed with sincere devotion, in a selfless manner, is also meditation. This can be gardening, being a caregiver, creating music, etc.

The mind is the most valuable possession of human beings. It sets us apart from other living creatures, helps us improve our lives, supports us in the process of evolution, and it makes us unique even among the human race. Because no two people think identical thoughts all the time.

Being the powerful tool that it is, the mind governs our existence and is largely responsible for the quality of the lives we lead. It can be used to help one attain success or it can take one to the depths of failure. To get the most out of life it is critical to learn to use the mind to its optimal level. In short, the mind is the key to success.

Eventually any form of mediation is an exercise of controlling the mind and focussing. Anyone who can achieve this single-minded focus while engaged in any activity is a yogi. Once the mind has been disciplined, then gaining control of the senses is a simple next step.

Krishna touches upon the following in this chapter:

- conquering the mind
- mind—the best friend and the worst enemy
- knowledge—its acquisition and application
- mastering equanimity and impartiality
- being non-judgemental and neutral
- the perils of gluttony and insomnia
- self-discipline
- channelising energies for self-improvement
- qualities of a yogi—consciousness merged with the divine, seeing God in everything, united with God despite being engaged in day-to-day activities
- the fate of the unsuccessful yogi

Most of the points here are along expected lines, but one stands out for its apparent connect, more to the body than the mind: gluttony and insomnia.

Gluttony has many masters. Eating while celebrating, eating when depressed, eating in company, eating when alone, eating for the sake of eating—a glutton finds a reason to gorge on food. Other than the obvious adverse effects on physical health, this is a clear sign of complete lack of control of the mind.

Insomnia, unless diagnosed as a physical condition, has its roots in a troubled mind. It thrives on a mind that is tormented, perturbed, agitated and restless. A calm ventilated mind can go a long way in affording good sleep for the body.

The last idea too, the fate of the unsuccessful yogi, may be of interest to many, as most of us, at some point or the other, undertake vows, take up new year resolutions, make promises to ourselves and to loved ones, but are unable to see these through or sustain the change permanently. And this could well happen even in situations where our intentions were sincere and honest to start with.

Similarly, Arjuna asks, what is the fate of those whose spiritual journey gets interrupted and remains incomplete? There could be many reasons for a spiritual sojourn being cut short, some beyond an individual's control.

Krishna reassures him that no effort ever goes waste. Any amount of time and labour spent on an endeavour becomes part of our personality and enhances it. It also adds to our good karma and bears positive results sooner or later.

Therefore, the fear of failure or non-completion of a task must not deter us from starting work on a project. Apprehension of not reaching the destination must not deter one from initiating the journey.

As a leitmotif of Krishna's advice of conquering our thought processes, the following imagery of a lone leaf calmly floating in troubled waters, leaves a lasting impression.

For those who have conquered the mind, the mind is their best friend. For those who have failed to do so, the mind remains the greatest enemy.

—Verse 6.06

chapter 6

Dhyana Yoga
Yoga as Meditation

6. 06–6. 09

बन्धुरात्मात्मनस्तस्य येनात्मैवात्मना जितः |
अनात्मनस्तु शत्रुत्वे वर्ते तात्मैव शत्रुवत् || 6||
जितात्मनः प्रशान्तस्य परमात्मा समाहितः |
शीतोष्णसुखदुःखेषु तथा मानापमानयोः || 7||
ज्ञानविज्ञानतृप्तात्मा कूटस्थो विजितेन्द्रियः |
युक्त इत्युच्यते योगी समलोष्टाश्मकाञ्चनः || 8||
सुहृन्मित्रार्युदासीनमध्यस्थद्वेष्यबन्धुषु |
साधुष्वपि च पापेषु समबुद्धिर्विशिष्यते || 9||

6.06: For those who have conquered the mind, it is their best friend. For those who have failed to do so, the mind remains the greatest enemy.

6.07: For the yogis who have conquered the mind, cold and heat, joy and sorrow, honour and dishonour are all the same. Such yogis find peace, and are constant in their devotion to the Supreme Soul.

6.08: The yogi who has both acquired knowledge and realised the same, and has conquered the senses, remains in control in all circumstances. For such a person dirt, stones, and gold, are all the same.

6.09: The yogi looks upon all, well-wishers, friends, foes, the pious and the sinners, with equal equanimity. The yogi who takes an impartial view of friend, companion and foe, remains neutral among enemies and relatives, and non-judgemental between the righteous and sinful, is considered to be distinguished among humans.

In these four verses Krishna elaborates on the qualities of a yogi. The purpose of practising yoga is to control the mind. Till such time as we conquer our mind we shall be dictated by lust, anger, illusion, envy, avarice and greed. These affect our judgement and lead to inappropriate actions, resulting in hatred, tension, stress, anxiety and depression. A mind driven by these forces is troubled, restless and makes a person weak and irresolute. Such an uncontrolled mind is one's greatest enemy.

On the other hand, a calm and peaceful mind is a source of constant strength, helping us take correct decisions, and walk the right path. A controlled mind is thus our best friend and guide. We are the ones to decide how we want our mind to evolve—as our best friend or our worst enemy. Whatever choice we make, we cannot escape its outcomes, as our mind is always active and determines the way we live our life.

Yogis who have truly conquered the mind are not unduly affected by either ordinary or extreme situations. They experience cold and heat, joy and sorrow with equal ease. What is viewed as honour and dishonour in human terms fails to perturb them. The yogi who conquers the mind is able to see these earthly perceptions as an outcome of the bodily senses. As he has completely expelled these from his consciousness and focusses only on well-being of the immortal soul, he remains unmoved by them. Such an evolved yogi is determined to reach his ultimate destination, and unwavering, continues walking on the chosen path.

A yogi who has acquired knowledge and then applied it to himself begins to see everything in relation to God. Equipped with wisdom he understands that material energy is hollow and eventually infructuous. And so neither does gold lure him nor does dirt repulse him. Confronted with precious gems or a mere stone, he views both with equal calm and dignity. As the yogi is in possession of gyan, or knowledge, these objects have no value for him and the only aspiration he may entertain would be the next higher level of learning, leading to Ultimate Knowledge.

The evolved yogi is able to see all living beings with equality of vision, and more importantly sees God in everything and everyone. Every living entity, be it friend, companion, enemy or adversary, a yogi can deal with all with equanimity. Surrounded by the righteous or the unrighteous, the ethical or the unethical, a yogi can see them all as God's creation, and thus none is shunned, rejected or favoured.

Thus a person who is non-judgemental, nonplussed, balanced and consistently maintains equanimity is a true yogi. Such a yogi who has attained exalted levels of knowledge, applied the knowledge appropriately, and has put it to good use, is a distinguished individual.

Anyone who can gain mastery over all of these while living in a materialistic world is certain to attract the attention, and receive the affections of the Supreme Lord. It is this level of calm, clarity and composure that every human being must strive for, and make all efforts to accomplish.

6. 16, 6. 17 & 6. 18

नात्यश्नतस्तु योगोऽस्ति न चैकान्तमनश्नतः |
न चाति स्वप्नशीलस्य जाग्रतो नैव चार्जुन || 16||
युक्ताहारविहारस्य युक्तचेष्टस्य कर्मसु |
युक्तस्वप्नावबोधस्य योगो भवति दुःखहा || 17||
यदा विनियतं चित्तमात्मन्येवावतिष्ठते |
निःस्पृहः सर्वकामेभ्यो युक्त इत्युच्यते तदा || 18||

6. 16: O Arjuna, those who eat too much or eat too little, sleep too much or too little, cannot attain success in yoga.

6. 17: But those who can regulate eating and recreation, be balanced in work, and disciplined in sleep, can conquer all sorrows by practising yoga.

6. 18: With all round discipline, they learn to withdraw the mind from sensory cravings and channelise energies on the improvement of the self. Such persons are said to be in yoga, and are free from all yearning of the senses.

After describing the objectives of meditation and the purpose behind it, Krishna now goes on to articulate some do's and dont's to be adhered to, for finding the perfect balance. He says that those who do not maintain their bodies well cannot be successful in yoga.

Even though it is the soul that needs to be nurtured for its eventual journey, the soul resides in the human form, and hence it is equally important to take care of the body. It is only when someone inhabits a clean house that the person can live a healthy and complete life. On the other hand, no matter how pure one may be on the inside, a person living in filth and squalor is unlikely to either receive or relay positive energy.

The *Vedas* lay great emphasis on the maintenance of physical health and hygiene. Krishna says that extreme of anything is not recommended, and any extreme behaviour or practice is an impediment to yoga. Excessive eating can be as self-defeating as not eating enough. It is imperative to striking the right balance of eating, sleeping and work. Eating nutritious food, getting good sleep, exercising the body, will all contribute to productivity and equanimity. If any of these is ignored or excessively pandered to, the balance will be lost and chances of attaining any degree of yogic expertise will be endangered. Vedic dictums lay special emphasis on yogasan, *pranayama* and the importance of light, nutritious diet.

The opposite of yoga is *bhog*. As opposed to a yogi, a *bhogi* is one who indulges in sensual pleasures, and has no self-control. Such individuals eventually succumb and become victims of *rog*, i.e., disease. If the body is diseased it can no longer practise yoga and this diminishes its chances of attaining the ultimate blissful state of mind.

When an individual is in complete control of his mind, channelizes all energies towards improving oneself, weans himself away from cravings and desires with single-minded focus on God, it can be said that he has successfully mastered the practice of yoga.

6. 29, 6. 30 & 6. 31

सर्वभूतस्थमात्मानं सर्वभूतानि चात्मनि |
ईक्षते योगयुक्तात्मा सर्वत्र समदर्शनः || 29||
यो मां पश्यति सर्वत्र सर्वं च मयि पश्यति |
तस्याहं न प्रणश्यामि स च मे न प्रणश्यति || 30||
सर्वभूतस्थितं यो मां भजत्येकत्वमास्थितः |
सर्वथा वर्तमानोऽपि स योगी मयि वर्तते || 31||

6. 29: The true yogis, having united their consciousness with God, see equally, all living beings in God, and God in all living beings.

6. 30: For those who see me everywhere and see all things in me, I am never lost, nor are they ever lost to me.

6. 31: The yogi who is established in union with me, and worships me as the Supreme Soul residing in all beings, dwells only in me, in spite of being engaged in all kinds of activities.

Those who have perfected yoga are referred to as yogis. Having merged their consciousness with that of the Supreme Power they become like the sun, giving light to all living beings equally. Just as Mother Nature is impartial and does not differentiate between its children, so does an enlightened yogi view all forms of life equally.

A true yogi perceives a wide horizon and can view and assess situations holistically. As the vision of a yogi expands so does the conviction that God exists everywhere. Krishna here tells Arjuna that he is all-pervading and always present everywhere and in everything.

Those who can sense his presence all around them never lose sight of the Lord, and nor does the Lord lose sight of them. A yogi may continue to be engaged in essential earthly activities, but he remains united with the Supreme Soul, unwavering in his devotion and unflinching in crises.

These maxims may sound simple and uncomplicated (and we've all heard them before) but they are the most difficult to adhere to. Perhaps for some, keeping their mind and body healthy, eating nutritious food, getting good sleep, exercising and maintaining desirable work-life balance may be the easy part. To view each person through the prism of equality may actually be the tougher challenge.

What Sri Krishna is suggesting here is actually the ultimate lesson in modern day concepts of life skills. In these times of continued discrimination and inequality the message here becomes more relevant than ever. However, this may be easier said than done. To have the conviction to

- get rid of notions of class, caste, colour, gender, ethnicity, and disability
- act impartially and be non-judgemental
- react in an unbiased manner
- delete the word prejudice from one's vocabulary and take decisions accordingly, and
- be intolerant of injustice in any form

are guiding principles few can boast of following. The long term challenge is of course of not just embracing these in a transactional manner, but being true to them always, in every situation.

In short, it is only when the idea of basic equality and its real life daily implementation gets integrated into our muscle memory, only then can we say that yoga has been mastered. Till such time as we see the world through uninformed human eyes with an average world view, we remain ordinary mortals.

It is when we evolve into someone who has internalised and indeed acts upon the ideals of social, religious, and cultural equality that we graduate to becoming exalted beings, inching closer to God. With each unbiased act, borne out of genuine belief in and conviction of equality, we find ourselves walking on the path to the desired destination.

6. 41, 6. 42 & 6. 43

प्राप्य पुण्यकृतां लोकानुषित्वा शाश्वती: समा: |
शुचीनां श्रीमतां गेहे योगभ्रष्टोऽभिजायते || 41||
अथवा योगिनामेव कुले भवति धीमताम् |
एतद्धि दुर्लभतरं लोके जन्म यदीदृशम् || 42||
तत्र तं बुद्धिसंयोगं लभते पौर्वदेहिकम् |
यतते च ततो भूय: संसिद्धौ कुरुनन्दन || 43||

6.41–6.42: The unsuccessful yogis, upon death, go to the abodes of the virtuous. After dwelling there for many ages, they are reborn in the earth plane, into a family of pious and prosperous people. Else, if unsuccessful after long practise of yoga, they are born into a family endowed with divine wisdom. Such a birth is difficult to attain in this world.

6. 43: On taking such a birth, O descendant of Kurus, they reawaken the wisdom of their previous lives, and strive even harder towards perfection in yoga.

In a previous verse (6.37) Arjuna asks Krishna, 'What is the fate of the unsuccessful yogi who begins by walking on the right path with all sincerity, but who does not endeavour sufficiently. Eventually failing to gain full control over his thoughts and desires he is unable to reach the goal of yoga in this life?'

To this Krishna responds saying that no effort goes waste. Unsuccessful yogis are divided into two categories:

- those who have drifted after a brief period of practice
- others who have practised yoga for a significant length of time.

The soul of the yogi who quickly deviates from the path and succumbs to *bhog*, i.e., material pleasures, is awarded residence in celestial abodes. These are higher planets where pious souls reside. God, like an indulgent parent, taking into cognisance the days spent in pursuing yoga—however brief that period may have been—gives the fallen yogi a chance to remain immersed in *bhog* in blissful surroundings, and fulfil his desires.

However, the drifted soul soon realises the futility of these activities (*bhog*) and seeing through the transient nature of all, understands that these do not satiate the inner yearning he was initially experiencing. Once the soul is ready with this acceptance it is given another opportunity to complete its spiritual journey and walk on the path leading to permanent bliss.

To facilitate the completion of the spiritual pursuit, these souls are then born into prosperous, well-to-do families. This makes it easy for the soul to accomplish the task it had drifted away from, in an earlier life. Being reborn into a prosperous family is significant because the person does not have to worry about the basic issues of living, does not have to spend all waking hours wondering where the next meal is coming from, or in utilising all positive energy in making both ends meet. Thus a person from a financially comfortable family has enough time and resources to pursue a higher calling. Having lived a life of comfort, and having satiated all material desires, the reborn soul easily switches back to the spiritual path and works towards attaining yogic perfection.

On the other hand, those who have spent considerable time practising yoga but could not reach the desired destination, do not have to spend time learning how to gain control over their senses, as they have already conquered the desire for worldly pleasures.

Pleased with their efforts and supportive of helping them complete their journey the Supreme Lord gives them rebirth in a family endowed with divine wisdom. Being born in a family with a spiritual bent of mind provides its members with an inherent impetus to follow spirituality. Such people have a natural advantage over others on account of the environment they grow up in. Compare this to the life of a family that lives on the streets or is illiterate and homeless. Do such children have the luxury of developing finer instincts towards the arts, the sciences, theology, etc.?

The circumstances, situation, and family of our birth have an important bearing upon the course of our lives. Being born into a wise, evolved family is like being nurtured in a nursery of future philosophers, thinkers, writers, artists etc., and having a headstart over others on the path of spirituality.

From our parents we inherit not just physical characteristics, but also social and moral placement. This can be an advantage or a disadvantage depending on the family one is born into. Thus, the place and family of our birth directly impacts the direction our lives take, and our achievements in life.

In keeping with the law of karma, the spiritual assets gained by the unsuccessful yogi in the previous life bear fruit in the next. Accordingly, those yogis who had traversed quite a distance, and developed and mastered equanimity are not sent to celestial abodes as an intervening grace period prolonging the cycle of birth and rebirth. They are given birth in a spiritually advanced family, to facilitate the continuation of their journey. Such a birth provides natural advantage because educated, evolved parents inculcate divine wisdom in the child right from its birth.

This is what is referred to as *sanskar*, or what a child receives and learns from the environment that it grows up in. These *sanskars* largely determine the path one adopts in life, and subsequent successes or failures while negotiating the complex journey of life.

The above explains Arjuna's question in great detail. We see here that God is watchful and just. Whatever spiritual assets we have accumulated in a past life—self-control, detachment, wisdom, devotion, faith, tolerance, determination, etc. are all known to him and taken into account. At the appropriate time, we receive the fruits of our past efforts. We sometimes see materialistic individuals suddenly turning deeply spiritual. When spiritual *sanskars* awaken within, they get the benefit of their *sadhana* of previous lives.

If on a long journey we stop and take a break, it does not mean that we have to start from the point of origin all over again. Our journey is temporarily discontinued and then we move again to cover the remaining distance.

Similarly, the deeds of our past lives are our assets, that shorten the journey in the present life as we build on what we had started in an earlier life. Therefore, no work done in any life is ever wasted or unaccounted for.

ॐ

Knowledge, Judgement
and Discernment

The seventh chapter, which is also the beginning of the second segment of the *Gita* describing the glories of bhakti, i.e., devotion, Krishna reveals himself as the origin of all material and spiritual energy. But his material and spiritual dimensions are unique and not driven by traits of goodness, passion or ignorance, as in the case of humans.

Krishna reiterates that he is the origin of the entire creation and it is into him that everything ultimately dissolves. He is present in water, fire, space, sun, moon, earth, and the planets, and rules them all. An acceptance of this presence in the human mind puts into perspective the ancient practice of offering obeisance to Nature.

Even today, trees, rivers and mountains are revered, and indeed worshipped on different occasions. Perhaps the first ever lesson in ecological preservation that has been well learned!

Describing the kind of people who surrender unto him, and those who don't, it is well established that only genuine devotees can arrive at their desired final destination. At some point or the other in life, most of us turn to God for solace. But this brief need-based dalliance does not quite amount to devotion, as it is driven more by apprehension or fear of the unknown.

The ignorant, those who encourage their baser instincts, people with deluded intellect, and those who owe allegiance to evil, do not turn to the Supreme Power.

On the other hand, the knowledgeable, those in pursuit of knowledge, those desirous of material wealth, and the distressed seek to submit themselves to the Supreme Lord. The knowledgeable are aware that the only way of being liberated from old age, death and the endless cycle of rebirth is to tread on the spiritual path.

Krishna also tells Arjuna that

- the Supreme Power is the fulcrum that holds the world together
- only one in thousands can hope to attain perfection
- those who use their intelligence are dear to the Lord and are the closest to him
- those who use their knowledge to make correct judgements and to discern right from wrong are superior to other mortals
- those seeking liberation from old age, disease and death can hope to find it only by choosing the correct spiritual path
- knowledge of the absolute and wisdom acquired from realisation are the twin keys to salvation.

No story can have just a beginning and an end, it is the middle of the narrative that connects the two, and without it the two ends of the spectrum have no purpose. Similarly, if there were to be just creation of the universe immediately followed by annihilation, it would be a meaningless exercise, much like a child building a house with building blocks just to dismantle it as soon as it is done.

> *No story can have just a beginning and an end—it is the middle of the narrative that connects the two, and without it the two ends of the spectrum have no purpose.*

Once created, the universe must grow, thrive and sustain itself. The source of this sustenance is also the Lord himself who ensures that every life, irrespective of its species, is born, lives for a given period of time, and then dies. All stages must be lived through and experienced so as to complete the designated time period in this world. Each of these motions takes place at the will of the creator, who is also the preserver and the annihilator, and without whose will nothing can be born, remain alive or even die.

Most of us might believe the above, but still have to occasionally grapple with the intangible aspect of the Creator. This could partly emanate from the maxim we have been taught since our childhood— seeing is believing.

Being the absolute power and the Ultimate Truth of the entire creation, Krishna seems to be aware of this challenge for ordinary mortals. Putting any doubts to rest he gives an illustration of how the Supreme Power holds the universe in place.

O Arjuna, the conqueror of wealth, there is no truth superior to me. Everything rests upon me, as beads strung on a thread.

–Verse 7.07

chapter 7

Jnana—Vijnana Yoga
Yoga as Knowledge and Judgement

7.03

मनुष्याणां सहस्रेषु कश्चिद्यतति सिद्धये |
यततामपि सिद्धानां कश्चिन्मां वेत्ति तत्त्वतः || 3||

7.03: Out of many thousands among men, one may endeavour for perfection; and among those who have achieved perfection, hardly one knows me in truth.

The chapter starts with Krishna telling Arjuna that by practising yoga and by fully concentrating on the Supreme Power ordinary mortals can transcend to the ultimate level of consciousness.

Of the innumerable souls only a small number is fortunate enough to be born as a human being. Of these, most fritter away their lives engaged in basic activities like eating and sleeping. There may be others who are involved in a higher order of activities but these may not be selfless acts. Thus, very few individuals fully realise the opportunity they have as human beings to attain ultimate consciousness.

Krishna discloses that rarely does anyone attain *siddhi* or spiritual perfection. Neither karma yoga, gyan yoga nor hatha yoga comes to fruition without pure devotion to God. Therefore those who do not include *sadhana* or meditation in their journey are unable to understand the Absolute Truth in full measure.

Krishna has stated in this verse that only one among numerous humans knows Him in totality. This also explains the continuous cycle of birth and rebirth, as the soul is rarely able to merge with the Supreme One and earn respite from this cyclic tedium.

In the next verse, Krishna goes on to describe the material and spiritual dimensions of his energies.

7.07

मत्तः परतरं नान्यत्किञ्चिदस्ति धनञ्जय |
मयि सर्वमिदं प्रोतं सूत्रे मणिगणा इव || 7||

7.07: O Arjuna, the conqueror of wealth, there is no truth superior to me. Everything rests upon me, as beads strung on a thread.

Addressing Arjuna as conqueror of wealth, Krishna discloses that no one is superior to him in the entire universe. Putting to rest any ambiguity or equivocacy, he establishes that he is the Supreme Lord, who is eternal, omniscient, and optimally blissful. He is without beginning and end, he is the origin of all, and it is he who orchestrates all action.

Using the analogy of beads strung on a thread, he says he is the thread that runs through each living being, and nurtures them all, providing strength, balance, comfort and security. While the beads are independent of each other, are free to move in their given place, have their individuality and independent identity, yet they are bound to the thread. Without the thread, the beads, no matter how valuable or precious, fail to make a mark or find a sought after placement. It is the thread that makes the beads come alive and adorn a place of pride.

Just as the beads rest on the thread, the entire creation exists with the Supreme Lord at its core. He is the Creator, the Sustainer, and the Annihilator. Without the Supreme Lord holding the universe together everything will fall apart.

Interestingly, the thread, though critical to the beads' remaining together, and gaining an identity as a necklace, always remains invisible. As a matter of fact if the thread were to be visible the string might be considered a shoddy piece of work!

7.08 (74)

रसोऽहमप्सु कौन्तेय प्रभास्मि शशिसूर्यंयो: |
प्रणव: सर्ववेदेषु शब्द: खे पौरुषं नृषु || 8||

7.08: I am the taste in water, O son of Kunti, and the radiance of the sun and the moon. I am the sacred syllable *Om* in the Vedic mantras; I am the sound in space, and the ability in humans.

In the previous verse, Krishna had said that the way a thread strings pearls together, it is he is who is the sustainer and the basis of all that exists in this world. Now, he continues to explain it further in the following four verses.

Interestingly, Krishna says he is the taste in water. This can be seen at many levels.

- At one level this obviously means he is water itself, and as water is a life-giving element his presence in water is obvious and well understood. But he is saying more—he is the taste in water. What could that mean? Especially as water hardly has any taste of its own.

- One implication, of course is that when we, are really thirsty it is only water that can quench our thirst. No other liquid can do what water can when the thirst is intense. This also means that when an individual's desire for knowledge is genuine and persistent it is only knowledge of the Supreme Power that can satisfy that quest for gyan, or knowledge.

- On another plane this means more. Water has no taste of its own yet other forms of matter, i.e., solids need liquids to carry their taste. For instance, it is impossible to make your favourite drink without water, no food can be cooked without water, and the taste of fruit is brought out by the presence of water in it. Thus nothing can have any taste unless water lends itself to it, to bring out its flavour. Our saliva which helps us discern flavour, also is largely composed of water.

- In other words, our taste buds cannot be satisfied by any food or drink in the absence of water in each of them. All foods—liquid, solid or frozen—are attractive to us and keep us alive because of the presence of water. Just as no aspect of life has any meaning without the presence of God in it.

- Another interpretation is that though water is essential for our existence, we can consume it only in its purest form. For instance, sea water is of no use for drinking, neither is dirty or contaminated water. To have a focus in life is good, but that should be on something clean and pure, and not something that is unclean and impure, and eventually of no real use.
  A thirsty man standing by the sea, might feel good, but the saline water is of no use for quenching his thirst.

Thus, without water, there can be no taste, without water there can be no food, and so without clean and pure water there can be no life.

Krishna goes on to say that he is the light of both the sun and the moon, and also the source and basis of all ability, aptitude and intellect in humans.

Amongst the various sounds, Krishna resides in the sacred Vedic syllable *Om*, which in itself is life-giving and life-sustaining.

Space acts as the vehicle for sound. Though space has no sound of its own it allows sound to form and travel. If sound has no space to travel, it will either not be formed at all or will return (as in an echo chamber).

Thus to make sound possible, Krishna is space itself, and the sound in space is formed by his energy. This in turn allows evolution of languages, music and all forms of sounds that enrich human life. Sound travel allows knowledge to be shared, and taken forward from guru to shishya. It is when the sound of a new born enters our ears that we are reassured that life is born.

7.09–7.11

पुण्यो गन्ध: पृथिव्यां च तेजश्चास्मि विभावसौ |
जीवनं सर्वभूतेषु तपश्चास्मि तपस्विषु || 9||
बीजं मां सर्वभूतानां विद्धि पार्थ सनातनम् |
बुद्धिर्बुद्धिमतामस्मि तेजस्तेजस्विनामहम् || 10||
बलं बलवतां चाहं कामरागविवर्जितम् |
धर्माविरुद्धो भूतेषु कामोऽस्मि भरतर्षभ || 11||

7.09: I am the original fragrance of the Earth, and the brilliance in fire. I am the life-force in all beings, and the penance of the ascetics.

7.10: O son of Pritha, know that I am the original seed of all beings. I am the intelligence of the intelligent, and the prowess of the powerful.

7.11: I am the strength of the strong, devoid of desire and passion. I am all sexual activity not conflicting with virtue or scriptural prescriptions, O best of the Bharatas.

In continuation of the previous verses, Krishna tells Arjuna, that the entire universe originates from him. He is the original fragrance of the earth, and the brilliance and heat in fire is him.

He is the source and the most essential ingredient of everything, and the entire universe is an extension of his opulence and grandeur. On earth, he is the life force behind both the non-living and the living.

He is also the force behind ascetics who deny themselves bodily pleasures and perform austerities for self-improvement and purification. This requires a lot of physical and moral resilience. Krishna says it is he who gives them the energy to sustain themselves on this gruelling path fraught with hardships.

As it is said, every forest grows from a seed. And so when Krishna says that he is the seed of all creation, he is implying that not only has all creation come from him, but it can go forward only because of him. This is not true only of organic growth, it applies elsewhere too. Water is the seed for rain, fire is the seed for warmth, intelligence is the seed for knowledge, and knowledge is the seed for salvation.

In addition to being the seed, Krishna is also intelligence of the mind, and power in the powerful. Those in whom he resides may be more intelligent than an average person, they may be intellectuals. Similarly power, both of the body and of the mind, also emanates from the Supreme Power. Exceptional qualities of head and heart in certain individuals do not happen by accident, but by the largesse bestowed on them by a superior being. He is the subtle force behind the intelligent and the glorious. Those who are humble and wise understand this and acknowledge it saying that they are just the tools chosen by God to produce a brilliant body of work.

Physical desire is a reality for all human beings, and is natural and necessary for the process of procreation. Krishna says that he is very much present in sexual activity too. But this must be performed within societal norms and for the purposes of reproduction. It is an inherent duty and natural desire of all species to procreate to keep one's species alive, and to ensure that the cycle of birth and death remains intact.

The words *kāma-rāga-vivarjitam* here mean devoid of passion and attachment. It is critically important to differentiate between sex performed as a dutiful act, and sex as an outcome of lust. Here passion and indulgence have a larger meaning and stand for indulgence in sexual activity that is driven by lust, resulting in pain, abuse, violence, misogyny, misuse of power and disregard for social structures, and all of these are strongly condemned.

When sexual activity happens for the sake of sensual pleasure alone, it is animal-like and lustful. On the other hand, sex within the institution of marriage, or in some societies and cultures as a statement of pure love and a culmination of that sentiment, finds the Supreme Power himself present in it.

7.15

न मां दुष्कृतिनो मूढा: प्रपद्यन्ते नराधमा: |
माययापहृतज्ञाना आसुरं भावमाश्रिता: || 15||

7.15: Four kinds of people do not surrender unto me—those ignorant of knowledge, those who (follow their basest instincts) and are lowest amongst humankind though capable of knowing me, those with deluded intellect, and those with a demonic nature.

There are four categories of people who do not surrender to God. They are

- the ignorant. These people are devoid of any spiritual knowledge. Their lack of knowledge and desire to learn prevents them from adopting the path of devotion.
- the lazy. These people pander to their baser instincts. They might be aware of what they ought to be doing, but are too lazy to make the effort. Pampering themselves and their earthly desires, they spend their entire lives in a state of inertia and inaction.
- those with deluded intellect. Such people are proud, egoistical, and over confident of their capabilities. They believe themselves to be invincible and too superior to accept a power higher than themselves.
- those with demonic nature. These people are aware of the presence of God but work at cross purposes, as they are consciously inclined towards evil. Their philosophy of life is diametrically opposed to the spiritual path and so they actively engage in activities that belie God's name, and work at misleading the vulnerable.

7.16

चतुर्विधा भजन्ते मां जनाः सुकृतिनोऽर्जुन |
आर्तो जिज्ञासुरर्थार्थी ज्ञानी च भरतर्षभ || 16||

7.16: O great one amongst the Bharatas, four kinds of pious people engage in my devotion—the distressed, the seekers of knowledge, the seekers of material gains, and those who are situated in knowledge.

Krishna now talks of those who take refuge in him. They are:

- the distressed. Often, people turn to God for strength and sustenance when facing challenging situations and when realisation dawns that there are no positive options available anymore. This is the only source that provides courage to the meek, hope to the hopeless, and strength to the weak. This is also the only source that is a great equaliser, available to rich and poor alike.

  There are times when doctors attending on a critical patient ask the family to pray and wish for a miracle. Men of science have been known to pray in certain distressful situations.

- A majority of people, including the sceptics, do turn to God some time or the other in their lifetimes. How long this devotion lasts, whether it becomes a lifelong engagement, or is transactional in nature, differs from person to person.

  Seekers of knowledge. Some follow the godly path out of curiosity and their inquisitiveness to know more about this invisible power. Hearing of the solace others derive from a spiritual pursuit, they tread on the same.

- Seekers of worldly possessions. People often pray for more power or money, status or other worldly possession. This devotion can be pure in its purpose, but the purpose itself is not particularly an exalted one. This could fall in the realm of conditional devotion.

- Those who are situated in knowledge. There are those people whose purpose in life is to remain devoted to the Lord and for whom this is the sole purpose of existence. This is the purest form of devotion, where spirituality is both a means and an end.

7.29

जरामरणमोक्षाय मामाश्रित्य यतन्ति ये |
ते ब्रह्म तद्विदुः कृत्स्नमध्यात्मं कर्म चाखिलम् || 29||

7.29: Those who take shelter in me, striving for liberation from old age and death, the individual self, and the entire field of karmic action, are actually Brahman.

After having described in detail his opulence and omnipresence, Krishna now tells us who is a Brahman. It is important to understand here first that in this context Brahman does not refer to the caste Brahmin as we know it today. Brahman here means the one with knowledge, or the intelligent one amongst the human race.

Birth, death, old age and disease come to the physical body, but the spiritual body, i.e., the soul, remains unaffected. And so when the physical body starts to see itself as an embodiment of the soul these earthly issues fail to perplex it. He who reaches the stage of first believing and then internalising the concept *Aham brahmasmi*, meaning 'I am spirit' is a Brahman, or a spiritual soul.

Thus when one takes shelter in the Lord, one is elevated to being a Brahman, a spiritual soul. A Brahman is liberated forever from the highs and lows of earthly life, mortal pain of old age and disease, and constant fear of death. These elevated souls thus remain unaffected by the vagaries of day-to-day existence, and find deliverance from extremes of joy and sorrow, in this life itself.

८

The Light of Liberation &
the Darkness of Doom

'You are today where your thoughts have brought you; you will be tomorrow where your thoughts take you'.

'You are today where your thoughts have brought you; you will be tomorrow where your thoughts take you'.

Whosoever wrote these words may well be describing the underlying message of the eighth chapter of the *Bhagavad Gita*. In the previous chapter Krishna introduced the word Brahman. As earlier, it is important to understand here too that in this context Brahman does not refer to the caste Brahmin as we know it today. Brahman here means the one with knowledge or the intelligent one amongst the human race.

Arjuna understands here that a learned person is one who is constantly aware of the Ultimate Truth, and is cognisant of it even at the time of death. Such a person realises that death alone does not mean salvation, only knowledge and correct action can help us attain that. The thoughts uppermost in our minds at the time of death play a significant role in the outcome of the onward journey, and thus it is important to remain connected with the ultimate reality at all times.

The juxtaposition of the concept of darkness with light is mutually complementary, and effectively brings out the sharpness of both. Perfect counterfoils to one another, the presence of black makes white appear whiter, while the presence of white makes black look blacker than ever.

Making liberal use of this metaphor, Krishna explains to Arjuna the difference between, and the consequences of, encouraging either knowledge or ignoranace. Knowledge and its appropriate application brings forth the light of liberation. Ignorance and inaction on the other hand, can only lead to the darkness of doom. Constant upgradation of knowledge is thus important. To shun ignorance and sloth is equally important.

Whatever we achieve in life, good, bad or average, is a result of the thoughts we nurture in our minds. Good and positive thoughts naturally bear good fruit, while the fruit borne of bad and negative thoughts is bound to be rotten. In the words of the Buddha, 'We are what we think. All that we are arises with our thoughts. With our thoughts we make the world.'

Krishna also explains the critical significance of

- Different paths of passing away from the world
- Death occurring during the northern solstice
- Death occurring during the southern solstice
- Positive thoughts at the end of life
- Liberation and deliverance
- Making the right choices

In almost all cultures and religions, when a person is dying holy verses are chanted, soothing music may be played etc. and the person made as comfortable as possible. All these are efforts to ease the soul gently into its forthcoming journey.

Ancient Egyptians are known to have buried their dead along with their favourite day-to-day items including gold and precious jewellery, while Hindus even today put drops of *Ganga jal,* or water from the holy River Ganga, in the mouth of a dying person. (Ganga is believed to have descended from the heavens, and as water is constantly evaporating to the skies and again returning to earth, a drop of its water is said to guide the soul in its journey into the unknown.)

As is encapsulated in the following verse, whatever are our predominant thoughts at the time of death will determine our destination. If the thoughts are of all that one is leaving behind, the soul may remain tormented and embroiled in earthly matters even after leaving the body. But if the mind is engaged with the ultimate reality, then it shall liberate the soul and allow it to merge with the Supreme Soul.

Krishna clearly says:

Whatever one remembers upon giving up the body at the time of death, O son of Kunti, one attains that state, without fail.

–Verse 8.06

chapter 8

Aksara Brahma Yoga
Yoga as Imperishable Knowledge

8.05 & 8.06

अन्तकाले च मामेव स्मरन्मुक्त्वा कलेवरम् |
य: प्रयाति स मद्भावं याति नास्त्यत्र संशय: || 5||
यं यं वापि स्मरन्भावं त्यजत्यन्ते कलेवरम् |
तं तमेवैति कौन्तेय सदा तद्भावभावित: || 6||

8.05: Those who relinquish the body while remembering me at the moment of death will come to me. This is certain, and there is no doubt about this.

8.06: Whatever one remembers upon giving up the body at the time of death, O son of Kunti, one attains that state, without fail.

Here (8.05) Krishna is responding to Arjuna's question in the previous verse. Addressing Krishna as Madhusudana (so named as Krishna had once slayed a demon called Madhu) Arjuna asks, how can those engaged in devotional service know you at the time of death?

Krishna here stresses on the importance of a higher consciousness saying that those who remember the Supreme Lord at the time of death are sure to find him. The word *smaran* meaning to remember, is important here as is the phrase *mad bhavamin*, which means god-like nature. Thus, if one's consciousness is absorbed in God at the moment of death, one attains him, and becomes god-like in character.

Significantly, as the time of death is uncertain for every living being and no one has ever been known to pre-empt or predict it, Krishna's words also imply that it is important to remain in this state of exalted consciousness all the time, as the soul can relinquish the body at any given moment.

In the next verse (8.06) this state of consciousness is further encouraged but not as overtly. Krishna says that whatever or whoever is in our thoughts, or what or who we feel closest to at the time of death, is going to determine the nature of our rebirth. This pronouncement subtly asks human beings to reject impure thoughts, abandon material pursuits and detach oneself from worldly involvements when close to death. The more we remain embroiled in these, the more likelihood there is of us being reborn in the midst of what has been uppermost in our minds. This also helps us better understand *vanaprastha ashram*, the idea of giving up worldly life and retiring from active involvements, followed by *sanyas*, the final stage of life, which means renunciation of all material possessions and family life.

On the other hand, if one is focussed on the Supreme Power it is certain that there will be relief from the tedium of rebirth, as God shall take the elevated soul into his fold. One's thoughts during the course of life on earth accumulate to influence one's thoughts at the moment of death. Thus this life creates the next life. The seeds of our next life are sown in this life itself.

For one who lives a good, pure life, the chances of her or his thoughts being pure at all times are bright. Whereas, one who is engrossed in the undesirable aspects of life, it is unlikely that she or he may entertain pure thoughts at the time of death.

In a nutshell, a lifetime of goodness and good deeds is required to prepare for a desirable end of life. It is not possible to change tracks suddenly and expect to reap full benefits in equal measure.

Death is an unknown experience, and in moments of crisis it is assumed that the mind naturally gravitates to the thoughts that constitute one's inner nature. Only if we contemplate something continuously does it get internalised and manifests itself as part of the inner working of the mind. To conclude, what is being said here is that to make goodness our inner being, the Lord must be remembered, recollected, and contemplated upon at every moment of our life.

8.15

मामुपेत्य पुनर्जन्म दु:खालयमशाश्वतम् |
नाप्नुवन्ति महात्मान: संसिद्धिं परमां गता: || 15||

8.15: Having attained me, the great souls are no longer subject to rebirth in this world, which is transient and full of misery, because they have attained the highest order of perfection.

Taking forward what is being said in the previous verses, Krishna reaffirms that those who find God no longer go through the cycle of rebirth as their souls merge with the supreme soul and are granted eternal peace. Having attained perfection they are no longer subjected to the challenge of living in this imperfect world.

In Hindu philosophy, life in the material world is viewed as a testing time. We are sent to this world in a particular life form earned on the basis of our karma in the previous life, and are here to improve ourselves. The eventual goal of every soul is to extricate itself from this cycle and merge with the ultimate power.

While animals may live a seemingly simple life of eating, sleeping and reproducing, they are bereft of intellect and so have little chance of improving their karma and so may continue to be born as animals, which is considered a lower life form. Human beings on the other hand, are blessed with intellect and have the power to discern and choose. However, their lives are not easy as every individual goes through pain, and existential challenges. A child may lose her parents, an adult may lose his job, an older person may be tormented with disease, thus most people face difficulties at some time or the other in their lives. And all through life we live in eternal fear of death and what lies beyond. No human being can honestly claim to be at ease about death, even though it is a grim reality everyone is aware of.

The biggest challenge that humans face is having to choose a way of life, and most end up making the wrong choices without realising the consequences. These choices ultimately determine the outcome of this life, which in turn determines the fate of our soul, as it traverses through the universe in quest of the eternal abode.

8.23–26

यत्र काले त्वनावृत्तिमावृत्तिं चैव योगिन: |
प्रयाता यान्ति तं कालं वक्ष्यामि भरतर्षभ || 23||
अग्निर्ज्योतिरह: शुक्ल: षण्मासा उत्तरायणम् |
तत्र प्रयाता गच्छन्ति ब्रह्म ब्रह्मविदो जना: || 24||
धूमो रात्रिस्तथा कृष्ण: षण्मासा दक्षिणायनम् |
तत्र चान्द्रमसं ज्योतिर्योगी प्राप्य निवर्तते || 25||
शुक्लकृष्णे गती ह्येते जगत: शाश्वते मते |
एकया यात्यनावृत्तिमन्ययावर्तते पुन: || 26||

8.23–26: O best of the Bharatas, I shall now describe to you the different paths of passing away from this world, one of which leads to liberation, and the other leads to rebirth.

Those who know the Supreme Brahman, and who depart from this world, during the six months of the sun's northern course, during the bright fortnight of the moon, and during the bright part of the day, reach the Supreme destination.

The practitioners of Vedic rituals, who pass away during the six months of the sun's southern course, the dark fortnight of the moon, the time of smoke, the night, reach the celestial abodes. After enjoying celestial pleasures, they again return to earth.

These two, bright and dark paths, always exist in this world. The way of light leads to liberation, and the way of darkness leads to rebirth.

In these verses, Krishna continues with his answer to Arjuna's question asked in verse 8.02, how can those engaged in devotional service know you at the time of death?

He says that for committed devotees of the Supreme Lord the time and manner of leaving their human body is not important as their souls will merge with the Supreme Soul anyway. Also, when a yogi has attained perfection he can by the power of yoga, select the time and situation of leaving the material world.

Those who have not reached that level of commitment and surrender, but have adopted the path of karma yoga, jnana yoga or hatha yoga as a way of life must leave the body at a suitable time. This will determine the subsequent journey of the soul.

Krishna says that there are two paths, the path of light and the path of darkness. Interestingly, these paths are not purely abstract but are supported by the movement of the earth itself, namely, the northern solstice and the southern solstice.

The six months leading to the northern solstice when the sun is on its northern course, the bright fortnight of the moon, and the bright part of the day, are all characterised by light. Light is symbolic of knowledge, while darkness is symbolic of ignorance. On the other hand, the six months leading to the southern solstice when the sun is on its southern course, the dark fortnight of the moon, and the night, all these have the commonality of darkness.

The significance of these earmarked times is both symbolic and physical. Therefore, those who leave the body at a time when all signs are indicative of light will easily reach the supreme destination. While those who depart in darkness will find brief solace in celestial abodes, but will eventually return in a life form as per the cycle of rebirth.

Those whose consciousness is well ensconced in God, and are detached from sensual pursuits, these individuals depart by the path of light which stands for cognizance and knowledge. Being thus situated, they attain the Supreme Abode of God, and are released from the wheel of *samsara* i.e., the material world. But those, whose consciousness is attached to the world, depart by the path of darkness which stands for oblivion and ignorance.

Unable to extricate themselves from the physical web of life and its attractions, they continue rotating in the cycle of life and death. In case they have performed some positive activities in their lifetime they are temporarily granted stay at the celestial abodes, but sooner or later, have to return to planet earth.

Therefore, all human beings have to take one of these two paths after death. Ultimately it depends on their karma, whether they align themselves to the path of brightness or the path of darkness.

৫

The Supreme Secret

The ninth chapter opens with Krishna sharing a secret with a receptive Arjuna. Reassuring his protege of the simplicity of what he is going to disclose, Krishna says it is the Ultimate Truth which is easy to understand, simple to adopt and apply, and is everlasting and imperishable in nature. He tells Arjuna that the Supreme Power is present in

- spirit and matter
- all living beings
- offerings and sacrifice
- all elements of the universe
- birth and death

and it is

- the eternal seed—immortal and indestructible
- the origin and the end
- the father and the mother
- mentor and guide
- master and friend

Those who are learned and wise understand this and devote themselves to move in a spiritual direction, leading to this divine destination.

As you sow so shall you reap!

There is an adage we are all familiar with—as you sow so shall you reap. The phrase is simple and self-explanatory. Viewed in a larger sense it can touch upon other aspects of life too.

Whosoever we choose as our role model in life, consciously or unconsciously, we try to emulate that person. With long and concentrated efforts, we might even transform and develop similar character traits. Therefore, we must select our heroes carefully and make informed choices.

For instance, those influenced by philanthropists are likely to develop an inclination towards charity and social work, while those attracted by the bright lights of the world of glamour will work on their looks and personality, in the hope of mesmerizing the world with their starry performances.

Similarly, whosoever we worship in life we are likely to find ourselves with them in our after-life. Those who worship the gods could reach the bright gates of the celestial abode, while others engaged in invoking evil spirits, ghosts and demons might soon be reduced to being one of them, and be condemned to a murky existence in a dark bottomless pit in the next life.

Chapter 9 also contains a verse that throws light on who qualifies for attainment of moksha. Contrary to expectations of a class and caste-ridden society, Krishna here declares in no uncertain terms that every human being is entitled to salvation, and is indeed worthy of it provided the devotion is pure and sincere.

This includes all sections of society including traders and those engaged in business, women, as well as those who perform manual labour. This declaration comes as a welcome statement in view of the later discriminatory social developments. One is left wondering at what point in time the understanding of this straightforward utterance started to mean something quite different.

Removing another popular misconception, Krishna talks of rituals, sacrifices and elaborate ceremonies. Rather unequivocally he declares that the grand scale at which these are performed is not consequential. What is, however, of absolute importance is the degree of sincerity and purity of devotion with which any prayer is offered. Honesty of intent here far outweighs the scale and size of its content.

The following verse puts to rest any misconceptions we may have of ostentatious ceremonies being a sign of our faith and dedication. Flamboyant offerings only serve the purpose for which they are made, i.e., to gain social recognition and prominence in the peer group. It does not necessarily translate into a proportionate advancement on the humble path of devotion.

If one offers to me a leaf, a flower, a fruit, or even water, with love and pure devotion, I will accept it.

–Verse 9.26

chapter 5

Raja Vidya Raja Guhya Yoga
Yoga as Supreme Knowledge & Supreme Secret

9.02 & 9.10

राजविद्या राजगुह्यं पवित्रमिदमुत्तमम् ।
प्रत्यक्षावगमं धर्म्यं सुसुखं कर्तुमव्ययम् ॥ 2॥
मयाध्यक्षेण प्रकृतिः सूयते सचराचरम् ।
हेतुनानेन कौन्तेय जगद्विपरिवर्तते ॥ 10॥

9.02: This knowledge is the king of learning and the most profound of all secrets. It purifies those who hear it. It is easily understood, directly perceptible and in accordance with dharma, easy to practise, and everlasting in effect.

9.10: Working under my direction, the material energy, brings into being all animate and inanimate forms, O son of Kunti. For this reason, the material world undergoes changes.

This chapter is called *Raj Vidya* or the king of all learning as the essence of all doctrines, including those explained earlier, is encapsulated here.

Krishna uses the metaphor *raja* to emphasise the paramount position of the knowledge he is going to reveal. He does not refer to his teachings as belonging to any particular religion, doctrine, or belief. He simply says that what he is going to describe to Arjuna is the king of all learning (*vidya*).

This knowledge is also the Supreme Secret (*guhya*) and is pure (*pavitram*). It is directly perceptible (*pratyaksha*), easy to practise (*kartum susukham*). An individual's devotion must be selfless without any desire for material rewards to make it virtuous (*dharmyam*).

Elsewhere in the *Gita*, Krishna has stated that of all living entities in different forms and species—'I am the father'. The Supreme Lord is also the supreme will and the very basis of the world we live in— which is the material manifestation of his creation. The world as per his will undergoes constant change, perpetuating the cycle of creation, maintenance, and dissolution.

God does not directly engage in the work of creating life forms. However, the entire cycle of birth, death, and possibly rebirth is regulated by him, and the cycle of life cannot move without his supreme will.

9.16–19

अहं क्रतुरहं यज्ञ: स्वधाहमहमौषधम् |
मन्त्रोऽहमहमेवाज्यमहमग्निरहं हुतम् || 16||
पिताहमस्य जगतो माता धाता पितामह: |
वेद्यं पवित्रमोङ्कार ऋक्साम यजुरेव च || 17||
गतिर्भर्ता प्रभु: साक्षी निवास: शरणं सुहृत् |
प्रभव: प्रलय: स्थानं निधानं बीजमव्ययम् || 18||
तपाम्यहमहं वर्षं निगृह्णाम्युत्सृजामि च |
अमृतं चैव मृत्युश्च सदसच्चाहमर्जुन || 19||

9.16: It is I who am the Vedic ritual, I am the sacrifice, and I am the oblation offered to ancestors. I am the healing herb, and I am the Vedic mantra. I am the clarified butter (ghee), I am the fire and the act of offering.

9.17: Of this universe, I am the father; I am also the mother, the sustainer, and the grandsire. I am the purifier, the goal of knowledge, the sacred syllable Om. I am the *Ṛig Veda, Sama Veda,* and *the Yajur Veda.*

9. 18: I am the goal of all living beings, and I am also their sustainer, master, witness, abode, shelter, and friend. I am the origin, end, and resting place of creation; I am the storehouse and eternal seed.

9.19: I radiate heat as the sun, and I withhold, as well as send forth rain. I am immortality and I am death personified, O Arjuna. I am the spirit and I am matter.

In the above verses, Krishna gives a glimpse into the various aspects of his infinite presence. He is present in all Vedic mantras and rituals as also in all sacrifices. All of these here can be looked upon in a larger sense with mantras and rituals being symbolic of the words we speak. Our day-to-day activities and sacrifices may symbolise acts of self-control. Krishna is the supreme healer as also the fire, the ghee that is poured on it, and all the offerings made. While on the one hand, he is fire which is warmth and purity, on the other, the Lord is the butter that keeps the flame burning, as do all our offerings, meaning that those who are pure will find further support from the Lord to remain on the path of purity.

Creation emanates from God, and hence he is its *pita*, father. Prior to creation, he holds the invisible material energy in his womb, and so he is also its *mata*, mother. He maintains the universe and nourishes it, and thus he is its sustainer. As he is the father of Brahma, who is the creator, he is also the grandsire of this universe. He is the answer to every quest for knowledge, and resides in the sacred syllable *Om*. Mentioning the *Vedas* by name, each perused by all eminent scholars, he states that he himself is the *Ṛig Veda, Sama Veda*, and the *Yajur Veda*.

Krishna goes on to say he is the ultimate goal of all living beings and he sustains everyone by not just being their master but also friend, who is witness to everything that is taking place right through our lives, as he is also the seed that brings us into existence. He offers shelter and refuge in time of need, as also the ultimate resting place. Parents, friends, partners and offspring may come and go from our lives but God always remains by our side—from before we are born, to being born, living on earth, and finally dying, and then while negotiating the final journey to the unknown it is only God who hand holds us right through—from before life to after life.

Being the sun himself, he radiates life sustaining heat, he makes the clouds rain, he is the spirit and he is also matter itself. Krishna clearly states that while on the one hand he is immortality, simultaneously he is also the personification of death.

9.25 (94)

यान्ति देवव्रता देवान्पितॄ न्यान्ति पितृव्रता: |
भूतानि यान्ति भूतेज्या यान्ति मद्याजिनोऽपि माम् ||25||

9.25: Those who worship celestial gods take birth amongst the celestial gods, those who worship ancestors go to ancestors, those who worship ghosts take birth amongst such beings, and my devotees come to me alone.

Reminiscent of the oft-given advice—be careful what you wish for, this verse suggests—be careful who you worship. And so the higher the leap (of faith) the longer is the jump, and the landing place.

In this verse, Krishna explains the outcomes of worshipping different entities. By going into this description he is suggesting we choose well and carefully while on this earth. The celestial gods or demigods, include the sun god, Surya, the rain god, Indra, the god of wealth, Kubera and many others. He says that those who worship them (or other demigods) shall find themselves in the celestial abodes for a while.

Similarly, it may be good to remember one's ancestors, but single-minded worship of ancestors shall take us to them after death and we might not be aware of this, or actively hoping for this, in our lifetimes. However, be it celestial abodes or being in proximity of ancestors, all this is temporary and will eventually end.

Some individuals, out of conviction or ignorance, worship ghosts and spirits. Some of us may be familiar with those who indulge in, what is popularly believed to be, black magic. Krishna says that persons who indulge in such activities and make this their focus, take birth amongst ghosts and spirits in their next life.

The most evolved devotees are those who attach their minds to the Supreme lord. They are resolute, and clear in their thoughts and pursuit. These exalted souls who remain steadfast and unwavering in their spiritual journey, go to his divine abode after death.

Krishna gives this knowledge to help us make informed choices, and not be treading on an imperfect path out of ignorance. To reach the highest destination, the roadmap has to be accurate, and these words clearly laying out various trajectories should leave no room for doubt in our minds, that to reach the highest level of spiritual evolution we must worship the one and only Supreme Power.

9.26

पत्रं पुष्पं फलं तोयं यो मे भक्त्या प्रयच्छति |
तदहं भक्त्युपहृतमश्रामि प्रयतात्मनः || 26||

9.26: If one offers to me a leaf, a flower, a fruit, or even water, with love and pure devotion, I will accept it.

This verse explains the Indian practice of offering flowers at holy places or while praying. Krishna makes it clear here that it is not the material value of what is offered to him, but the extent of devotion that is important. He suggests that whether it is a leaf, flower, fruit or even water, if offered with sincerity and true devotion it is acceptable.

He demonstrates this suitably while eating dry rice at his childhood friend Sudama's house. In another avatar as Shri Rama in *Ramayana*, when poor Shabari offers half eaten berries to the Lord—first tasting them herself to make sure each one was sweet, before offering them to him—he actually eats them.

While one implication of this is to do with the material value of offerings, or rather the insignificance of them, the other implication is to do with nature. Flowers, fruits, leaves and water are all symbols and products of nature, and so are dear to the Lord. These are also equally available and accessible to everyone. Elsewhere Krishna says—I accept the offerings of those whose hearts are pure.

But devotion cannot be limited to the time of prayers and offerings alone. In the next verse, Krishna goes on to say that each of our day-to-day actions must also be viewed as an offering to him.

Thus, all actions should also be offered to Him. In other words whatever social or professional duties one may be engaged in, it should be done with sincerity and conviction. Every act requires devotion, and when viewed as an offering to God, should naturally prompt us to do our best.

So devotion is not to be restricted to the confines of a temple; as a matter of fact it is to be constantly engaged with, and experienced every moment of our life.

Such an attitude transforms everyday activities of daily life into service of God. Just making offerings and chanting mantras at fixed times are not enough: it has to be embellished with performing each action with utmost honesty and sincerity.

9.32

मां हि पार्थ व्यपाश्रित्य येऽपि स्युः पापयोनयः |
स्त्रियो वैश्यास्तथा शूद्रास्तेऽपि यान्ति परां गतिम् || 32||

9.32: O Arjuna, son of Pritha, all those who take refuge in me, also those of low birth, women, business people and traders, and those who do manual labour, even they will attain the supreme destination.

After declaring that the most inexpensive of offerings, be it a leaf, flower, fruit, even water, is acceptable to him so long as it is offered with sincere devotion, Krishna now talks of devotees, and who qualifies to be one. It is made abundantly clear that where devotion is concerned, in the eyes of the Almighty, there is no distinction between those of high birth or low birth. Clearly these are manmade constructs and do not stand in the way of anyone involving oneself in devotion.

This verse breaks into stereotypical social paradigms that Krishna here emphatically disrupts. Lucid and explicit, he declares that irrespective of birth, gender, caste, or race, whoever takes complete refuge in him will attain the supreme goal. The gates of heaven are perennially open for those who live a pure life, no matter where they may be situated on the social ladder.

This puts a serious question mark on the subsequent emergence of discriminatory social practices based on birth. These condemnable practices eventually marginalised the majority of population under some criterion or other, ensuring the superiority of those born in privileged families. The exclusive boy's club fiercely guarded its own self-propounded rights and entitlements, which included ownership of land and entry into temples and other holy places. Sadly, many of these practices continue to be in play even today.

There is some debate that revolves around the use of the word *api*, in the verse above meaning 'even' or 'also', as being disdainful and supercilious vis-a-vis the persons in question. A positive interpretation, however, might establish this to actually be an indication and assertion of concepts of inclusivity and equality—a specific disruption of set norms.

It is important to remember here that Krishna is addressing Arjuna, who is himself a beneficiary of a skewed monarchical system. To drive home these progressive ideas and demolish accepted social norms, words have to be chosen carefully and spoken assertively.

Interestingly, young Krishna himself, though related to Arjuna through his mother, was brought up neither as a Brahmin (men of scriptures by birth) nor as a kshatriya (warriors by birth). In his early years he did not grow up in a palace or enjoy any advantages of being upper caste. As a consequence of a series of untoward events, he was brought up by foster parents of humble origins.

Reverting to the issue of the use of 'even' or 'also' being contemptuous or patronising, more needs to be said. The bracketing together of the business and trader class who tend to be the most prosperous in any society, with women and manual workers, should set to rest any such thought processes. This curious but specific clubbing together of well-to-do traders with other less fortunate groups could be an outcome of the desperation of the upper classes to preserve their self-declared superiority. Insecure in the face of the enormous wealth of the business community, it is possible that merchants and traders too were denied entry into the sanctum sanctorum, purely as an act of self-preservation.

The *Gita* rarely touches upon society, as the focus here is on the self, the journey of the soul and its eventual fate. This is one of the rare verses in which Krishna makes a statement based on accepted societal norms, and duly demolishes them.

Thus wiping the slate clean, Krishna seems to be setting a new precedent—could this too be one of the purposes of his taking birth on earth? To cleanse society of social hierarchies?

Be that as it may, this declaration of social equality is indeed gratifying and heartening. It clearly comes across as the thought process of a progressive mind that accurately identifies current issues and has a vision that is way ahead of its time.

Unfortunately, these teachings and ideas remain largely ignored to this day. Distorted and reconstructed to suit biased and prejudiced minds, society has been evolving in a dubious one-step-forward–two-steps-backwards mode for some time now.

ॐ

Omnipotent, Omniscient
and Omnipresent

In continuation of the previous chapter, Krishna goes on to describe his infinite glories and gives a detailed narration of his imperishable existence and all-pervading presence.

The 'Divine Power' has neither a past, present or future; nor a beginning, middle or end. However, in the context of his own creation which includes the entire universe, the Divine is everything, the beginning, the middle as well as the end.

The extent of his potency, his invincible strength and indestructible nature, in other words his omnipotence, omniscience, and omnipresence, when looked at holistically make up a fascinating whole.

In this chapter it is the poetic quality of the micro description of his own omnipresence that is truly enchanting. Both lyrical and artistic at the same time, the tenth chapter is replete with imagery that remains with the listener or reader, for a long, long time.

Krishna describes his presence in

- gods, demigods and Vedic scriptures
- sages and thinkers
- knowledge of spirituality
- logical and systematic conclusions

- reward and punishment
- silence and sound
- past, present and future
- seeds and trees
- in all characteristics and nature of living beings
- beginning, middle and end of all beings
- luminous bodies, planets and stars
- the five senses
- fire, water and mountains
- animals, birds, reptiles and water creatures
- months and seasons lakes, rivers and oceans

The Supreme Soul is a magnificent personification of splendour, power, beauty, opulence, knowledge and compassion. All roads for attainment of salvation lead to him. It is he who can grant peace of mind, unique satisfaction and bliss to those who remain in pursuit of excellence.

He bestows the qualities of non-violence, intelligence, austerity, contentment, truthfulness and equanimity upon living beings. As are emotions like joy and sorrow, fear and apprehension. Success and failure, fame and infamy, rise and fall, each of these takes place in our lives at the will of the Divine.

> *The Supreme Soul is a magnificent personification of splendour, power, beauty, opulence, knowledge and compassion. All roads for attainment of salvation lead to him. It is he who can grant peace of mind, unique satisfaction and bliss to those who remain in pursuit of excellence.*

This chapter also stands out for being one of the few where women find a specific mention. Interestingly, the qualities listed out here for women are not particularly what one might think of as essentially feminine or womanly. Certainly not in the divisive spirit in which masculine and feminine qualities came to be defined over a period of time.

In olden times, as roles in society were primarily dictated by the gender of an individual, there was rarely any over-lapping between the prescribed character traits of a man and that of a woman.

A close look reveals that each of the qualities mentioned here is completely gender agnostic, and is as desirable in men as in women. It is gratifying to discover that nowhere does a text as old and wise as the *Gita* lay down that a woman should be beautiful, fair, obedient, servile or in any way remain the 'disregarded' half of humankind all through her oppressed life.

Interesting as this is, it does make one wonder how and when, down the ages, did descriptors like beauty, deference, subservience and obedience, become the expected extensions of a woman's personality?

Describing himself in extreme terms, Krishna says that while on the one hand he is frightening and dreaded as Death itself, on the other hand he is very much present in the finer qualities of women.

I am all-devouring death, and I am the origin of those things that are yet to be.
Amongst women I am fame, prosperity, fine speech, memory, intelligence, courage, and forgiveness.

–Verse 10.34

chapter 10

Vibhuti Vistara Yoga
Yoga as Divine Manisfestation

10.04–05

बुद्धिर्ज्ञानमसम्मोहः क्षमा सत्यं दमः शमः |
सुखं दुःखं भवोऽभावो भयं चाभयमेव च || 4||
अहिंसा समता तुष्टिस्तपो दानं यशोऽयशः |
भवन्ति भावा भूतानां मत्त एव पृथग्विधाः || 5||

10.04–05: Intelligence, knowledge, clarity of thought, forgiveness, truthfulness, control over the senses and mind, joy and sorrow, birth and death, fear and courage, non-violence, equanimity, contentment, austerity, charity, fame, and infamy—all these qualities of living beings are created by me alone.

In these two verses, Krishna continues to confirm his supremacy over all that exists in creation. He mentions several emotions most of which human beings experience at some time or the other during the course of their lives. He declares that the various moods, characteristics, and dispositions of humankind emanate from him, and are determined by him.

Intelligence refers to the ability to analyse things in their proper perspective and knowledge refers to the ability to discriminate spiritual from material. This also implies that mere academic knowledge is not sufficient. Freedom from doubt and delusion, the ability to forgive those who have harmed us, the courage and conviction to declare the truth for the benefit of all, even when it might be inconvenient to some, all these qualities are bestowed upon us by the Lord himself.

The most essential power of self-control, both of mind and body, the ability to accept joy, sorrow, birth and death with the same grace and equanimity, and to be fearless and courageous against all odds are much sought after qualities.

To remain non-violent in the face of aggression, experience absolute contentment, observe austerity and discipline, these qualities come to us as blessings. To be generous in giving, and to be unaffected by either fame or infamy are characteristics of an exemplary human being.

Krishna states that all these qualities are present in individuals to the extent allowed by him alone. Hence, he is the source of all good and bad traits in living beings.

Whatever positive qualities we are blessed with now, are the outcome of our past karma. What we make of them in this life, whether we put them to positive use or negative, is borne out of how we use our intelligence and knowledge, and our power of discerning spiritual from material.

10.20–21

अहमात्मा गुडाकेश सर्वभूताशयस्थितः |
अहमादिश्च मध्यं च भूतानामन्त एव च || 20||
आदित्यानामहं विष्णुर्ज्योतिषां रविरंशुमान् |
मरीचिर्मरुतामस्मि नक्षत्राणामहं शशी || 21||

10.20: O Arjuna, I am seated in the heart of all living entities. I am the beginning, middle, and end of all beings.

10.21: Amongst the twelve sons of Aditi (Adityas) I am Vishnu; amongst luminous bodies I am the sun. Of the Maruts I am Marichi, and amongst the stars in the night sky I am the moon.

Significantly, in this verse Krishna addresses Arjuna as Gudakesha or the one who has conquered the darkness of sleep. For those who are asleep in the darkness of ignorance it is not possible to imbibe knowledge. But since Arjuna is above such darkness, his mind is open and accepting, and thus found fit by the Lord to impart knowledge to. The larger message here being that if we have closed minds even knowledge-givers may shun us, and we may remain bereft of the opportunity for self-improvement.

As the Supreme Lord is the creator and sustainer of this universe he is also the beginning, middle and end for all beings. We are born by his will, he preserves us and in the end we eventually go back to him.

From the *Puranas* we learn that Sage Kashyap had two wives—Aditi and Diti. From his first wife, Aditi, he fathered twelve celestial beings—Dhata, Mitra, Aryama, Shakra, Varun, Amsha, Bhaga, Vivasvan, Pusha, Savita, Twashta, and Vaman. Amongst these Adityas (twelve sons of Aditi), Krishna is Vaman, as Vaman was the avatar of the Supreme Lord Vishnu.

With his other wife Diti, Sage Kashyap fathered demons. Diti desired to have a son more powerful than Indra, the king of the celestial gods. So she kept her baby in her womb for a year. Feeling insecure, Indra then used a thunderbolt and split her foetus into many pieces, but it turned into many foetuses. These became the Maruts, or the 49 kinds of wind that flow in the universe, doing tremendous good wherever they flow. The major ones amongst them are Avaha, Pravaha,

Nivaha, Purvaha, Udvaha, Samvaha and Parivaha. The chief wind, known as Parivaha, also bears the name Marichi. Krishna states that his magnificence and power manifests itself in the wind called Marichi.

Amongst the luminous bodies, the sun is obviously supreme not because of the light it gives, but because it is life sustaining. All the might of the moon and stars put together is unable to dispel darkness, while the sun alone is enough to turn night into day.

In another context, the same is true of the moon where all the stars put together cannot light up the night. And so, Krishna says that amongst all the constellations and stars in the night sky, he is the moon because it best reveals his splendour.

10.22–23

वेदानां सामवेदोऽस्मि देवानामस्मि वासव: |
इन्द्रियाणां मनश्चास्मि भूतानामस्मि चेतना || 22||
रुद्राणां शङ्करश्चास्मि वित्तेशो यक्षरक्षसाम् |
वसूनां पावकश्चास्मि मेरु: शिखरिणामहम् || 23||

10.22: I am the *Sama Veda* amongst the *Vedas,* and Indra amongst the celestial gods. I am the mind amongst the senses; amongst the living beings I am consciousness.

10.23: Amongst the Rudras I am Lord Shankar; amongst the demi gods I am Kuber. I am Agni amongst the Vasus and Meru amongst the mountains.

Of the four *Vedas*—*Rig Veda, Yajur Veda, Sama Veda, Atharva Veda,* the *Sama Veda* describes God's magnificence. The *Sama Veda* is also the most musical and is sung in praise of the Lord. It is enchanting to those who listen to it, and encourages devotion amongst its listeners.

Among the gods, Indra is the chief and Vasava is another name for him. He is supreme in paradise, wields ultimate power, and holds a superior rank. Thus, Indra reflects the opulence of God himself.

The five senses play a critical role in determining how we live our lives. It is the mind that is responsible for and directs our actions and reactions, and regulates self-control. Thus amongst the faculties, it is the mind that is most superior and therefore Krishna resides in our minds. It is our intelligence and intellect that differentiates us from other species and establishes our superiority amongst living entities.

The *Puranas* have named eleven Rudras, i.e, the eleven forms of Lord Shiva—Hara, Bahurupa, Tryambaka, Aparajita, Vrisakapi, Shankar, Kapardi, Raivata, Mrigavyadha, Sarva, Kapali. Among these, says Krishna, Shankar is the original form of Lord Shiva in the universe and is synonymous with Krishna's own name.

Yakshas are semi-divine demons, and known for their love of acquiring wealth and hoarding it. Krishna resides in their leader, Kuber, who is the god of wealth and the treasurer of the celestial gods.

Land, water, fire, air, space, sun, moon, and stars are the eight Vasus that comprise the universe. Amongst these, fire gives warmth and energy to the rest of the elements. Thus, Krishna mentions fire as his special manifestation.

Situated in the celestial abodes, Meru is a mountain known for its rich natural resources. It is believed to be the axis around which many heavenly bodies rotate. Speaking of its glory, Krishna states that among mountains he resides in Meru.

10.24–25

पुरोधसां च मुख्यं मां विद्धि पार्थ बृहस्पतिम् |
सेनानीनामहं स्कन्दः सरसामस्मि सागरः || 24||
महर्षीणां भृगुरहं गिरामस्येकमक्षरम् |
यज्ञानां जपयज्ञोऽस्मि स्थावराणां हिमालयः || 25||

10.24: Of all priests, O Arjuna, I am Brihaspati; of all commanders, I am Kartikeya; and of all reservoirs of water I am the ocean.

10.25: Of the great sages I am Bhrigu, and amongst sounds I am Om. Amongst chants know me to be the chanting of the Holy Name; amongst immovable things I am the Himalayas.

Residing amongst the heavenly planets, Brihaspati is the chief priest in heaven. He is thus the senior most of all priests. Here, Krishna says that amongst all priests, he is Brihaspati.

Kartikeya, the son of Lord Shiva, who is also called Skanda, is the commander-in-chief of the celestial gods. He is thus the chief of all military commanders, and best reflects the might and strength of God and, so the Lord manifests himself in Kartikeya. Krishna further states that amongst all stagnant bodies of water, he is the mighty ocean which embraces the earth.

Brahma, the first living creature in the universe created several sons for the propagation of various species. Of these Bhrigu is the most powerful sage who possesses wisdom, glory, and devotion. Krishna's timeless glory is revealed best through him.

In a previous verse, Krishna had declared the syllable 'Om' to be a sacred sound. Considered most auspicious, it is often present in the beginning of Vedic mantras. This magical monosyllable is said to be the origin of the *Gayatri mantra*, and from this mantra eventually the *Vedas* were revealed.

Amongst the celestial mountains Krishna is Meru, but on earth amongst all immovable phenomenon, he is the Himalayas, a mountain range that lies at the north of India. From time immemorial, the Himalayas have fascinated and attracted people for different reasons. For mountaineers it is the ultimate challenge, and for those on a spiritual path it signifies the journey to nirvana. And so, of the multitude of mountain ranges in this world, the majestic Himalayas best display the might and expanse of the Supreme Power.

Krishna's choice of sacrificial offering is simple. Not laying stress on elaborate form and rituals, he says chanting the holy names of God is the most effective offering. This chanting can be repeated any number of times, and can be done anywhere and at any time, and is more purifying than any other form of offering.

10. 26–27 (105–106)

अश्वत्थ: सर्ववृक्षाणां देवर्षीणां च नारद: |
गन्धर्वाणां चित्ररथ: सिद्धानां कपिलो मुनि: || 26||
उच्चै:श्रवसमश्वानां विद्धि माममृतोद्भवम् |
ऐरावतं गजेन्द्राणां नराणां च नराधिपम् || 27||

10.26: Of all trees I am the peepul tree; of the celestial sages I am Narada. Amongst the Gandharvas I am Chitrath, and amongst those who have achieved perfection, I am the sage Kapil.

10.27: Amongst horses know me to be Ucchaihshrava, produced from the churning of the ocean of nectar. I am Airavata amongst all lordly elephants, and amongst humans I am the monarch.

The peepul is one the largest trees in the Indian sub-continent. It is sturdy, provides thick shade and has aerial roots that grow top down, back into the ground, making the tree tough and tenacious. Interestingly, the Buddha meditated and attained enlightenment under a peepul tree which later came to be known as the Bodhi tree. It is in this tree that Krishna chooses to manifest himself.

The celestial sage Narada is always engaged in singing praises of God and performing divine acts throughout the three worlds. He is often mistaken to be a mischief-maker though his actions are driven by his sincere desire to encourage self-introspection and purification. It is in Narada that Krishna finds the greatest devotee in the universe.

Amongst the Gandharvas, who sing beautifully, the best singer is Chitrarath, and it is in him we see the talent of Krishna himself. Amongst those yogis who have attained perfection Sage Kapila who revealed the *saankhya* system of philosophy is the most exalted. Considered to be an incarnation of God Krishna makes special mention of him as a manifestation of his glory.

Gods and demons once took part in *samudra manthan*, a churning of the ocean. From this churning, both nectar and poison were produced. Lord Shiva drank the poison, while the nectar produced many magnificent entities.

One of these was Ucchaihshrava, a celestial winged-horse, white in colour and the fastest horse in the universe. Another was Airavata, the majestic white elephant. Both these magnificent creatures, the best of their kind, served Indra.

While Krishna continues naming the most splendid in each category to reveal his glories to Arjuna, he says that amongst horses he manifests himself in Ucchaihshrava, and amongst elephants in Airavrata.

In a social set up, the king in any society is the most superior being and is said to be the representative of God on earth. Thus, in the human species Krishna resides in the king.

10.28–30 (107–109)

आयुधानामहं वज्रं धेनूनामस्मि कामधुक् |
प्रजनश्चास्मि कन्दर्पः सर्पाणामस्मि वासुकिः || 28||
अनन्तश्चास्मि नागानां वरुणो यादसामहम् |
पितॄणामर्यमा चास्मि यमः संयमतामहम् || 29||
प्रह्लादश्चास्मि दैत्यानां कालः कलयतामहम् |
मृगाणां च मृगेन्द्रोऽहं वैनतेयश्च पक्षिणाम् || 30||

10.28: I am thunderbolt amongst weapons and Kamadhenu amongst the cows. Amongst all acts of procreation I am Kaamdev, the god of love; amongst snakes I am Vasuki.

10.29: Amongst the many-hooded serpents I am Ananta; amongst aquatics I am Varun. Amongst the departed ancestors I am Aryama; amongst dispensers of law I am Yamraj, the lord of death.

10.30: I am Prahlad amongst demons; amongst all that controls I am time. Know me to be the lion amongst animals, and Garud amongst the birds.

Normally, one might not think of thunderbolt as a weapon but here Krishna identifies himself with it saying that of all weapons he is the thunderbolt, which is unbelievably powerful and deadly. The sub text here is also to not undermine the power of nature and natural forces. Krishna deliberately refers to this thunderbolt here as his representation, and pointedly positions it above the mace and disc that are always seen in the hands of Lord Vishnu.

Indulgence in sexual activity is encouraged for purposes of procreation and in this Kaamdev, the God of Love represents the Lord. When sexual activity happens for the sake of sensual pleasure alone, it is animal-like and lustful. On the other hand, sex within the institution of marriage, or in some societies and cultures as a statement of pure love and a culmination of that sentiment, finds the Supreme Power itself present in it. Earlier in verse 7.11, Krishna had declared that he himself is the sexual desire that is not in conflict with virtue and scriptural prescriptions.

Amongst snakes Krishna manifests himself in Vasuki, the unique snake that has a gem called *nagamani* on his head. Vasuki is well-known for coiling around Lord Shiva's neck, who blessed and wore him as an ornament.

Anant is the divine many-hooded serpent on whom Lord Vishnu rests. He possesses ten thousand hoods. It is believed that he has been describing the glories of God with each of his hoods since the beginning of time, and the description is not yet complete.

Varun is the celestial god of the ocean in whom Krishna manifests himself from amongst all aquatic beings. Aryama, the third son of Aditi is worshipped as the head of the departed ancestors, and represents the Lord himself.

Yamraj is the celestial god of death. It is he who takes charge of the soul, for the journey away from its mortal frame after death. Yamraj is known to dispassionately dispense justice on behalf of God on the basis of the soul's actions in this life, and granting punishment or reward in the next life.

Yamraj never deviates even the slightest from his duties, no matter how tedious and morbid these may be. For this perfection as the dispenser of justice he reflects the glory of God.

Though born as the son of the powerful demon king Hiranyakashipu, Prahlad turned out to be one of the greatest devotees of Lord Vishnu. Thus, amongst the demons, Prahlad best reflects God's glory.

As is often said, time is the best healer, and time and tide wait for no man. No matter how intense the pain, desire or ambition, with time all emotions get subdued. And so amongst subduing forces, time is supreme and is thus Krishna's choice of an equanimous phenomenon.

And of course the king of the jungle is the majestic lion, and amongst all animals the power of the Lord reveals itself in the mighty lion. Garud, the legendary bird or bird-like creature is the divine vehicle of Lord Vishnu, and the greatest amongst the birds. Garud is therefore the natural choice of Krishna as the most exalted of all birds.

10.31

पवन: पवतामस्मि राम: शस्त्रभृतामहम् |
झषाणां मकरश्चास्मि स्रोतसामस्मि जाह्नवी || 31||

10.31: Amongst purifiers I am the wind, and amongst wielders of weapons I am Lord Rama. Of water creatures I am the crocodile, and of flowing rivers I am Ganga.

Of the many purifiers of the environment, fresh air is the most important. Amongst purifiers Krishna manifests himself as wind as this performs the task of purification most effectively converting the impure to pure.

Lord Rama was the most powerful warrior on earth and much respected for his skills as a marksman. What also set him apart, was the fact that he never misused his skill for his own advantage. Each time he picked up the bow and arrow it was for some good. He was not only the best, he was also the most responsible wielder of weapons, and these qualities made him perfect. Rama was also an avatar of God, and thus Krishna feels one with him.

Of all the water creatures, Krishna mentions the crocodile which is dominant in aquatic life, and also greatly feared by other creatures, including human beings. The fact that it can survive outside water too makes it even more menacing. Amongst flowing water, Krishna is the Ganga. The river descended on earth from celestial abodes and did so with the purpose of rejuvenating the earth. It is therefore, greatly revered, enjoys unique spiritual sanctity, and is life sustaining. Even today the Ganga stands for purity, and is the life line for thousands of people who live in its proximity.

10.32 & 33

सर्गाणामादिरन्तश्च मध्यं चैवाहमर्जुन |
अध्यात्मविद्या विद्यानां वाद: प्रवदतामहम् || 32||
अक्षराणामकारोऽस्मि द्वन्द्व: सामासिकस्य च |
अहमेवाक्षय: कालो धाताहं विश्वतोमुख: || 33||

10.32: O Arjuna, I am the beginning, middle, and end of all creation. Amongst different paths of knowledge I am the knowledge of spirituality, and in debates I am the logical conclusion.

10.33: Of letters I am the first letter 'a'; I am the dual word in grammatical compounds. I am the endless Time, and amongst creators I am Brahma.

In verse 10.20, Krishna tells Arjuna that he is the beginning, middle and end of all living beings. Now, he says the same for all creation—I am the beginning—*adi*, the middle—*madhya*, and the end—*ant* of everything. These three stages are also referred to as creation, maintenance, and dissolution. None of these three can happen without his will.

To acquire exalted knowledge there are several sources—the four *Vedas*, their six supplements, the *Vedanta Sutra, the Puranas*, and innumerable books on logic and religiosity. All these offer varied kinds of knowledge, but of these the one that teaches spiritual knowledge, i.e., *adhyatama sutra* is *Vedanta Sutra*. It is this knowledge that Krishna values the most.

Logic is the basis for communication of ideas, and finding and establishing of truths. Among logicians there are different kinds of arguments. Supporting one's argument with evidence that also supports the opposing side is called *jalpa*. Merely trying to defeat one's opponent is called *vitanda*. The logical conclusion of the discussion is known as *vada*. This conclusive truth is the representation of Krishna. Thus the universal principles of logic are a manifestation of the power of God.

'A' is the first vowel of the alphabet, and since vowels are written before consonants 'a' is the beginning of sound. In Sanskrit, all letters are formed by combining a half-letter with 'a'. For example, म + अ = म (*m* + *a* = *ma*). Therefore, in Sanskrit alphabet the letter 'a' has special significance.

Another feature in Sanskrit language is combining two or more words to form compound words to acquire a new meaning.

Of the many formations, *dwandva* is the most superior because both words retain their prominence, while in the others, either one word becomes more prominent, or both words combine together to give the meaning of a third word. The dual word Radha-Krishna is an example of *dwandva*, while another example is Ram-Krishna. Krishna highlights *dwandva* or the dual word as the most worthy of grammatical formations.

Of all the long-lasting phenomena, time is everlasting. Even when we use the phrases 'the beginning of time' and 'the end of time' we are not sure exactly what that time is, as time has no beginning and no known end—just like Krishna himself.

Amongst the creators of the universe, Brahma, who has four heads, plays the most proactive role. Therefore, he is representative of the Supreme Lord. Krishna singles out the first-born Brahma, who created the entire universe, and states that among all creators, the creative ability of Brahma reflects the glory of God in the most befitting manner.

10.34

मृत्युः सर्वहरश्चाहमुद्भवश्च भविष्यताम् |
कीर्तिः श्रीर्वाक्च नारीणां स्मृतिर्मेधा धृतिः क्षमा || 34||

10.34: I am all-devouring death, and I am the origin of those things that are yet to be. Amongst women I am fame, prosperity, fine speech, memory, intelligence, courage, and forgiveness.

From the moment we are born, we prepare for death. Death is devouring every living being with each passing moment. Death is the only certainty in life, and yet no one is ever prepared for it. Krishna manifests himself in the supremacy of this certainty.

All living creatures go through six basic changes. The body is born, lives and dies, forever growing, ageing and changing till it finally ceases to exist.

God is present in each of these changes—he is the origin of all that is, and all that is yet to be, and he is also the all-devouring death that ultimately consumes us all. Death takes us back where we came from—from the end back to the beginning.

Traditionally, some qualities are viewed as masculine and some as feminine. Over time, these specific distinctions have blurred as we have moved towards gender equal or even gender neutral societies. Now we look at qualities simply as good, not so good, avoidable etc. Black and white have given way to several shades of grey. Today, a quality that is good for a man would be equally good for a woman, and vice versa.

There are seven desirable qualities in an individual that Krishna stresses upon here.

Fame—to earn a good name either professionally or otherwise. To be well known for something positive, to be sought after, to stand out amongst a crowd.

Prosperity—to create wealth, to live life in a manner where one improves on what one is born with; to make one's life better, prosperous and opulent.

Fine speech—the importance of communication skills cannot be undermined in any society or occupation. Be it a request, an order, compliance, expression of displeasure, display of affection or approval, when well-articulated and perfectly communicated ensures favourable outcomes.

Memory—a sharp memory, a knack for memorising facts and figures, the ability to remember and recall names, people and situations is a distinct advantage over peers both in daily life and in exceptional times of crisis, emergency or calamity.

Intelligence—the importance of being in possession of an intelligent mind need hardly be elaborated. An intelligent person, irrespective of class, gender, class or race has a natural advantage over others. Not only is an intelligent mind an asset for oneself, intelligence also contributes to evolution of societies and continues to add to humankind's superiority to other forms of life.

Courage—this is an essential ingredient for being a strong personality. A courageous person can overcome odds more effectively than others. Courage here does not necessarily mean physical bravery, it stands for something more subtle. It is an inner strength and conviction to speak one's mind, support truth no matter how inconvenient, adopt a stance and stay with it, empathise, recognise one's own shortcomings and failures, and stand with the weak and the underprivileged.

Forgiveness—this is a virtue but also one of the most difficult things to do. It is easy to pontificate and tell others to forgive and forget. But it is only a rare few who can actually do that.

Because to err is human, to forgive is divine.

10.35

बृहत्साम तथा साम्नां गायत्री छन्दसामहम् |
मासानां मार्गशीर्षोऽहमृतूनां कुसुमाकरः || 35||

10.35: Of the hymns in the *Sama Veda* I am the Brihatsama; of all poetry I am the *Gayatri mantra*. Of the twelve months I am Margasheersha, and of seasons I am spring, which brings forth flowers.

Earlier in verse 10.22, Krishna had said that of the *Vedas* he is the *Sama Veda*, which is rich with melodious devotional songs. Now he says that within the *Sama Veda*, he is the Brihatsama, which has an exquisite melody and is typically sung at midnight.

Like all languages, Sanskrit has its distinctive systems of rhymes and meters for writing poetry. The poetry of the *Vedas* is in many meters. Amongst regulated poetry, the *Gayatri mantra* is most attractive and melodious. It is also a deeply meaningful prayer:

bhūrbhuvahḥ swahḥ tatsaviturvarennyamṁ bhargo devasya dhīmahi dhiyo yo nahḥ prachodayāt

–(*Rig Veda* 3.62.10)[v31]

'We meditate upon the Lord who is illuminating the three worlds and is worthy of our worship. He is the remover of all sins and the destroyer of ignorance. May he illumine our intellects in the proper direction.'

The *Gayatri mantra* holds a special place in Vedic mantras. It is believed to be the sound incarnation of Lord Brahma who is its initiator, and passed down from him, generation after generation the *Gayatri mantra* has percolated down to us.

Margsheersha, the ninth month of the Hindu calendar, falls in November-December, when the weather is pleasant. The crops in the field are harvested at this time of the year, and so it is auspicious and fulfilling. There is an overall sense of well-being and most people love this time. Krishna who rejoices in the happiness of his creations identifies with this month.

Amongst the seasons, spring manifests God's opulence the most. *Basant*, the spring season, is known as *ritu raja*, or the king of seasons. It is a time when nature is literally and metaphorically blossoming with life. With many festivals celebrated in this season, it is a time of festivity and joy, alive with a sense of joie de vivre in the air.

10.36–37

दूतं छलयतामस्मि तेजस्तेजस्विनामहम् |
जयोऽस्मि व्यवसायोऽस्मि सत्त्वं सत्त्ववतामहम् || 36||
वृष्णीनां वासुदेवोऽस्मि पाण्डवानां धनञ्जयः |
मुनीनामप्यहं व्यासः कवीनामुशना कविः || 37||

10.36: Amongst cheats I am gambling, and of all that is splendid, I am the splendour. I am victory of the victorious, the spirit of the enterprising or adventurous, and the virtue of the virtuous.

10.37: Of the descendants of Vrishni, I am Vasudev, and amongst the Pandavas I am Arjuna. Know me to be Ved Vyas amongst the sages, and Shukracharya amongst the great thinkers.

Since God is present in everything he cannot be there only in the good. Heroes and villains, good samaritans and charlatans, saints and sinners are all creations of the same maker. As human beings are blessed with intelligence, they have the capability of making choices. Some may choose to use their intellect for duplicity and cheating. Thus God is present in these acts too.

Gambling is considered to be the ultimate in all acts of cheating, and so Krishna is present in it. His greatness and presence is not lopsided—he is omnipotent and omnipresent.

In other words, if Krishna were to cheat no one can surpass him. For example, in tech terms when a hacker gets to work he can wreck the most sophisticated of software.

Amongst the victorious Krishna is victory itself, and amongst the enterprising and adventurous, he is the enterprise and the adventure. He is the splendour of everything splendid and virtue of the virtuous. Krishna took birth on earth as the son of Devaki and Vasudev, and is the most glorious descendant of the Vrishni dynasty to which he belonged. Amongst the Pandavas, the five sons of Pandu, Yudhishthira, Bheema, Arjuna, Nakula, and Sahadeva, Arjuna was the most gifted and an archer par excellence, and it is in him that Krishna manifests himself. Arjuna is also known as Dhananjaya and this is how he is addressed here.

Of all sages, Ved Vyas occupies a special place. He revealed Vedic knowledge in various ways and wrote many scriptures for the understanding of common people. It is believed Ved Vyas was one of the many avatars of Krishna himself.

Shukracharya, the spiritual master of demons, was an exceptionally learned sage, known for his expertise, knowledge and understanding of ethics. Realising that the demons too need someone to show them the way, he accepts the role of their leader, guide and mentor. By virtue of his learning, superior intelligence and far sightedness, even though on the side of demons, he is considered a representative of God himself.

10.38–39

दण्डो दमयतामस्मि नीतिरस्मि जिगीषताम् |
मौनं चैवास्मि गुह्यानां ज्ञानं ज्ञानवतामहम् || 38||
यच्चापि सर्वभूतानां बीजं तदहमर्जुन |
न तदस्ति विना यत्स्यान्मया भूतं चराचरम् || 39||

10.38: Amongst the means of preventing lawlessness I am just punishment, and appropriate conduct amongst those who seek victory. Amongst secrets I am silence, and in the wise I am their wisdom.

10.39: I am the seed generating all living beings, O Arjuna. There is no creature moving or non-moving that can exist without me.

Though human beings are superior to many other species, the practice of reward and punishment seems to work as effectively with us as with some other life forms. The desire for reward and the fear of punishment is what motivates and deters most of us from performing or not performing certain acts. In a simple management principle of man management, we can see it happening around us as the practice of promotion and demotion in any work environment. To prevent wrong-doing, and to maintain balance and peace, the Lord is present in punishment too.

The desire to be victorious is natural, and understandably no one wants to lose, irrespective of the race. But the test lies, not in being victorious but in the means we adopt for reaching the victory stand. Were we ethical, fair and just? Did we indulge in any unacceptable behaviour along the way? Were our actions above board? Krishna says that in victory he represents appropriate conduct, righteousness and morality.

Once spoken nothing can remain a secret—the greatest secret is that which is wrapped in silence. Thus, when it comes to keeping a secret the Lord is silence itself.

Balance, maturity, knowledge and experience make a person wise. The wise can discriminate between the material and the spiritual. A person endowed with wisdom can see all events, persons, and objects in relation to God. This gives one the correct perspective and equanimity to live with the ups and downs of life, and not lose sight of the ultimate goal. Someone who can assimilate all this wisdom is considered wise, and it is in this wisdom that Krishna manifests himself.

Krishna goes on to say that he is omnipotent—the seed that generates everything on earth, and without his potency nothing can exist. Living beings are born in four ways. They are born from

- eggs, such as birds, snakes, and lizards
- the womb, such as humans, cows, dogs, and cats
- sweat, such as lice, ticks
- the earth, such as trees, creepers, grass, and corn.

Others, such as ghosts, evil spirits, illusionary and the supernatural, Krishna is the origin of all of them. Physical, metaphysical, material, spiritual, movable or immovable, everything is generated by the seed and will of the Lord, and cannot exist without it.

11

The Cosmic Form and
the Cosmic Vision

The conversation between Krishna and Arjuna continues. Now fully understanding the omnipotent, omniscient and the omnipresent quality of his 'charioteer', Arjuna is keen to see him in his cosmic form. Seeing that now Arjuna has understood the extent of his sheer magnitude and magnificence, Krishna describes what he is about to show him. The cosmic form.

'Behold my majestic opulence!' says Krishna. This majestic infinite entity includes

- the celestial gods
- everything moving and non-moving
- unlimited faces, eyes, arms and legs
- heavenly fragrances
- the brilliance of a thousand suns
- confluence of all gods and living entities
- and much else

Overwhelmed and overcome with the vision of 'the thousand-armed one' presenting itself to him, Arjuna asks Krishna to also reveal his 'four-armed form' as that might be less intimidating. Krishna thus shows his friend his many forms that even celestial gods have not had the occasion to behold.

It is here that Krishna says, 'I am mighty Time, the ultimate destroyer, that comes forth to annihilate the worlds.' This aspect of the Supreme Power needs to be thought over and understood for its depth and meaning.

Each one of us in our own small way is the creator and preserver of something. It can include something as simple as planting a seed, making a painting, or arranging papers in a file. Every piece of work requires some creativity and once done we take great pride in it, as in watering and protecting our plant, displaying our painting or keeping away a new file in a safe place.

Rarely, if ever, do we destroy our own plant, mutilate our own painting or destroy our own file. But the Supreme Power seems to be equally comfortable in first creating, then preserving and finally destroying. But why?

To understand the grand plan of creation and the inevitability of the churning of the cycle of time, continuously changing everything, it is important to understand this. Clearly, the larger picture of the universe and the purpose behind it is of essence here.

To keep the narrative moving on stage, actors must play their part and exit, and so everything must give in sooner or later. Or could it be like building a sand castle at the beach? Even a child knows her work will get washed away, but puts her heart and soul into building it anyway?

Each of us is aware of our mortality, but we choose to shut our eyes to it, and remain engaged in material acquisition. We are experts at surviving on the placebo that if we can't see it, it is not there.

This superhuman ability to destroy one's own creation is the ultimate example of detachment...

This superhuman ability to destroy one's own creation is the ultimate example of detachment—one which most human beings are sadly incapable of mastering. Anyone who can do this, without malice or evil intent, is certainly at an exalted level of existence.

Arjuna wishes to see the divine form but does not realise the naivety of his wish. Human eyes can only see earthly objects, that too within a certain distance and with reasonable light. To behold the cosmic form, what is required is cosmic vision.

Unable to resist the temptation of moving from the sublime to the ordinary, one may add that the situation is reminiscent of settling down to watch a 3D film. Yes, you certainly need those special glasses for viewing.

Aeons ago, Krishna said the same thing. The rest, as they say, is history.

But you cannot see my cosmic form with these human eyes of yours. Therefore, I grant you divine vision. Behold my majestic opulence!

–Verse 11.08

chapter 11

Vishvaroopa-Darshana Yoga
Yoga as Vision of Cosmic Form

11. 04–05

मन्यसे यदि तच्छक्यं मया द्रष्टमिति प्रभो |
योगेश्वर ततो मे त्वं दर्शयात्मानमव्ययम् || 4||

श्रीभगवानुवाच |
पश्य मे पार्थ रूपाणि शतशोऽथ सहस्रश: |
नानाविधानि दिव्यानि नानावर्णाकृतीनि च || 5||

11.04: O Yogeshwara, Lord of all mystic powers, if you think I am strong enough to behold it, then kindly reveal to me that eternal cosmic form.

11.05: The Supreme Lord said: Behold, O Partha, my hundreds and thousands of wonderful forms of various shapes, sizes, and colours.

In the previous verse, Arjuna desired to see the cosmic form of the Supreme Lord. Continuing with his request he now seeks his approval. But why does he say 'if you think I am strong enough'?

Arjuna has by now realised that human eyes can only see earthly forms and are unable to understand the extent of the infinite. So he leaves it to Krishna to reveal himself if he thinks Arjuna has the capability of seeing him in his cosmic form.

Previously, Arjuna addressed Krishna as yogi. Yoga is the science of uniting the individual soul with the Supreme soul, and those who practise this science are called yogis. The name Yogeshwara means lord of all yogis. By using the name Yogeshwara now Arjuna is acknowledging Krishna's stature.

Conceding to Arjuna's request, Krishna then asks him to behold his cosmic, infinite form. Although the form is one, it has unlimited features, and contains innumerable persons, multiple shapes and countless colours. In addition to these, celestial gods and other wonderful sights are also visible in the unique cosmic form.

11.06

पश्यादित्यान्वसून् रुद्रानश्विनौ मरुतस्तथा |
बहून्यदृष्टपूर्वाणि पश्याश्चर्याणि भारत || 6||

11.06: Behold in me, O scion of the Bharatas, the sons of Aditi, the Vasus, the Rudras, the Ashwini Kumars, as well as the Maruts and many more marvels never revealed before.

Krishna goes on to reveal that the celestial gods are all part of his divine form; he shows Arjuna the twelve sons of Aditi collectively known as Adityas, the eight Vasus, the eleven forms of Rudras, the twin Ashwini Kumars, as well as the forty-nine Maruts within himself.

Thus, the universal form of the Lord not only contains wonders that exist on earth but also those that exist in the entire universe. Very rarely, if ever, are all these sights seen as a single whole.

The twelve sons of Aditi are: Dhata, Mitra, Aryama, Shakra, Varun, Amsha, Bhaga, Vivasvan, Pusha, Savita, Tvashta, Vaman.

The eight Vasus are: Dara, Dhruv, Soma, Ahah, Anila, Anala, Pratyush, Prabhas.

The eleven Rudras are: Hara, Bahurupa, Tryambaka, Aparajita, Vrisakapi, Shambhu, Kapardi, Raivata, Mrigavyadha, Sarva, Kapali.

The two Ashwini Kumars are the twin-born physicians of the gods.

The forty-nine Maruts (wind gods) are: Sattvajyoti, Aditya, Satyajyoti, Tiryagjyoti, Sajyoti, Jyotishman, Harita, Ritajit, Satyajit, Sushena, Senajit, Satyamitra, Abhimitra, Harimitra, Krita, Satya, Dhruv, Dharta, Vidharta, Vidharaya, Dhvanta, Dhuni, Ugra, Bhima, Abhiyu, Sakshipa, Idrik, Anyadrik, Yadrik, Pratikrit, Rik, Samiti, Samrambha, Idriksha, Purusha, Anyadriksha, Chetasa, Samita, Samidriksha, Pratidriksha, Maruti, Sarata, Deva, Disha, Yajuh, Anudrik, Sama, Manusha, and Vish.

11.07–08

इहैकस्थं जगत्कृत्स्नं पश्याद्य सचराचरम् |
मम देहे गुडाकेश यच्चान्यद्द्रष्टुमिच्छसि || 7||
न तु मां शक्यसे द्रष्टुमनेनैव स्वचक्षुषा |
दिव्यं ददामि ते चक्षुः पश्य मे योगमैश्वरम् || 8||

11.07: With everything moving and non-moving, assembled together in my universal form, behold now, Arjuna, the entire universe. Whatever else you wish to see, observe it all within this universal form.

11.08: But you cannot see my cosmic form with these human eyes of yours. Therefore, I grant you divine vision. Behold my majestic opulence!

No one can see the entire universe at the same time, certainly not a mere human being. But Arjuna, who from being a friend has now become a devotee of Krishna is given the unique opportunity of being able to see anything and everything from the past, present and future. He will see every aspect of the universe, including its many parts, whether moving or non-moving.

Very soon, Arjuna will also see the victory of the Pandavas and the defeat of the Kauravas as an event that is going to happen in the near future.

When the Supreme Lord appears in an avatar on earth, only his material or earthly form is visible to people. The real cosmic form that does justice to his all-encompassing presence and Supreme Power is visible only to those with divine vision. As Arjuna is an ordinary mortal he is unable to see the true opulence of Krishna with his human eyes, and his mortal intellect fails to comprehend the universal form. As a human being he is bedazzled, confused and shaken, and physically incapable of grasping the grand scale of the Lord.

This reiterates Krishna's words earlier on (verse 9.11) when he says that ignorant persons are unable to recognise him when he descends on earth in a human form, failing to see the transcendental nature of his personality, i.e. as the Supreme Lord of all creation. Thus, Krishna now says that he will grant divine vision to Arjuna with which it will become possible for him to behold the Lord's universal form in all its brilliance.

In a larger sense this means that when God wishes to bestow his kindness on a devotee's soul, he adds his divine eyes to the soul's material eyes; he adds his divine mind to the soul's material mind; he adds his divine intellect to the soul's material intellect. Thus enhanced with the divine senses, mind, and intellect of God, the devotee's soul can see the Lord's divine form, focus on it, and comprehend it.

11.10–13

अनेकवक्त्रनयनमनेकाद्भुतदर्शनम् |
अनेकदिव्याभरणं दिव्यानेकोद्यतायुधम् || 10||
दिव्यमाल्याम्बरधरं दिव्यगन्धानुलेपनम् |
सर्वाश्चर्यमयं देवमनन्तं विश्वतोमुखम् || 11||
दिवि सूर्यसहस्रस्य भवेद्युगपदुत्थिता |
यदि भाः सदृशी सा स्याद्भासस्तस्य महात्मनः || 12||
तत्रैकस्थं जगत्कृत्स्नं प्रविभक्तमनेकधा |
अपश्यद्देवदेवस्य शरीरे पाण्डवस्तदा || 13||

11.10: Arjuna saw unlimited faces and eyes in that cosmic form, unlimited brilliant visions, decorated with innumerable celestial ornaments and wielding many kinds of divine weapons.

11.11: He wore celestial garments and many garlands on his body, and was anointed with numerous sweet-smelling heavenly fragrances. He revealed himself as the wonderful and infinite Lord, the brilliance of whose face is all-pervading.

11.12: If hundreds and thousands of suns were to blaze forth together in the sky, they would not match the effulgence of that great form.

11.13: There Arjuna could see the entire universe in totality situated in one place, in that cosmic body of the God of gods.

In these verses Sanjaya is describing to Dhritarashtra the divine visuals he is seeing. Sanjaya was specially blessed by Ved Vyas with a boon of being able to see anything anywhere, from near or far, and thus is able to see the battlefield as he sits miles away.

As he speaks, the repeated use of the words *aneka* (many) and *anant* (unlimited) indicates that there was no limit to the number faces, eyes, mouths, shapes, colours, and forms that he was seeing.

These manifestations were distributed throughout the universe, but by the grace of the Lord and the special vision received, Arjuna could see them all at once. In normal course, the human mind is incapable of grasping anything even remotely of this magnitude. The cosmic form of God revealed unusual wonders, marvels, and miracles across limitations of space and time, and is nothing short of being a magical wonder.

Running short of words to convey what he was witnessing Sanjaya tries describing the effulgence of the universal form. As nothing ever seen before could be comparable to the brilliant radiance, he compares it to thousand suns blazing simultaneously in the midday sky. Perhaps even this was an understatement as no words could do justice to the unparalleled splendour and grandeur of the cosmic form.

After describing the dazzling brilliance of the Supreme Lord, Sanjaya says that the unique vision encompassed the entire universe. Arjuna experiences the good fortune of seeing the entire creation in its totality in Krishna's body, which included infinite universes, their multiple galaxies and planetary systems.

According to Vedic scriptures of the several universes and many planets, some are made of earth, some of jewels, some of gold, while others are not so magnificent. Seated on his chariot on the battlefield Arjuna could see them all with the divine eyes and intellect, granted to him by Krishna.

11.15–16

अर्जुन उवाच |

पश्यामि देवांस्तव देव देहे
सर्वांस्तथा भूतविशेषसङ्घान् |
ब्रह्माणमीशं कमलासनस्थ-
मृषींश्च सर्वानुरगांश्च दिव्यान् || 15||
अनेकबाहूदरवक्त्रनेत्रं
पश्यामि त्वां सर्वतोऽनन्तरूपम् |
नान्तं न मध्यं न पुनस्तवादिं
पश्यामि विश्वेश्वर विश्वरूप || 16||

11.15 : Arjuna said: O Krishna, I behold within your body a special confluence all the gods and living entities. I see Brahma seated on the lotus flower; I see Shiva, all the sages, and the divine serpents.

11.16: O Lord of the universe, I see your infinite form from all sides, with countless arms, stomachs, faces, and eyes, whose form is the universe itself, I do not see in you any beginning, middle, or end.

On being granted divine vision Arjuna can now see the cosmic form of Krishna. Unable to contain his sense of wonder Arjuna exclaims that he was seeing a confluence of many entities. He saw multitudes of beings from all the three worlds, including gods of celestial abodes. He sees Lord Brahma, the creator, sitting on the lotus, Lord Shiva, all sages, and divine serpents such as Vasuki.

Addressing Krishna as *vishweshwar*, controller of the universe, and *vishwarup*, universal form, Arjuna increasingly realises the Lord's true opulence and magnificence. He says that he is seeing countless forms within the one cosmic form, but he is unable to find any beginning, middle or end of the magnificent sight.

11.17–18

किरीटिनं गदिनं चक्रिणं च
तेजोराशिं सर्वतो दीप्तिमन्तम् |
पश्यामि त्वां दुर्निरीक्ष्यं समन्ताद्
दीप्तानलार्कद्युतिमप्रमेयम् || 17||
त्वमक्षरं परमं वेदितव्यं
त्वमस्य विश्वस्य परं निधानम् |
त्वमव्यय: शाश्वतधर्मगोप्ता
सनातनस्त्वं पुरुषो मतो मे || 18||

11.17: Adorned with a crown, armed with the club and disc, I see your form, shining everywhere like an abode of splendour. It is difficult to look upon you in the blazing fire of your effulgence. Like the blazing fire of the sun, your form shines forth in all directions.

11.18: You are the supreme indestructible being, the Ultimate Truth to be understood by the scriptures. You are the basis of all creation; you are the eternal protector of religion; and you are the everlasting Supreme Divine Being.

The cosmic form that Arjuna sees is a personification of splendour itself. Human eyes are unable to bear the brightness of the vision as the brilliance exceeded the light of thousands of blazing suns. Blessed with divine sight, Arjuna is able to see this unique vision.

Within the universal form, Arjuna sees the four-armed Lord Vishnu, adorned with a crown and with the emblems special to him—mace, disc, and lotus flower.

Arjuna recognises the sovereignty of Krishna as the Supreme Lord, who is the basis of all creation. It is possible to understand the magnificence of the Lord by studying the Vedic scriptures. The aim of the scriptures is to lead us to the right path. Now seeing Krishna in all his brilliance Arjuna realises that this is the destination for which the sacred texts prepare us.

11.19–23

अनादिमध्यान्तमनन्तवीर्य-
मनन्तबाहुं शशिसूर्यनेत्रम् |
पश्यामि त्वां दीप्तहुताशवक्त्रं-
स्वतेजसा विश्वमिदं तपन्तम् || 19||
द्यावापृथिव्योरिदमन्तरं हि
व्याप्तं त्वयैकेन दिशश्च सर्वाः |
दृष्ट्वाद्भुतं रूपमुग्रं तवेदं
लोकत्रयं प्रव्यथितं महात्मन् || 20||
अमी हि त्वां सुरसङ्घा विशन्ति
केचिद्भीताः प्राञ्जलयो गृणन्ति |
स्वस्तीत्युक्त्वा महर्षिसिद्धसङ्घाः
स्तुवन्ति त्वां स्तुतिभिः पुष्कलाभिः || 21||
रुद्रादित्या वसवो ये च साध्या
विश्वेऽश्विनौ मरुतश्चोष्मपाश्च |
गन्धर्वयक्षासुरसिद्धसङ्घा
वीक्षन्ते त्वां विस्मिताश्चैव सर्वे || 22||
रूपं महत्ते बहुवक्त्रनेत्रं

महाबाहो बहुबाहूरुपादम् ।
बहूदरं बहुदंष्ट्राकरालं
दृष्ट्वा लोकाः प्रव्यथितास्तथाहम् ॥ 23॥

11.19: You are without beginning, middle, or end; your power is unlimited. Your arms are infinite; the sun and the moon are like your eyes. I see fire blazing forth from your mouth and warming the entire creation with your radiance.

11.20: The entire outer space is pervaded by you alone. Seeing your wondrous and terrible form, I see the three worlds trembling in fear, O greatest of all beings.

11.21: All celestial gods are seeking your shelter by entering into you. In awe and wonder, some are praising you with folded hands. The great sages and perfected beings are praising you by singing auspicious hymns and prayers.

11.22: All the manifestations of Lord Shiva, the Rudras, Adityas, Vasus, Sadhyas, Vishvadevas, Ashwini Kumars, Maruts, Gandharvas, Yakshas, Asuras, and Siddhas and ancestors are all beholding you in wonder.

11.23: O mighty-armed Lord, your imposing magnificent form with its innumerable mouths, eyes, arms, thighs, legs, bellies, and terrifying teeth, intimidates all planets and even celestial gods. All the worlds in the universe are awestruck, and so am I.

Fascinated by what he could see Arjuna now repeats that the Lord is without beginning, middle, or end. If one were to put oneself in Arjuna's place it is not difficult to understand his sense of wonder and amazement. Let us for a minute imagine seeing a form which is unending and unlimited, which does not seem to start or end anywhere. Chances are we might find ourselves being repetitive and awestruck.

Reiteration and repetition of the Lord's glory is not a flaw or weakness, it is an unconscious process of internalisation of the unbelievable. The Supreme Power is indeed, without a beginning and end, as all space and time are within him, and he is beyond the measure of material limits. The sun and moon are like the eyes of the Lord who has fire blazing from his mouth, keeping the universe alive and warm.

Omnipresent across space, the all-pervading form generates fear and awe. Even the celestial gods seek shelter in the Lord and sing his praise with folded hands. Revered sages, learned men and women, indeed, every entity hopes and prays to be accepted by the Supreme Being and melt into its infinite form.

Continuing to repeat himself, Arjuna says that all manifestations of Lord Shiva, the Adityas, Vasus, Sadhyas, Vishvadevas, Ashwini Kumars, Maruts, Gandharvas, Yakshas, Asuras, and Siddhas and ancestors are looking at the Lord in wonder and amazement. The innumerable mouths, eyes, arms, thighs, legs, bellies, and terrifying teeth all add up to an unparalleled spectre never seen earlier. Be it the gods or mere mortals, all tremble in fear and realize their insignificance in the face of the Supreme Power. Along with all other entities, Arjuna is himself awestruck.

11.26–27

अमी च त्वां धृतराष्ट्रस्य पुत्रा:
सर्वे सहैवावनिपालसङ्घै: |
भीष्मो द्रोण: सूतपुत्रस्तथासौ
सहास्मदीयैरपि योधमुख्यै: || 26||
वक्त्राणि ते त्वरमाणा विशन्ति
दंष्ट्राकरालानि भयानकानि |
केचिद्विलग्ना दशनान्तरेषु
संदृश्यन्ते चूर्णितैरुत्तमाङ्गै: || 27||

11.26–27: I see all the sons of Dhritarashtra, along with their allied kings, including Bhishma, Dronacharya, Karna, and also some generals from our side, rushing headlong into your fearsome mouths. I see some with their heads smashed between your terrible teeth.

The wonderous spectacle that Arjuna sees now is a glimpse of the future. Just as the Lord has no beginning, middle or end, similarly the Supreme Power also has no past, present or future. And so along with his existing opulence, Arjuna also sees what the future holds.

Beholding the imminent future in the divine form, Arjuna sees the great Kaurava generals–Bhishma, Dronacharya, and Karna, as well as many of the Pandava generals entering the mouth of the Lord and being ground between his teeth. Teeth here symbolise tools of destruction. We see those on the side of evil being devoured by the Lord, literally being chewed to pieces before they are annihilated. This is the purpose for which the Lord has taken birth in human form—to restore goodness, and to rid the earth of evil.

Bhishma was the son of Shantanu and Ganga, and to facilitate his father's wish for remarriage and to allow his future child to be the heir, Bhishma takes a vow of celibacy, thus disrupting the natural line of succession. Bhishma also takes a vow to always protect the throne of Hastinapur—irrespective of who occupied it, and so many years later, much to his dissatisfaction, finds himself on the side of Duryodhana as he is the son of the ruling king, Dhritarashtra. Eventually Bhishma has to pay the price for the vows he took in his youth, and be defeated and die in the war.

Bhishma is well aware that he is siding with evil in the battle against good, but being a man of his word, he cannot go back on his vow. The fact that the Kauravas had treated the Pandavas unfairly caused him great anguish and pain, but as someone loyal to the throne he is helpless. In his final days, he lies on a bed of arrows on the battlefield till death takes him.

Dronacharya was the guru of martial arts for both the Kauravas and the Pandavas. He was known for his loyalty to the royal family and even went to the extent of teaching more to Arjuna than to his own son, Ashwatthama. In another instance, he asks Eklavya, an able student but from a lower social class, who was more gifted than Arjuna, to cut off his thumb and give it to Dronacharya as *guru dakshina* (offering to teacher). He thus ensured that no contemporary of Arjuna surpassed him in archery and warfare.

Later Dronacharya has to be with Kauravas as he was dependent on Duryodhana for his livelihood and social status. Thus, Dronacharya too was destined to die in the war. Knowing that no one could defeat him he himself tells the Pandavas the way in which he could be overcome and killed. His teaching skills, knowledge, and loyalty are legendary and even today Dronacharya is quoted as an example of exemplary teaching and mentoring.

Karna was Kunti's eldest son born before her marriage, and so was abandoned by her as a newborn. Brought up as a foundling by a lower caste couple, Karna lives a life of deprivation and faces constant ridicule of the upper castes. Duryodhana is the only one who acknowledges Karna's exceptional qualities as an archer, a great warrior, and a good human being. He honours Karna and makes him king of a small kingdom, Anga. Karna is thus beholden to Duryodhana and cannot go against him knowing fully well that his mentor is on the side of evil.

Karna is known as *daanveer* for his legendary generosity, and later on, even when he knows that he is a kshatriya by birth, and that Pandavas are his brothers, he does not disclose this so as to keep his mother's honour. To date, Karna is revered as a man of exceptional qualities of head and heart. Ironically, in this battle he finds himself on the wrong side, and so willingly gives up his life to fight for his friend Duryodhana, and die at the hands of the Pandavas. He allows himself to be killed by Arjuna so that his younger brother could emerge victorious.

Thus we see three exceptional characters, Bhishma, Dronacharya and Karna, good men but on the side of evil, paying a price for the choices they had to make. However, of the entire army of the Kauravas, it is these three who are till today looked upon with respect and awe for their loyalty, sacrifice, and the rare quality of standing by their commitment, knowing fully well that they are hurtling along on the path to disaster. Death and destruction await them, but they do not for a moment consider going back on their word.

11.28–31

यथा नदीनां बहवोऽम्बुवेगाः
समुद्रमेवाभिमुखा द्रवन्ति |
तथा तवामी नरलोकवीरा
विशन्ति वक्त्राण्यभिविज्वलन्ति || 28||
यथा प्रदीप्तं ज्वलनं पतङ्गा
विशन्ति नाशाय समृद्धवेगाः |
तथैव नाशाय विशन्ति लोका-
स्तवापि वक्त्राणि समृद्धवेगाः || 29||
लेलिह्यसे ग्रसमानः समन्ता-
ल्लोकान्समग्रान्वदनैर्ज्वलद्भिः |
तेजोभिरापूर्य जगत्समग्रं
भासस्तवोग्राः प्रतपन्ति विष्णो || 30||
आख्याहि मे को भवानुग्ररूपो
नमोऽस्तु ते देववर प्रसीद |
विज्ञातुमिच्छामि भवन्तमाद्यं
न हि प्रजानामि तव प्रवृत्तिम् || 31||

11.28–29: Like river waters flowing rapidly into the ocean, so are all these great warriors entering your blazing mouths. Like moths rush speedily into the fire to perish, so are all these armies entering your mouths with great speed.

11.30: The flaming tongues of your many mouths are licking people from all sides and devouring them. O Vishnu, you are scorching the entire universe with the fierce, all-pervading rays of your effulgence.

11.31: O God of gods, so fierce of form, tell me who you are. I bow before you; please bestow your mercy on me. You, who are the origin, I wish to know who you are, for I do not understand your nature and your purpose.

Arjuna sees people from both armies slipping into the cosmic form. The final journey is the same for all as they are devoured by death, but based on their deeds in life the reasons for the end and pathways adopted are different. The likes of Bhishma, Drona and Karna are merging with the Lord as a natural progression, much like the rivers that flow on their course and merge with the ocean, which is their ultimate destination.

On the other hand, there are those who were driven by self-interest, greed and misplaced ambition. Arjuna compares them to moths who get lured by the warmth and light of the fire, and out of ignorance get scorched by its blistering heat.

The description that Arjuna goes on to give of the sight he is beholding is indeed brutal and unnerving. Here the cosmic form appears dragon-like in its ferocity. The angry mouths are seen spewing fire while long blazing tongues lick living entities to a gory, blistering end.

The Lord appears as an all-devouring force lapping up Arjuna's friends and allies from both sides. Nothing, and no one can escape the ferocious omnipresent power that eventually annihilates all that it creates.

Now that his wish has been granted and the Lord has revealed himself, Arjuna begins to see the enormity of the sight that confronts him. Unable to understand the infinite proportions of the cosmic form, he is at a loss and feels agitated. He now wants to know of God's nature and purpose. Therefore, he asks the question, 'Who are you and what is your purpose?'

11.32–33 (143–44)

श्रीभगवानुवाच |

कालोऽस्मि लोकक्षयकृत्प्रवृद्धो
लोकान्समाहर्तुमिह प्रवृत्त: |
ऋतेऽपि त्वां न भविष्यन्ति सर्वे
येऽवस्थिता: प्रत्यनीकेषु योधा: || 32||
तस्मात्त्वमुत्तिष्ठ यशो लभस्व
जित्वा शत्रून्भुङ् क्ष्व राज्यं समृद्धम् |
मयैवैते निहता: पूर्वमेव
निमित्तमात्रं भव सव्यसाचिन् || 33||

11.32: The Supreme Lord said: I am mighty Time, the ultimate destroyer, that comes forth to annihilate the worlds. Even without your participation, the warriors in the opposing army shall be destroyed.

11.33: Therefore, arise and prepare to fight and attain honour! Conquer your foes and enjoy the gains of a flourishing kingdom. These warriors are already slain by me, and you, O Sabyasachi, will only be an instrument of my work.

Earlier on Krishna says that when considering phenomena that is long lasting, time is endless and therefore most superior in terms of being infinite. Adding further to it he now tells Arjuna that time is mighty and is the ultimate destroyer. So time is the greatest healer, time never stops for anyone, once gone time never comes back, and time also eventually finishes everyone and everything. As the Supreme Power,

Krishna declares that he is Time itself and ultimately no one can escape from the might and reach of time.

Admonishing Arjuna, Krishna then tells him that whether he participates in the battle or not, the warriors on the other side are destined to be destroyed, as they are on the side of evil. This is also the purpose for which the Divine has taken birth on earth.

Krishna then apprises Arjuna of the opportunity that is presenting itself to him of proving himself on the battlefield. He asks Arjuna to get up and fight and finish the enemy. This is the perfect moment for him to attain glory as a fighter, and establish himself as a warrior par excellence. The Lord asks Arjuna to decimate the enemy, and prepare for a life of peace and prosperity while he rules over his kingdom. Significantly, here he addresses Arjuna as Sabyasachi, which means ambidextrous, or the one who can use both hands efficiently, telling him that the future is already known to him and Arjuna cannot change it, but he can be instrumental in fructifying it.

This gives an interesting insight into what we might view as our achievements as individuals. In the grand scheme of things, birth, life and death are pre-determined and so are life–changing events—both positive and negative—based on our deeds of past life. God does not need us to make his plans work, but he does give us the choice and the opportunity to participate and contribute in moving towards destined milestones, and thus achieve glory on earth. Therefore, opportunities that come to us must not be frittered away as these are God's way of giving us a chance to support him in making his plans a reality.

By addressing him as Sabyasachi, Krishna also reminds Arjuna of the special talents he has, and that he must make use of these. Each one of us is blessed with something special. Some can sing, some can write, while others can paint, and so on. Some of us optimise on our talents, feel grateful for being blessed with them, and make full use of these.

This is the simplest way of pleasing the Divine as it is he who has given us these gifts.

On the other hand, there are those who fritter away opportunities and allow their talents to remain unexplored, thus invoking God's displeasure. The gifts we are blessed with and the choices we are faced with, must be made best use of. This way we earn name and fame on earth, and also please the Lord who has generously bestowed both talents and opportunities on us.

11.34

द्रोणं च भीष्मं च जयद्रथं च
कर्णं तथान्यानपि योधवीरान् |
मया हतांस्त्वं जहि मा व्यथिष्ठा
युध्यस्व जेतासि रणे सपत्नान् || 34||

11.34: Dronacharya, Bhishma, Jayadratha, Karna, and other brave warriors have already been killed by me. So slay them without feeling disturbed. Fight and you will be victorious over your enemies in battle.

Like a fond parent helping a young child hold a pen in her hand to write, Krishna is intent on helping Arjuna achieve glory on earth.

The way the parent allows the child to believe that she has written the alphabet, while actually it is the strong guiding hand that has done the writing, Krishna has already determined the fate of those fighting on the side of evil. But he is keen that Arjuna gets credit for it. Being the exceptional warrior that he is, it is possible only for Arjuna to decimate such a powerful enemy.

Dronacharya, Bhishma, Jayadratha and Karna are known for their prowess and mastery in warfare. Each one of them is a good human being, but through a complicated development of circumstances finds himself on the side of the Kauravas. It is therefore preordained that they shall have to pay a price for making this choice, and eventually succumb in the battle.

Annihilation of evil is the primary purpose for which God appears on earth from time to time, to cleanse the system of impurity, dishonesty, malpractices and exploitation. By ensuring defeat of the Kauravas, Krishna is putting that intent to action, and is initiating the process of cleansing of the world.

In disclosing to Arjuna the pre-determined fate of his relatives on the other side, Krishna is actively reducing his cousin's guilt and remorse at having to kill his own people. Simultaneously, he is also making sure Arjuna's name becomes part of folklore, after effectively putting down such formidable counterparts.

Apart from fearlessly fighting the enemy, the underlying message here is also that, one, it is important to recognise an opportunity when it is knocking on the door, and two, to optimise on what it has to offer. It could well be a once-in-a-life time chance to establish oneself as the best in one's field of work.

As they say, some opportunities that come our way are godsent. In Arjuna's case this is absolutely true.

11.39

वायुर्यमोऽग्निर्वरुण: शशाङ्क:
प्रजापतिस्त्वं प्रपितामहश्च |
नमो नमस्तेऽस्तु सहस्रकृत्व:
पुनश्च भूयोऽपि नमो नमस्ते || 39||

11.39: You are Vayu (the god of wind), Yamraj (the god of death), Agni (the god of fire), Varun (the god of water), and Chandra (the moon-God). You are the creator Brahma, and the ancestor of all beings. I offer my respectful salutations unto you a thousand times, again and yet again!

On realizing the omnipotence of Krishna, Arjuna offers obeisance to him. He understands that all sources of life and power are manifestations of the same Lord. He says that be it Vayu, the god of wind, Yamraj, the god of death, Agni, the god of fire, Varun, the god of water, or Chandra, the moon god, all are but manifestations of the Supreme Lord. Krishna is Brahma, the creator of the universe and the ancestor of all living entities. Arjuna is completely beholden to the glories of the Lord. Being in a state of awe he is repetitious, and offers respectful salutations over and over again.

11.41–42

सखेति मत्वा प्रसभं यदुक्तं
हे कृष्ण हे यादव हे सखेति ।
अजानता महिमानं तवेदं
मया प्रमादात्प्रणयेन वापि ॥ 41॥
यच्चावहासार्थमसत्कृतोऽसि
विहारशय्यासनभोजनेषु ।
एकोऽथवाप्यच्युत तत्समक्षं
तत्क्षामये त्वामहमप्रमेयम् ॥ 42॥

11.41–42: Thinking of you as my friend, I addressed you informally as, 'O Krishna,' 'O Yadav,' 'O my dear mate.' Your majesty was not known to me, resulting in my being negligent and displaying inappropriate affection. And if, in jest, I treated you with disrespect, while playing, resting, sitting, eating, when alone, or in presence of others—for all that I beg forgiveness.

As Krishna's status increasingly dawns on him, Arjuna is recalling the times they have spent together as friends and cousins. Shocked and awkward now, Arjuna realises that he has been addressing Krishna by his name, or as his buddy, or even as Yadava—a playful reference to Krishna's caste. He now begs forgiveness for all the times he has indulged in friendly bantering with Krishna during their growing up years.

We can see here how the dynamics between the two has undergone a complete transformation in a relatively short time. From being friends and cousins for years, Arjuna and Krishna become warrior and charioteer. Krishna then goes on to adopt the role of mentor, guide and counsellor when Arjuna starts to lose his nerve at the battlefield. And now we see the two—one as the Divine Power in all its glory and the other as the humble devotee kneeling at his feet.

An interesting reality emerges here as we realise that relationships need not always be static. As we grow, roles are constantly redefined—a friend can become a guide, the strong could experience moments of weakness, and a childhood friend you assumed you knew all about, turns out to be much more than who she or he appeared to be. A case in point that nothing in life is permanent and everything is constantly changing and evolving, and that we must accept new realities graciously, and with humility.

11. 46–47

किरीटिनं गदिनं चक्रहस्त-
मिच्छामि त्वां द्रष्टमहं तथैव |
तेनैव रूपेण चतुर्भुजेन
सहस्रबाहो भव विश्वमूर्ते || 46||

श्रीभगवानुवाच |
मया प्रसन्नेन तवार्जुनेदं
रूपं परं दर्शितमात्मयोगात् |
तेजोमयं विश्वमनन्तमाद्यं
यन्मे त्वदन्येन न दृष्टपूर्वम् || 47||

11.46–47: O thousand-armed one, I wish to see you in your four-armed form, carrying the mace and disc, and wearing the crown. The Supreme Lord said: Arjuna, being pleased with you, by my yogic power, I gave you a vision of my original cosmic form. No one before you has ever seen this resplendent, unlimited form.

Having seen the rare cosmic form on being blessed with divine vision, Arjuna realises that who he thought was a friend and cousin, was actually the Lord himself. He has seen what no human being gets to see, and the sight is daunting and intimidating. Faced with the usually invisible form, Arjuna is shaken and awestruck, and finds it challenging to maintain his composure and balance.

Finding it difficult to relate to this supremely majestic form he prefers to see the Lord in the human form. Addressing Krishna as the thousand-armed, *sahasra baho*, he requests him to reveal his four-armed form, *chatur bhuj rup*, which he feels he might be more comfortable with as it is closer to the human body in appearance.

Seeing that Arjuna was shaken and perturbed, Krishna accedes to his request. He assures Arjuna that he has not revealed his overwhelming personality in its totality to frighten or punish Arjuna. As a matter of fact, he has done it as he is pleased with Arjuna and has given him a glimpse of a sight that no human being has ever had the good fortune of beholding. Arjuna is, therefore, the first one to set eyes on this breathtaking vision which the Lord has manifested using his ultimate yogic power.

11.51–53

अर्जुन उवाच |
दृष्ट्वेदं मानुषं रूपं तव सौम्यं जनार्दन |
इदानीमस्मि संवृत्त: सचेता: प्रकृतिं गत: || 51||

श्रीभगवानुवाच |
सुदुर्दर्शमिदं रूपं दृष्ट्वानसि यन्मम |
देवा अप्यस्य रूपस्य नित्यं दर्शनकाङ्क्षिण: || 52||
नाहं वेदैर्न तपसा न दानेन न चेज्यया |
शक्य एवंविधो द्रष्टुं दृष्ट्वानसि मां यथा || 53||

11.51: Arjuna said: O Krishna, seeing your gentle human form, I have regained my composure and my mind is now restored to normal.

11.52–53: The Supreme Lord said: this form of mine that you are seeing is difficult to behold. Even the celestial gods are eager to see it. Neither by the study of the *Vedas*, nor by penance, charity, or fire sacrifices, can I be seen as you have seen me.

From the cosmic form and its thousands of arms, Krishna now appears in his four-armed form. This comes as a relief for Arjuna who found it difficult to view the intimidating infinite form with no beginning, middle or end. This is closer to the human form, and makes Arjuna feel comfortable helping him regain his composure and once again be in control of himself.

However, Krishna is careful to remind Arjuna not to take this form lightly either, as it is very rarely that anyone gets to see this. Even the celestial gods yearn to have a glimpse of God in the human form as he is now visible to Arjuna. Krishna stresses that no amount of Vedic studies, austerities, or fire sacrifices are enough for a devotee to be granted this vision of the Lord.

While human beings might make sincere and genuine efforts to reach this state of bliss, it can happen only when the Lord decides to reveal himself in some form. In other words, human beings can only strive to come face to face with the Supreme Power, but the actual revelation and manifestation will happen only when it is God's own will. No amount of spiritual pursuits and intellectual activities are enough, what is ultimately required is God's kindly disposition towards the devotee.

11.54–55

भक्त्या त्वनन्यया शक्य अहमेवंविधोऽर्जुन |
ज्ञातुं द्रष्टु च तत्त्वेन प्रवेष्टु च परन्तप || 54||
मत्कर्मकृन्मत्परमो मद्भक्त: सङ्गवर्जित: |
निर्वैर: सर्वभूतेषु य: स मामेति पाण्डव || 55||

11.54: O Arjuna, by pure devotion alone can I be known as I am, standing before you. Thereby, on receiving my divine vision, O mighty armed one, one can enter into union with me.

11.55: Those who perform all their duties for my sake, who depend upon me and are devoted to me, who are free from attachment, and are without malice toward all beings, such devotees certainly come to me.

In this verse, Krishna emphasises on devotion as the means to attain him. He reiterates that this rare form of his can be seen only through bhakti. Those who are truly devoted are dear to the Lord. No matter how much one might practise detachment, renunciation and remain in pursuit of knowledge, without devotion these are like a job half done.

In the next verse, Krishna describes what bhakti is. He underscores five aspects of devotion that form the basis of what appeals to him.

- All duties must be performed for the sake of the Almighty. Duties cannot be divided into material and spiritual, personal and professional. Every action must be taken and performed as an offering to the Lord.

- Devotees must understand that their ultimate success is dependent on the Lord's will. And so they must not assume that their own acts are sufficient to see them through. They must have complete faith in his grace and be cognisant of the fact that their devotion is merely a beginning.

- Devotion must be pure, unconditional and unwavering. Right through the trials and tribulations of life faith in the Almighty must remain unshaken and strong.

- Freedom from attachment is essential. If the mind is attached to worldly possessions devotion cannot be single-minded. Material attachment gives rise to conflicting thoughts, and creates havoc with the order of our priorities.

- Anyone who harbours ill-feeling, jealousy, envy and malice towards one's fellow beings cannot be a true devotee. Unless our hearts and minds are freed of all these inter-personal negativities, we cannot rise above petty pursuits.

12

The Power of Love
and Devotion

One of the shortest chapters of the *Gita*, the stress here is on devotion and dedication. People dedicate themselves to different missions and each one of us has a unique way of being devoted. While some may work for the needy by actually visiting their homes, others may raise funds for them, sitting in their own homes. Doctors cure patients by prescribing medicines but scientists help in the process by researching on drugs.

People from varied cultures have their own way of praying, and follow different protocols for worship or offering prayers. All paths of bhakti, or devotion, that are adopted lead to the same destination; the routes, however, may be different from one another and thus give way to misconceptions about the goal of the journey.

Some of the areas Krishna throws light on in the conversation here are:

- the significance of focus
- visible vs. invisible
- degrees of devotion
- devotees and devotion
- meditation as a tool
- deliverance as a reward
- restraining the mind
- striving for perfection

A phrase often used in translation is 'surrendering of the intellect'. It may be useful to clarify here that, this by no means implies taking leave of one's senses or indulging in mindless devotion. What surrender here stands for is complete acceptance and confluence of thought processes to focus on one idea, or reality.

Human beings are favourably inclined towards creating symbols for ideas. We go to the extent of personifying abstractions and emotions and like to keep photographs of loved ones close to us as we find this reassuring and heart-warming, especially so in case of those who may be far away, and, over a period of time the once familiar faces may start to become hazy in our minds.

A case in point is the ever-growing popularity of audio-visual learning for children. Present day learning outcomes are a considerable improvement on the days of yore when a black and white textbook was the only source of learning for children.

Does the same hold good for keeping faith, and focusing on the greatest abstraction of them all—God himself? Probably yes. This explains the tendency to hold sacred a stone, a river or a mountain— indeed sometimes entire cities. Humanisation of the gods seems to work for us because that is the only form we can identify with and make our own.

So far so good. But trouble starts when we want our neighbour to also see divinity in the same tree as we do, or to feed the same animal that we do. We frequently forget and fail to understand, that others could be having their own symbols that could be as sacred to them as ours are to us.

Creating symbols for the purpose of better focus and identification is an innocuous activity per se. But it can become problematic when we try to convince the world that our symbol is better than theirs. If each devotee were to nurture a particular image of God and keep it strictly personal, the world might be a better place to live in.

Creating symbols for the purpose of better focus and identification is an innocuous activity per se. But it can become problematic when we try to convince the world that our symbol is better than theirs. If each devotee were to nurture a particular image of God and keep it strictly personal, the world might be a better place to live in.

Reverting to the narrative, by now Arjuna has recovered from his state of nervousness and despondency, and wants to know more from the fountain of knowledge, Krishna.

In the twelfth chapter, Krishna elaborates on the visible versus the invisible in response to Arjuna's question.

Arjuna enquires : Which is preferred—those who are sincerely devoted to your worship or those who worship the unmanifested form? Who do you consider to be more perfect in yoga?

–Verse 12.01

chapter 12

The Power of Love & Devotion
Yoga as Devotion and Dedication

12.01

अर्जुन उवाच |
एवं सततयुक्ता ये भक्तास्त्वां पर्युपासते |
ये चाप्यक्षरमव्यक्तं तेषां के योगवित्तमाः || 1||

12.01: Arjuna enquired: Which is preferred—those who are sincerely devoted to your worship or those who worship the unmanifested form? Who do you consider to be more perfect in yoga?

In the previous chapter, Arjuna sees the cosmic form of the Lord, which encompasses the entire universe. Fascinating though the sight was, Arjuna is overwhelmed and he voices his preference for the more human form of the Lord and his wish is granted.

Regaining his composure and accepting the reality that his friend Krishna was much more than what he appeared to be, now Arjuna wishes to know about the kind of devotees Krishna looks at more favourably. Some individuals worship the visible form of the Supreme Power as he appears on earth. As an extension of this, they may also see God in everything around them. Belief in idol worship, offering prayers to trees, rivers and nature as a whole are well-known phenomena.

There are others who do not follow this path and focus on the invisible, the unmanifested form of God. Such devotees may create their own image of the Lord, or simply pray to the invisible Force and chart their own path of devotion.

Arjuna is curious to know which of these devotees Krishna prefers, and subsequently bestows his blessings on. God has both aspects—the omnipresent and omniscient power, as also the incarnation in human form on earth. The latter has a specific palpable form which for mere mortals might be easier to relate to, while the former is invisible and thus for some might be difficult to focus on.

This duality could well be compared to our own existence. While no one has ever seen or felt the soul, the human body is tangible and can be seen, felt and heard and so appears more real than the soul. But the reality is that both exist, the body and soul.

12.05

क्लेशोऽधिकतरस्तेषामव्यक्तासक्तचेतसाम् ॥
अव्यक्ता हि गतिर्दुःखं देहवद्भिरवाप्यते ॥ 5॥

12.05: For those whose minds are attached to the unmanifested, the path of realisation is full of tribulations. For embodied beings, worship of the unmanifest is difficult.

As Krishna is the creator he understands his creation, i.e., human beings and the working of their minds well. He knows both their capabilities and their shortcomings. He understands that not everyone can find solace in a power that is invisible.

For instance, when a child cries, she wants her mother to hold her and make her feel safe and cared for. She is bound to feel lost and insecure, if the mother is far away, and she cannot see or touch her, and maybe even questions the mother's very existence. As the mother and child spend more time together, the physical bond grows and gradually evolves into the strongest and purest form of love and devotion.

Similarly, not all human beings can focus on something they cannot see. And so might find it challenging to nurture devotion to an impersonal form. Striving to establish a bond with the invisible might be tough, and this path could even prove frustrating and endless with no goalposts in sight.

Understanding this human imperfection, Krishna recommends focussing on his human, or personal form, as this path of devotion is easier to sustain, and as the bonding grows devotees eventually arrive at a stage of perfection in their dedication to the Supreme Power. As a matter of fact, this is also one of the purposes for which God manifests human form.

When we feed the human body we are helping keep the body and soul together. Similarly, as we worship the visible we are gently led to the invisible, till the two merge to become one.

12.06–07

ये तु सर्वाणि कर्माणि मयि संन्यस्य मत्परः |
अनन्येनैव योगेन मां ध्यायन्त उपासते || 6||
तेषामहं समुद्धर्ता मृत्युसंसारसागरात् |
भवामि नचिरात्पार्थ मय्यावेशितचेतसाम् || 7||

12.06-07: But those who dedicate all their actions to me, and worship me without distraction, and with focussed mind meditate on me with exclusive devotion, O Partha, I swiftly deliver them from the ocean of birth and death, as their consciousness is merged with me.

Taking the discourse forward, Krishna reiterates that his devotees reach him easily. Having chosen to worship the visible form of the Supreme Power, devotees can seamlessly focus their mind and senses on the Lord. All their actions and activities are performed for the same purpose as they bask in the glory of their chosen one. Having a tangible form that they identify as the Lord, the consciousness of the sincere devotee quickly merges with that of God.

Krishna on his part ensures a smooth journey for his devotees, and they cover the distance between themselves and their destination unperturbed and uninterrupted. God helps remove their doubts, hand-holds them as they walk from darkness to light, and clears obstacles from their path from time to time.

This way they cross the ocean between this world and the next, and God swiftly delivers them from the tedious and painful cycle of birth and death. As the devotee is already clear in his objectives and has performed positive actions in support of the same ultimate objective of reaching God, his consciousness merges with that of the Supreme Soul without any roadblocks.

12.08–10

मय्येव मन आधत्स्व मयि बुद्धिं निवेशय |
निवसिष्यसि मय्येव अत ऊर्ध्वं न संशयः || 8||
अथ चित्तं समाधातुं न शक्नोषि मयि स्थिरम् |
अभ्यासयोगेन ततो मामिच्छाप्तुं धनञ्जय || 9||
अभ्यासेऽप्यसमर्थोऽसि मत्कर्मपरमो भव |
मदर्थमपि कर्माणि कुर्वन्सिद्धिमवाप्स्यसि || 10||

12.08: Fix your mind on me alone, and surrender your intellect to me. Without doubt, this way you will always live in me.

12.09: O Arjuna, the conqueror of wealth, if you are unable to steadily fix your mind on me, then constantly practise restraining the mind from worldly affairs. This way you will develop a desire to attain me.

12.10: If you cannot practise remembering me with devotion, then just try to work for me. Thus, performing devotional service to me, you shall achieve perfection.

Having explained that worship of the personal form is preferred, Krishna now begins to explain how to worship him. He suggests fixing the mind on God, and surrendering the intellect to him. It is the mind that thinks all kinds of thoughts and experiences varied desires. These thoughts may not always be of the highest order, and on occasions we may find ourselves having thoughts that we might not be very proud of, or may not readily want to share with anyone.

It is our intellect that guides us and helps us discern and choose. Thus the mind performs more basic functions while our intelligence sets us apart from other species and mediocre human beings as well.

Krishna suggests focussing on the Supreme Power both with mind and intellect, and this convergence opens all doors for us and ensures that we stay with divine consciousness forever.

There may be many who might find it difficult to put this convergence to practice. Krishna suggests that such people must start with withdrawing from material desires and worldly affairs. This withdrawal will gradually give way to more exalted thoughts and actions, and direct them to the right path.

There may still be some who are unable to wean themselves away from worldly pursuits. This is natural and expected, as most human beings are ordinary mortals fully invested in their material existence. Krishna suggests it would be good for them to often remember the Lord with devotion. Whatever actions they perform, or whatever activities they like to be involved with, must be done as a dedication to God.

Any job performed to the best of one's ability is as good as devotional service. Be it household work, professional duties or recreational activities, every act must be performed as if we are doing it for God. If we put our heart and soul into every action, and perform each one with honesty and sincerity, every job well done will take us closer to the Supreme Power.

13

The Palpable and the Impalpable

If you can think it, you can do it. This is a nugget of wisdom we have often been exposed to especially during motivational sessions. Nothing could be closer to the truth as all inventions, discoveries and creative work are basically an outcome of a thought in someone's mind. Even a flight of fancy, perhaps.

> *If you can think it, you can do it.*

The thirteenth chapter marks the beginning of the third, and the final segment of the *Gita*. The last six chapters focus on knowledge and its role in finding and walking on the right spiritual path. This chapter explores the relationship between body and soul, examining how the two work in tandem with one another, and the manner in which this combination determines our thoughts and actions.

Our body is not just a palpable composition of living cells, but also includes our mind, intelligence, thoughts etc. The physiological and the psychological make us what and who we are. The soul, residing within this unique organism carries its own past experiences and makes its contributions in shaping our personality for as long as we are alive. In turn, how we live our lives affects the soul's onward journey once it exits the body.

Taking the conversation forward, Krishna explains this interaction between body and soul. He then talks of preferable human attributes and qualities that support us in self-improvement and spiritual evolution.

It may be worth mentioning the resemblance the list below has with Gandhi's philosophy of life. The *Bhagavad Gita*'s influence on Gandhi and the role it played in defining the way he lived his life is more than apparent here.

In order to live an exemplary life Krishna suggests the following qualities:

- cleanliness of body and mind
- detachment and devotion
- equanimity and humility
- freedom from ego
- non-violence
- preference for peace and quiet
- pursuit of knowledge and truth
- renunciation of material pursuits and their rewards
- self-control
- simplicity
- tolerance

Tolerance appears at the end here only because the list is in alphabetical order to avoid any subjective prioritisation. Tolerance and inclusivity have been at the core of being a good human being, and are considered basic to being an evolved individual.

One mind can only think as much as a single mind can. It is only when there is a confluence and convergence of ideas, thoughts and philosophies from varied sources that the human species can evolve positively.

A case in point is the rapid technological advancement made in the last few years. Who 'invented' technology as we see it around us today? It is hard to think of a single name simply because it is building on one another's ideas, and cross learning that has contributed to this constantly evolving phenomenon.

The beauty of the *Bhagavad Gita* and the Vedic scriptures is that they realise this inherent variety amongst human beings and accommodate it in their instructions. So in the realm of spiritual practice as well, it is appreciated that not all are attracted to the same kind of practices.

Different people have different ideas, and all must be accepted and appreciated. The following verse encapsulates the philosophy of tolerance and inclusivity.

Some perceive the Supreme Soul within themselves through meditation, others do so by acquiring knowledge, while still others strive to achieve by performing selfless service.

–Verse 13.25

chapter 13

Kshetra Kshetrajna Vibhaga Yoga
Yoga as Matter and Spirit

13.01–02 (163–64)

अर्जुन उवाच |

प्रकृतिं पुरुषं चैव क्षेत्रं क्षेत्रज्ञमेव च |
एतद्वेदितुमिच्छामि ज्ञानं ज्ञेयं च केशव || 1||

श्रीभगवानुवाच |

इदं शरीरं कौन्तेय क्षेत्रमित्यभिधीयते |
एतद्यो वेत्ति तं प्राहु: क्षेत्रज्ञ इति तद्विद: || 2||

13.01: Arjuna said, O Keshava (the slayer of the demon Keshi), I wish to understand what are nature (*prakriti*) and its beneficiaries (*purush*), and what are field (*kshetra*) and field of activities (*ksṣhetrajña*)? I also wish to know what is true knowledge, and what is the goal of this knowledge?

13.02: The Supreme Divine Lord said: O Arjuna, this body is termed as *kshetra* (the field of activities), and the one who knows this body is called *kshetrajña* (the knower of the field) by the sages who know the truth about both.

Addressing Krishna as Keshav, the slayer of the demon Keshi, Arjuna says he is curious to understand nature, *prakriti*, and humankind, *purush*; field, *kshetra* and field of activities, *kshetrajna*. Arjuna is also keen to understand knowledge and what its object is.

Everything that we see around us in its pure original form is nature or a natural product. All flora and fauna is included in nature, i.e., *prakriti*. *Purush*, i.e., the human species is the most intelligent creation of nature. All other creations follow the cycle of nature, and involuntarily abide by it. But humans, by virtue of their intelligent minds and armed with the option of choices, occasionally try to alter the course of nature, paying a heavy price for it. It is important for humans to remember that they are but another creation of nature, and can never become superior to their creator.

The spiritual context in which Arjuna is asking the question, the field, i.e., *kshetra*, is the soul, and the field of activities, i.e., *kshetrajna*, is the body. Krishna begins by explaining the distinction between the body and soul, and their requirements and activities.

The soul is divine and invisible, and can neither eat, see, smell, hear, taste nor touch. The body on the other hand, is material and physical, and thus cannot function perfectly without eating, seeing, smelling, hearing, tasting or touching. These are essential capabilities that keep the body alive and active. Even though the soul does not per se need these to exist as it is eternal, to keep the connect between soul and body, these physical activities gain significance. This is reminiscent of the oft-used phrase—keeping body and soul together—in other words keeping oneself alive.

The spiritual context in which Arjun is asking the question, the field, i.e., *kshetra*, is the soul and the field of activities, i.e., *kshetrajna*, is the body. Krishna begins by explaining the distinction between the body and soul and their requirements and activities.

Anyone who understands this connection is knowledgeable. The goal of this knowledge is to nurture the soul by keeping the body healthy and active, and to provide the soul with a befitting embodiment.

13.06

महाभूतान्यङ्कारो बुद्धिरव्यक्त मेव च |
इन्द्रियाणि दशैकं च पञ्च चेन्द्रियगोचरा: || 6||

13.6: The field of activities is composed five great elements—ego, intellect, the unmanifested, the eleven senses (five knowledge senses, five working senses, and mind), and five objects of the senses.

Krishna goes on to explain the twenty-four elements that constitute the field of activities:

- *prakriti*: the unmanifested, intellect, ego
- *pancha mahabhuta*: five physical elements—earth, water, fire, air, space
- *pancha tanmaatras*: five sense objects—taste, touch, smell, sight, sound
- five knowledge senses: ears, eyes, tongue, skin, nose
- five working senses: voice, hands, legs, genitals, anus
- *dashaikam*: last but not least, the mind is put above all.

Earlier, in verse 10.22 Krishna had declared that the mind is the most superior of all senses. The five senses play a critical role in determining how we live our lives. It is the mind that is responsible for, and directs our actions and reactions, and regulates self-control while the 24 elements collectively establish the connect between the field and the field of activities.

Thus amongst the faculties it is the mind that is most superior, and therefore Krishna resides in our minds. It is our intelligence and intellect that differentiates us from other species, and establishes our superiority amongst living entities.

13. 07

इच्छा द्वेष: सुखं दु:खं सङ्घातश्चेतना धृति: |
एतत्क्षेत्रं समासेन सविकारमुदाहृतम् || 7||

13.07: Desire and hatred, happiness and misery, the body, consciousness, and the will—all these are the field and its modifications.

Having described the *kshetram* or the field of activities Krishna now elucidates the attributes of the *kshetra* or the field itself and what comprises it.

As explained in verse 13.02, the primary constituent of the field of activities is the body. The body is born, grows, lives and dies, and, all this while it embodies the soul within it. Some of the major drivers that keep the body active are desire, hatred, happiness and misery.

Each human being experiences desire and hatred and these are not emotions to be condemned in totality. It is what we desire or what we hate that is important. To desire knowledge, charity, sharing etc. is welcome. Similarly, to nurture hatred for violence, greed, lust or envy is how one should live one's life. Thus, it is acceptable to experience desire and hatred, but these are unacceptable if directed inappropriately.

Happiness and misery are an intrinsic part of life, and each one of us experiences these in some measure, at different points of time. Once again, the critical point here is what determines our joys and sorrows. Also does constant search for happiness make one a better person or worse? Does misery make one bitter and cynical? Or does it make one empathetic to others?

Human beings have been endowed with some special gifts, and two significant ones are consciousness and free will. It is these that set us apart, not only from other species, but from fellow humans too.

What are our uppermost thoughts? Our actions and reactions, our motivations, our philosophy of life, our aspirations, and our life goals? All these are a part of our consciousness. Which of these do we act upon, how we live our lives and what are the key driving factors that determine our day-to-day actions, all these depend on how we exercise our free will.

13. 08–12

अमानित्वमदम्भित्वमहिंसा क्षान्तिरार्जवम् |
आचार्योपासनं शौचं स्थैर्यमात्मविनिग्रहः || 8||
इन्द्रियार्थेषु वैराग्यमनहङ्कार एव च |
जन्ममृत्युजराव्याधिदुःखदोषानुदर्शनम् || 9||
असक्तिरनभिष्वङ्गः पुत्रदारगृहादिषु |
नित्यं च समचित्तत्वमिष्टानिष्टोपपत्तिषु || 10||
मयि चानन्ययोगेन भक्तिरव्यभिचारिणी |
विविक्तदेशसेवित्वमरतिर्जनसंसदि || 11||
अध्यात्मज्ञाननित्यत्वं तत्त्वज्ञानार्थदर्शनम् |
एतज्ज्ञानमिति प्रोक्तमज्ञानं यदतोऽन्यथा || 12||

13.08-12: Humility; freedom from false pride; non-violence; tolerance; simplicity; service of a guru; cleanliness of body and mind; being steady; self-control; renunciation of the objects of the senses; absence of false ego; perception of the evils of birth, disease, old age, and death; non-attachment; absence of association with spouse, children, home, and so on; even-mindedness amidst pleasant and unpleasant events in life; constant and exclusive devotion toward me; aspiring to live in a solitary place, an aversion to people in general; constancy in spiritual knowledge; and philosophical pursuit of the Absolute Truth—all these I declare to be knowledge, and besides this whatever there may be, is ignorance.

What Krishna declares here as knowledge is nothing to do with information acquired from books and scriptures. Not a single book is prescribed for reading, in this lengthy discourse. What are laid down here are qualities, more instinctive, inherent and spiritual. None of the human attributes included here is likely to be imbibed merely by pouring over hefty volumes of scriptures. Most of these characteristics are inborn, though there are many people who work on themselves, evolve and self-improve.

Humility, absence of misplaced pride and ego, non-violence, tolerance and simplicity are recommended. Then Krishna goes on to say that it is important to associate with a guru. In a larger context, a guru could well mean a guide, mentor, role model, leader or any aspirational figure that one might relate to. Krishna himself is seen in these multiple roles vis-à-vis Arjuna, both in the battlefield and later.

Amongst all these sublime qualities it is significant that personal hygiene, both of body and mind, finds a mention along with withdrawal from and renunciation of sensory pleasures and worldly attachment. Self-control and steady and consistent behaviour, are obviously linked to this state of existence.

For one to be able to perceive birth, death, disease, old age, and all the ups and downs of life with equanimity is a tough call. To eventually withdraw from family life and social engagements could be positive signs of having chosen the path to salvation. Those on this path will naturally disengage from people at large and find solace in steady pursuit of spiritual knowledge and Ultimate Truth.

All the virtues and attitudes described above make a person knowledgeable and wise. False pride, over-confidence, excessive involvement with worldly pleasures, egotistical behaviour, living in filth and squalor, entertaining inappropriate thoughts and giving in to violence, avarice, greed, lust and deceit are the anti-thesis to all that is endorsed by the Lord himself.

In a nutshell, this is the sum total of knowledge as defined by Krishna, and anyone who chooses to walk on a contrary path is ignorant and clearly heading towards eventual disaster.

13.25

ध्यानेनात्मनि पश्यन्ति केचिदात्मानमात्मना |
अन्ये साङ् ख्येन योगेन कर्मयोगेन चापरे || 25||

13.25: Some perceive the Supreme Soul within themselves through meditation, others do so by acquiring knowledge, while still others strive to achieve by performing selfless service.

Devotees, philosophers and those engaged in discharging their duties in the best way possible, are all working towards attainment of the same goal. Just like no two fingers are alike despite belonging to the same hand, similarly there are many ways of treading the path of spirituality.

Some search for the Lord within themselves, by focussing all their energies in meditation. For them the search is the ultimate source of joy and satisfaction.

There are others who are in the quest of truth through acquisition of knowledge. Exercising their intellect, and remaining in pursuit of gyan is their way of being spiritual. Self-improvement, and search and sharing of knowledge, is what such people thrive on. Cultivating knowledge is perceived by them as a form of devotion.

There is yet another category of people who remain constantly engaged in work—they do this for the sake of it, and not in the hope of any return. All these are simply different kinds of devotion, and none is superior or inferior to the other. Meaningful action and optimising on talents bestowed on them could be some people's mission in life.

Every soul is unique and the body it resides in is an individual with particular traits. A combination of both, body and soul, plays a part in determining the path of choice. Different experiences of the soul through its many previous journeys, and the physical realities of the body in the material world creates distinct perceptions. Adopted of free will and performed with sincerity, all paths are equally good, and are simply different routes to the same destination.

14

Human nature and Evolution of Thought Processes

The previous chapter clearly drew the distinction between the soul and the earthly body. In this chapter Krishna delves into the three *gunas*—modes of material nature—or simply put, the different characteristics of human nature. It is believed that understanding these three categories is the key to self-improvement, and takes one on the path to liberation.

Over the years, science has successfully addressed several challenges posed by Mother Nature, but despite some spectacular advancements and inventions it has not quite been able to completely decode the human brain, or the complex workings of the human mind.

It is still not clear why and how we dream, why we remember some insignificant things so clearly, and entirely forget more important things. Why we are magically drawn to some people, and can just about bear to be with others?

Why do some of us like to work in the mornings and others late at night? Why are some attracted to money and the world of glamour, while there are others who shun it entirely?

The day being the same twenty-four hours for all of us, how is it that some manage to get so much done each day, while others are always running short of time?

How do siblings, born and brought up in the same environment, sometimes turn out so different? Why are some of us trouble makers, while there are others who are constant trouble shooters?

A close understanding of the three modes of human nature can perhaps provide some answers.

These are the modes of

- goodness
- passion
- ignorance

Our predominant *guna* determines our behaviour and actions. By and large, there is a pattern to our individual nature, and each of us falls under a certain personality type.

That being said however, the three *gunas* cannot be put in water-tight boxes. The complexity of the human mind makes this near impossible. On a physiological plain every human body is identical and performs bodily functions in the same way.

But when it comes to thinking, thought processes, imagination, fantasy, creativity, likes and dislikes, each one of us is unique. It may not be inaccurate to say that no two minds work in exactly the same way, at all times.

The human mind can be erratic and unpredictable. Sometimes it disappoints by falling short of expectations, and at others it surprises with an unforeseen move.

After much detailing of human nature and its particular drivers, Krishna introduces the twist in the tale. At times we do unexpected things, or look back to some event and ask ourselves with disbelief or satisfaction (as the case may be)—was it really me who did that? How could I have? These are the times when the personality type we supposedly fall under seems to take the back seat, and we end up doing something contrary to our accepted nature.

The human mind can be erratic and unpredictable. Sometimes it disappoints by falling short of expectations, and at others it surprises with an unforeseen move. Krishna touches upon this aspect of human nature in the following verse.

Sometimes goodness prevails over passion and ignorance, O descendant of Bharata. At other times, passion dominates over goodness and ignorance, and on some occasions, ignorance overcomes goodness and passion.

–Verse 14.10

chapter 14

Gunatraya Vibhaga Yoga
Yoga as Human Nature

14.05

सत्त्वं रजस्तम इति गुणा: प्रकृतिसम्भवा: |
निबध्नन्ति महाबाहो देहे देहिनमव्ययम् || 5||

14.05: O mighty-armed Arjuna, the material energy consists of three modes—goodness, passion, and ignorance. These modes bind the eternal soul to the perishable body.

In the thirteenth chapter Krishna explained how, by working on knowledge enhancement, we can find the desired path to salvation. The body and soul are intertwined and the acts performed by the body determine the soul's future trajectory.

In this chapter, Krishna talks of how each one of us is driven by a specific mode of material energy. These modes fall in three categories or *gunas*—*sattva* or goodness, *rajah* or passion, *tamah* or ignorance. Whichever of these three is predominant in a person, it shall govern her thoughts and actions accordingly. It is this that determines our personality and makes us who we are.

Nourishment of the soul and its journey is largely affected by the particular *guna* that is the driving force of the body that the soul inhabits.

14.06–08

तत्र सत्त्वं निर्मलत्वात्प्रकाशकमनामयम् |
सुखसङ्गेन बध्नाति ज्ञानसङ्गेन चानघ || 6||
रजो रागात्मकं विद्धि तृष्णासङ्गसमुद्भवम् |
तन्निबध्नाति कौन्तेय कर्मसङ्गेन देहिनम् || 7||
तमस्त्वज्ञानजं विद्धि मोहनं सर्वदेहिनाम् |
प्रमादालस्यनिद्राभिस्तन्निबध्नाति भारत || 8||

14.06: Amongst these, *sattva guṇa*, the mode of goodness, being purer than the others, is illuminating and free from impurity. O sinless one, it illuminates the soul and attaches it to the body by creating a sense of happiness and knowledge.

14.07: O Arjuna, son of Kunti, *rajo guṇa* is of the nature of passion. It is borne out of worldly desires and affections, and binds the soul through attachment to fruitful actions.

14.08: O Arjuna, *tamo guṇa*, which is borne of ignorance, is the cause of illusion for the embodied souls. It deludes all living beings through negligence, laziness, and sleep.

In these verses Krishna explains the modes that characterise material energy in living beings. First and foremost is *sattva guna*, the mode of goodness, which is the most superior. Those who are steeped in goodness are free from sinful and impure thoughts and actions. Their minds are illuminated, they are serene and content, and strive towards knowledge and purity. They work and serve selflessly, and are not desirous of monetary returns for their actions since the source of their happiness lies elsewhere. The soul is happily ensconced in such a mind and body, and flourishes with inputs from enhanced knowledge, or gyan.

Those in whom *rajo guna,* the mode of passion, is predominant, are engrossed in the worldly pursuit of wealth, status, position and visible symbols of power, prosperity and wellbeing. They choose to perform actions that result in palpable outcomes, and can be measured in material terms. Frequently indulging in sensual gratification they thrive on physical and material pleasures. Attachment to worldly things is the guiding force of such people. *Rajo guna* increases lust and desires, which in turn further fuel an increase of the mode of passion. It is a vicious cycle of desire and gratification which keeps the person active, while the soul is trapped inside a body driven by passion and desire.

If *sattva guna* is one end of the yardstick, *tamo guna* is the other. Those influenced by it derive pleasure from sleep, procrastination, sloth, intoxication, violence, deceit and gambling. They fail to discriminate between right and wrong, are unethical and are people of low or zero integrity. They naturally slip into an immoral life, neglecting their duties and responsibilities. *Tamo guna,* the mode of ignorance, leads the person deeper into a bottomless pit of darkness and ignorance. As the soul within gets progressively removed from knowledge and light, it sinks into a dark hole of oblivion and ignominy.

14.09

सत्त्वं सुखे सञ्जयति रज: कर्मणि भारत |
ज्ञानमावृत्य तु तम: प्रमादे सञ्जयत्युत || 9||

14.09: O Arjuna, descendant of Bharata, *sattva* brings happiness and satisfaction; *rajas* propels the soul toward actions; and *tamas* puts a cover on knowledge and traps one in delusion.

Having explained the three modes of human nature Krishna now tells Arjuna of the kind of overall pattern of life one can expect from each. A person driven by *sattva,* finds satisfaction in intellectual pursuits, knowledge enhancement, in making new discoveries and even establishing new maxims for ordinary mortals to follow. Such persons are not reluctant to share knowledge, and believe in doing good for society as a whole. They are not overly ambitious and are content with their life and work.

Those in whom *rajas,* or the mode of passion, is predominant are work-oriented and actively engaged in worldly activities. Social status and recognition, prestige, wealth, physical comfort and a celebratory approach to life are the markers that set them apart from others. It is these people driven by passion who make the world a joyous and happy place to live in. However, it is the very same people who often cross a line and allow ambition and greed to determine their actions. This inevitably becomes problematic for themselves and for those directly or indirectly affected by these behaviour patterns.

Tamo guna, the mode of ignorance, adversely affects the intellect and seriously impairs judgement and the ability to discern. These individuals live in an illusionary world and refuse to accept reality, or look at truth in the eye.

Living all their lives with myopic vision and short-term perspectives, they are not open to suggestions either of self-improvement or of doing something constructive in life. Such people leave behind them a legacy of delusion, and a wasted life lived in a stagnant, make-believe world.

14.10

रजस्तमश्चाभिभूय सत्त्वं भवति भारत |
रज: सत्त्वं तमश्चैव तम: सत्त्वं रजस्तथा || 10||

14.10: Sometimes goodness prevails over passion and ignorance, O descendant of Bharata. At other times, passion dominates over goodness and ignorance, and on some occasions, ignorance overcomes goodness and passion.

While the three *gunas* are clearly defined, it does not mean that every aspect of a person conforms to it all the time. Different people react differently to adversities in life, and many are known to go through a sea change in their personality once they attain name and fame.

It is impossible to put the human mind in a box and label it as good, passionate, or ignorant. There are bound to be grey areas when people's behaviour is, what might be termed as, 'out of character'.

At times, good people are seen to be committing the most reprehensible of acts, and the worst criminal does something saintly. On an impulse, a charlatan may give away his earnings in charity, and someone obsessed with physical comfort might decide to sleep on the floor for a few days.

This happens when an individual swings from one personality kind to another, and this is not unusual. Being empathetic, and having a complete understanding of human nature, Krishna says, people can be unpredictable and irresolute, and thus vacillate from one behaviour pattern to another. This depends on which *guna* gains control of our minds at a given point of time.

14.14–15

यदा सत्त्वे प्रवृद्धे तु प्रलयं याति देहभृत् |
तदोत्तमविदां लोकानमलान्प्रतिपद्यते || 14||
रजसि प्रलयं गत्वा कर्मसङ्गिषु जायते |
तथा प्रलीनस्तमसि मूढयोनिषु जायते || 15||

14.14–15: Those who die in the mode of goodness reach the exalted abodes of the learned. When those driven by the mode of passion die, they are born among people driven by fruitful activity, while those dying in the mode of ignorance take birth in an animal species.

Having explained the three *gunas*, and the related propensity created by each, Krishna now moves to the next stage where he discloses elements of respective soul's journey after completing its time on earth. What we do while living out our lives, how we act, behave and perform in this life determines the subsequent destiny of the soul.

Sattva guna: Those who live a virtuous life, remain focussed on knowledge enhancement, and are productively engaged in pursuit of goodness, may be rewarded with entry into a celestial abode after death. Alternately, they are reborn in families of scholars and intellectuals. The environment in these families or the new surroundings would be conducive to learning, where piety, empathy and social good are at the core of day-to-day life.

Rajo guna: Driven by greed, avarice, jealousy and avarice some people are engaged only in activities that can translate into material gain. Physical desire and sensual pleasures dominate their thought processes. Consequently, they are reborn in families engaged in material pursuits and are in possession of an average intellect.

Tamo guna: This category of people while away their time on earth enveloped in sloth, intoxication, inactivity and procrastination. They belittle the opportunities that life has to offer. Consequently, they may well find themselves going down the ladder, and be reborn as an animal, devoid of the gift of intelligence that only human beings are blessed with.

These verses clearly lay out the future trajectory of souls ensconced in different material modes. One interesting aspect that emerges here is that the life form that one is born into is not always progressive or evolutionary. In other words, a soul taking birth as a human once is no guarantee for repeated rebirths as humans. Depending on how this life is lived, the next birth could be progressive or even regressive. That is to say, a human could be reborn as an animal if this life is frittered away, and no efforts are made at self-improvement.

Thus the soul can move up in the evolutionary ladder, could be static, i.e., retain the same level, or go down, based on the choices it makes, the actions it performs and the opportunities it avails of in the given life.

14.16–18

कर्मण: सुकृतस्याहु: सात्त्विकं निर्मलं फलम् |
रजसस्तु फलं दु:खमज्ञानं तमस: फलम् || 16||
सत्त्वात्सञ्जायते ज्ञानं रजसो लोभ एव च |
प्रमादमोहौ तमसो भवतोऽज्ञानमेव च || 17||
ऊर्ध्वं गच्छन्ति सत्त्वस्था मध्ये तिष्ठन्ति राजसा: |
जघन्यगुणवृत्तिस्था अधो गच्छन्ति तामसा: || 18||

14.16: It is said the fruit of actions performed in the mode of goodness bring about pure results. Actions done in the mode of passion bring pain, while those performed in the mode of ignorance lead to darkness.

14.17: From the mode of goodness knowledge develops, from the mode of passion arises greed, and the mode of ignorance gives way to negligence and delusion.

14.18: Those situated in the mode of goodness rise upward; those in the mode of passion stay on earthly planets, and those in the mode of ignorance go downward to hellish worlds.

After having described the onward journey of the soul based on the *guna* that a body aligns itself to in its life on earth, Krishna goes on to elaborate on the outcomes of each. The reincarnation of the soul in its next birth is linked to the *guna* that dominates its personality. Upon completion of its time in the present life, the soul reaches a place which is in sync with its *guna*.

For the mode of goodness, positive results are assured. As these people are engaged in virtuous acts and their thoughts and intentions are pure, they acquire knowledge, and gain mastery and expertise in one or more fields. They are content and satisfied, and find happiness in intellectual pursuits. In after life too, their journey is an ascending one where they move closer to the Supreme Power.

The mode of passion unravels itself quite differently, and inevitably brings pain. Each of the pursuits is driven by material desire, and the gains and losses are mapped to earthly standards. Passion is difficult to satiate, and can only lead to further acts of depravity and decadence. As a result, the soul soon finds itself back on earth as it is unable to extricate itself from the web of materialism.

The mode of ignorance quite naturally leads to negativity. Complete inaction, lack of motivation and a life of inertia is just the beginning of a downward spiral. After lazing through life, the body meets its end, but having achieved nothing condemns the soul to descend to the netherworld which is best known for its misery and darkness.

Thus those who are in *sattva guṇa* gloriously enter the higher celestial abodes; those who are in *rajo guṇa*, return to earth; and those who are in *tamo guṇa*, are condemned to the underworld.

14. 20–21

गुणानेतानतीत्य त्रीन्देही देहसमुद्भवान् |
जन्ममृत्युजरादुःखैर्विमुक्तोऽमृतमश्रुते || 20||

अर्जुन उवाच |
कैर्लिङ्गैस्त्रीनगुणानेतानतीतो भवति प्रभो |
किमाचारः कथं चैतांस्त्रीन्गुणानतिवर्तते || 21||

14.20: By transcending the three qualities of the body, one becomes free from birth, death, disease, old age, and misery, and attains immortality.

14.21: Arjuna asked : What are the characteristics of those who have gone beyond the three qualities of material nature, O Lord? How do they conduct themselves? How do they transcend?

Having described how our predominant character traits govern our lives, the outcome of respective actions, and the consequent onward journey of souls, Krishna now says that those who can transcend above the three modes of material existence are granted immortality. Thus they leave behind them the cycle of birth and rebirth, all the pain, suffering, disease, misery of old age, and the over-arching fear of death. They attain salvation, and are relieved from the obvious tedium of life, or several lives on earth.

Arjuna has now understood the distinction between the modes of material life, and the manner in which these affect life and after life. He now wants to know from Krishna how to identify those who have transcended the three *gunas*. What is the manner in which they conduct themselves and live their lives on earth, and eventually how do they transcend to another world? In the next verse Krishna explains this in detail.

14.22–25

श्रीभगवानुवाच |

प्रकाशं च प्रवृत्तिं च मोहमेव च पाण्डव |
न द्वेष्टि सम्प्रवृत्तानि न निवृत्तानि काङ् क्षति || 22||
उदासीनवदासीनो गुणैर्यो न विचाल्यते |
गुणा वर्तन्त इत्येवं योऽवतिष्ठति नेङ्गते || 23||
समदुःखसुखः स्वस्थः समलोष्टाश्मकाञ्चनः |
तुल्यप्रियाप्रियो धीरस्तुल्यनिन्दात्मसंस्तुतिः || 24||
मानापमानयोस्तुल्यस्तुल्यो मित्रारिपक्षयोः |
सर्वारम्भपरित्यागी गुणातीतः स उच्यते || 25||

14.22-23: Krishna said: O son of Pandu, Arjuna! They who do not hate illumination, nor attachment, nor even delusion when these are abundantly present, nor do they long for them when they are absent, being aware that these are just manifestations of the three modes. They remain neutral to the modes of nature and are not agitated by them. Knowing it is only the *gunas* that act, unwavering they stay established in the self.

14.24-25: Those who are alike in happiness and distress; who are established in the self; who look upon soil, stone, and gold as of equal value; who remain the same amidst pleasant and unpleasant events; who are intelligent; who accept both blame and praise with equanimity; who remain the same in situations of honour and dishonour; who treat both friend and foe alike; and who have abandoned all earthly endeavours—they are said to have risen above the three *gunas*.

In response to Arjuna's question on how to identify transcended souls, Krishna now elaborates on the traits of those who have risen above the three *gunas*. He says such individuals are not agitated when they see the modes of material nature functioning in the world. They observe the effects manifested in persons and situations around them, but remain unaffected by these.

Living in the midst of greed, indolence, avarice, gluttony and other negative outcomes that frequently come into play, they remain composed and balanced, secure in the knowledge that the *gunas* are at work. They might dislike and disprove of these but are evolved enough not to dislike or hate the person concerned.

The enlightened souls also work towards making the world a better place, and in contributing to society for the larger good. However, they never lose sight of the fact that as humans one can only try, the ultimate action is in the hands of the Almighty. Devoid of any ego or ideas of self-aggrandisement, they work selflessly and tirelessly, and sometimes even anonymously.

Such people do not experience any extreme reactions and take joy and sorrow, honour and dishonour, fame and infamy with the same degree of equanimity.

Being on the transcendental platform they master the art of not getting overly involved in day-to-day situations. Composed in pain as well as in pleasure, uncomplaining in heat and cold, poverty and prosperity, these self-realised souls accept the dualities of existence on earth, but remain above them all.

Material possessions have no value for them as they can view a lump of soil, a stone, or a piece of gold equally dispassionately. Bouquets and brickbats, profit and loss, success and failure, none of these can affect the balance and composure of these exalted minds and bodies. Such transcendental souls are also described as *nirguna*, i.e., one who has no *gunas*, or is above the effect of the *gunas*.

15

The Supreme Self

Ever held a road map upside down, and tried to navigate your way to an unknown destination? And when the journey takes longer than expected you wonder what happened. But surely, this is the correct map, so why am I not reaching my goal? You've been following all instructions correctly, driving carefully, going at a steady speed, but still seem to be reaching nowhere.

And then the penny drops, so to speak, when you realise that what you thought of as home was actually the destination, and what was showing as destination turned out to be home after all. A classic case of decoding the map upside down.

In a similar vein, Krishna draws the most powerful imagery of the *Gita* in the fifteenth chapter. The upside-down tree is an analogy of our origin and subsequent existence on earth. Confusing the soul for the body, we forget that our soul's journey begins from above and not on this earth as we assume. Neither does it end here, as the soul travels back, continuing to make its way beyond this earthly life.

Apart from the multiple interpretations that can be derived from this idea, an important learning is to develop a capability of taking an aerial view of life and situations. This could well be the first step towards material detachment.

A view from the top can certainly be exhilarating, but at the same time could also be a humbling experience. When perspectives start to overlap, when world view contracts to being a myopic one, and when the future spreads itself out like an endless bumpy road, an aerial view of the situation could sort ruffled feathers.

Seeing ourselves from a vantage point, which lies above the plane of our bodily existence not only results in an immediate distancing from earthly circumstances, but also drives home our own insignificance in the larger scheme of things. An eye opener indeed when we realise

> *...we realize that we are but a speck in the grand plan that is at work and constantly playing itself out...*

that we are but a speck in the grand plan of things that is at work, and is constantly playing itself out.

In this chapter Krishna also talks of:

- the perishable or the fallible, and
- the imperishable or the infallible

All humans start their journey as perishable beings, who must cease to exist one day. That being said, it is possible to translate oneself to the imperishable by living an exemplary life driven by sublime spiritual norms.

All that we see around us—inventions, discoveries, atrocities, oppression, philanthropy, art and literature, social structures and political systems, are products of the human mind. The mind has a huge capability of thinking the good and the bad, and alas, both in equal measure.

The first step towards this is accepting the supremacy of the mind and understanding that it determines the nature of the self. Gaining control over one's own mind, and maintaining balance and composure at all times is by no means an easy task. Indeed, it is a constant struggle to be able to do so.

Krishna touches upon this aspect of life in this chapter.

All souls embodied in living entities in this material world are my eternal fragmented parts.
But bound by material nature, they are struggling with the six senses, including the mind.

–Verse 15.07

chapter 15

Purushottama Yoga
Yoga as the Supreme Self

15.01

श्रीभगवानुवाच |
ऊर्ध्वमूलमध:शाखमश्वत्थं प्राहुरव्ययम् |
छन्दांसि यस्य पर्णानि यस्तं वेद स वेदवित् || 1||

15.01: The supreme Divine Power said: It is said that there is an imperishable tree that has its roots growing upwards and branches downwards, and whose leaves are the Vedic hymns. The one who understands the significance of this tree is said to be truly knowledgeable of the *Vedas*.

The fifteenth chapter begins on a rather mysterious, fantastical note. After having explained the different modes of nature and possible ways of extricating oneself from material entanglement, Krishna now talks of an upside down tree.

There is an eternal, imperishable tree, he says with its roots above and branches below, it is called the *ashvattha* tree. The word *ashvatth* also means that which will not remain the same even the next day, or something which is constantly changing. This can also be understood as symbolic of life and the world around us as these too are constantly changing, and are never the same on any two days. Therefore, the world we live in is temporary, or *ashvatth*.

While our body is born on earth and lives and dies here, the soul's journey starts elsewhere. For the soul which is eternal, the sojourn into the world can well be seen as the inverted *ashvattha* tree, whose roots originate from God and are supported and nourished by him.

The trunk and branches extending downwards, encompass all the life-forms and living entities in the material realm. Its innumerable leaves are the Vedic mantras which describe rituals, ceremonies, and rewards. Our effort remains active till the action runs out its time cycle, and eventually gives way to another, much like the fresh green leaves that are borne of the tree, serve their purpose, turn yellow and drop off. Even before the old leaves detach themselves from the branch, the process for new leaves has started within the tree, just like one day of our lives gives way to the next, while today is ending, tomorrow is already beginning.

This constant cycle of the leaves of the *ashvattha* tree nourishes the material existence of the soul and perpetuates the continuous cycle of life and death. Due to this continuity, the beginning and the end are not experienced by the soul, just like the shedding of leaves does not affect the existence of the tree.

A tree which is nurtured and well taken care of becomes stronger, starts to grow aerial roots that grow back to its origin, and its goodness is further replenished. As it receives nourishment and care from God, its trunk thickens, its leaves multiply and its foliage becomes more dense and thick.

This is reminiscent of a peepul tree that grows aerial roots as it grows. These roots wrap themselves around the trunk, making it thicker, wider and stronger. Similarly, the banyan tree (both peepul and banyan are considered sacred) also grows aerial roots, but these grow perpendicular to the trunk penetrating fresh ground. This results in increasing the coverage of the tree and providing it greater nourishment and balance. The aerial root system of providing nourishment to the tree is akin to the evaporation cycle where water from the earth turns to clouds, and the clouds again turn into rain and return to earth.

A tree that does not quite perform the role it was sent out to do, experiences no exceptional growth, merely survives for the duration for its lifecycle, and then one day simply ceases to exist. Its end is not likely to change much in the world.

While a tree, that has actively performed its duties, has enriched itself from its time on earth, been helpful to others and stood out as an epitome of strength, wisdom and compassion, will be sorely missed by the world when its time is over, and it withdraws from the material world to merge with the Supreme Soul.

This way, an exceptional tree or soul, is relieved from rebirth, but while it is residing in a body also leaves behind it an indelible mark in the world that it inhabits.

To believe the analogy of this upside down tree is to fully comprehend the cycle of finite life and death of the body, as well as the infinite journey of the soul.

15.02

अधश्चोर्ध्वं प्रसृतास्तस्य शाखा
गुणप्रवृद्धा विषयप्रवाला: |
अधश्च मूलान्यनुसन्ततानि
कर्मानुबन्धीनि मनुष्यलोके || 2||

15.02: The branches extend upward and downward, nourished by the three modes of material nature. The twigs are the objects of the senses. The roots grow downward, keeping the flow of actions in motion in the world of humans.

Carrying forward the analogy of the upside tree Krishna now goes on to detail the similarities between the human form and its existence, and the *ashvattha* tree. Whatever is our predominant nature—goodness (*sattva*), passion (*rajas*) or ignorance (*tamas*) determines the growth of the tree.

Those driven by passion might focus their energies on material embellishments, in other words, be like a flowering tree which attracts attention because of its beautiful flowers. But this can only be for a limited period of time, and thus amounts to temporary gains. As soon as the season changes the tree loses its beauty as well as its admirers. It is significant here that a flowering tree does not have deep roots nor does it have a long lifespan. Such trees can be said to be *rajas* in their attitude.

On the other hand, those driven by goodness, the *sattvik*, and wisdom are not interested in outward manifestation of what is, in any case, a temporary phenomenon. They can see the hollowness of it all, and remain focussed on strengthening their roots and drawing sustenance for a long and healthy lifespan. Such people continue to nurture the roots, enrich themselves with divine inputs and live an exemplary life. As the roots grow older and stronger, aerial roots begin to grow further reinforcing the origin of the tree. Interestingly, the peepul tree is known to live for centuries, and can easily outlive several human generations. As the tree adds in years it gains respect and sometimes is even worshipped as a symbol of God.

And then we also have trees that have neither strong roots nor any exceptional leaves or flowers. Such trees live out their lives without making a mark in any way. These trees are akin to people who are ignorant and unwilling to learn and improve. Not known for or looked up to for anything in particular, they fall in the category of *tamas* and remain static both in mind and body. Unheard and unsung, they just slip out of the world, and having put their lives to no tangible good are destined to remain entangled in the cycle of rebirth.

15.03–04

न रूपमस्येह तथोपलभ्यते
नान्तो न चादिर्न च सम्प्रतिष्ठा |
अश्वत्थमेनं सुविरूढमूल
मसङ्गशस्त्रेण दृढेन छित्त्वा || 3||
तत: पदं तत्परिमार्गितव्यं
यस्मिन्गता न निवर्तन्ति भूय: |
तमेव चाद्यं पुरुषं प्रपद्ये
यत: प्रवृत्ति: प्रसृता पुराणी || 4||

15.03-04: The real form of this tree is not perceived in this world, neither its beginning nor end, nor its continued existence. But with determination, one must cut down this deep-rooted tree with a strong axe of detachment. Then one must search out the base of the tree, which is the Supreme Lord, from whom the activity of the universe came into being a long time ago. Upon taking refuge in him, one will not return to this world again.

Speaking further about the *ashvattha* tree, Krishna says it is not easy for those in human form to understand this concept, as there are too many distractions in the material world. For an ordinary mortal, seeing is believing and what cannot be seen is hard to believe. Most people have this simplistic mindset, and thus remain embroiled in the razzle-dazzle of the world. Thus for most individuals the buds and flowers of the tree become things to aspire for, and so they neglect to nurture the roots. Needless to add that if one keeps plucking the flowers and forgets to water the roots, eventually the flowers will stop blooming and the tree will wither.

Krishna recommends a constant search for the roots of the tree. Human beings should never forget the origin of their creation, and must engage in searching for the roots of the tree, i.e., their soul. It is here that the Supreme Lord is to be found. Earlier on too Krishna had said that he is the source of both material and spiritual creation, and everything big and small emanates from him. Finding the source and following his instructions is the surest way of ultimately merging with the Supreme Soul. For this we might be required to completely disengage from the buds and the flowers, and immerse ourselves in single-minded devotion.

In the words of the Lord, what is required is the use of 'a strong axe of detachment' whereby all links with worldly pleasures and rewards may be cut off. This requires extreme determination, courage of conviction and perseverance. But the efforts will be worth its while as it will result in deliverance from the tedium of birth and rebirth of the soul, and having to repeatedly live through the pain and suffering of life on earth.

15.07

ममैवांशो जीवलोके जीवभूत: सनातन: |
मन:षष्ठानीन्द्रियाणि प्रकृतिस्थानि कर्षति || 7||

15.07: All souls embodied in living entities in this material world are my eternal fragmented parts. But bound by material nature, they are struggling with the six senses including the mind.

All liberated souls find the Lord and merge with the Supreme Soul. However, Krishna assures Arjuna that this does not mean that those still in the loop of birth, death and rebirth have been spurned by the creator. All souls residing in human bodies are a part of the Lord, and are never forgotten or abandoned by him. He is simply waiting for them to strive and reach him, while he is there guiding them all along.

While on earth, these souls are dealing with the five senses, i.e., sight, sound, smell, taste and touch. Interestingly, to these accepted five senses Krishna here adds one more—the mind—which perhaps is the most difficult to understand and control.

It has often been said, that which consumes your mind controls your life. In this context it is important to note the use of the word *karshati,* which means, to struggle. In this verse this word is used to describe the soul's journey, while it is on earth, and its constant struggle with the human mind.

While the five senses need to be controlled too, the key to all five lies in controlling and conditioning the mind. Once this has been accomplished, the rest falls in place. All the while the soul co-exists in the body it is struggling to keep the mind in check and on the right path. Given human propensity to stray and deviate, this is not always an easy task.

15.16

द्वाविमौ पुरुषौ लोके क्षरश्चाक्षर एव च |
क्षर: सर्वाणि भूतानि कूटस्थोऽक्षर उच्यते || 16||

15.16: There are two kinds of beings in the world, the perishable and the imperishable. All beings in the material realm are perishable. Those living beings who are liberated become imperishable.

In this verse Krishna says that there are two kinds of beings; the perishable (*kṣhara*) and the imperishable (*akṣhara*). No matter which life form or species we may choose to consider, all beings in the material realm are perishable. Those who find liberation merge with the Supreme Soul, and become imperishable.

For living beings, more specifically human beings, life is a constant struggle as it is ever changing. Every living being must go through the six stages of existence, conception as foetus, birth, growth, reproduction, old age, and finally death. The transition from one stage to another is not always smooth, and each stage comes with its own baggage of troubles. All through our lives we are dealing with issues related to one of these stages of growth.

Human beings are blessed with five senses but keeping them in check is a perpetual challenge. No matter how genuine the effort may be at exercising self-control, we do slip up every now and then, and often tell ourselves, or each other, 'It's okay, we're human after all'. This is true, and the fact that we are human makes us prone to making mistakes.

However, the lapse may seem minor at that point in time and we may even forget about it, but eventually it all adds up, and in the final tally it may cost us dearly. Our mistakes ensure that we have to go through the repetitive cycle of birth and death of the material body, and forever be *kshara*, or perishable.

But those of us who can evolve to being *akshara*, or imperishable by living pure lives, merge with the supreme soul, and become free from the cycle of birth and death. In the spiritual world the body does not change, and there is a constant state of oneness. For the imperishable there is no birth, no disease, no old age and no death, and they reside forever in the divine realm, the Abode of God.

This luxury of being in a constant state of peace and calm can be ours only if we strive to self-improve, and distinguish ourselves from ordinary mortals and work towards moving closer to the divine.

15.18

यस्मात्क्षरमतीतोऽहमक्षरादपि चोत्तमः |
अतोऽस्मि लोके वेदे च प्रथितः पुरुषोत्तमः || 18||

15.18: I am transcendental to the perishable world of matter, and also to the imperishable soul; hence I am celebrated, in the *Vedas* as the Supreme One.

In this verse Krishna refers to himself as Purushottama, or the one who is most superior to all. Having described in detail his opulence and his all-pervading presence, not just on earth but in the universe, he now informs Arjuna that he is the most superior even among imperishable souls.

All the perishable and fallible beings aspire to become imperishable and infallible. In other words, to evolve from being *kshara* to *akshara*. Once a soul becomes *akshara*, or imperishable, it hopes to merge with the Supreme Soul, which is Krishna himself, in all his magnificence and glory.

Krishna is thus transcendental and divine, is universally celebrated for his multi-faced personality, and worshipped for his all-encompassing powers. All the *Vedas* and sacred texts endorse this reality encouraging humans to emulate Krishna in their daily lives.

16

The Divine and the Demoniac

Right from the day we hear our first story there is always a play between the good and the evil in the plot. In these days of more refined sensibilities, this may not be so stark in children's stories, but the use of contrast to set one off against the other is an age-old artistic technique.

Sadly, it is not merely a writing technique, it is a reflection of the reality around us. The story may be mythological, fantastical or an allegory, but the dramatis personae are invariably based on real human characters. Art, as we know, is an imitation of life. And this might not always be limited to the aesthetic aspects of existence.

Most ancient texts are replete with stories of *sur* or *devata* (angel) versus *asur* or *daanav* (devil), and the constant friction for supremacy between the two. Invariably, good wins over evil, peace and calm is restored, and good is forever revered. This is where the likeness with real life ends, as the outcome of the sparring groups might not always be so in reality.

In the sixteenth chapter of the *Gita*, Krishna talks of the qualities to aspire for and those to be avoided. Ironically, there are 26 good qualities and only six evil ones. But time and again the deadly six—hypocrisy, arrogance, conceit, harsh speech, anger and ignorance—seem to overpower the benign twenty-six in the eternal drama of good versus bad.

So what do demoniac qualities turn us into? What do they make us do? The three larger-than-life outcomes of nurturing demoniac qualities are

- lust
- anger
- greed

It is these three that repeatedly propel individuals to indulge in performing unacceptable, evil deeds. One or the other of these is the leitmotif that characterises almost every criminal act and anti-social behaviour.

In the *Gita* Krishna comes across mostly as a guru, advisor, counsellor, strategist or patient, empathetic teacher.

But it is when he talks of the fate of those who encourage demoniac qualities in themselves and in others, and allows these to determine their actions, that we see another side of him. Angry, incensed and infuriated, Krishna describes such people as the basest of the entire human race— the proverbial dirty fish that goes about dirtying the entire pond.

As an act of punishment and castigation, and to set an example to others treading on a similar path, these demoniac persons are condemned to remain forever trapped in the cycle of birth and rebirth.

Making it abundantly clear that this is not enough chastisement for the guilty in question, he adds that each time rebirth happens from another demoniac womb it ensures that the tarnished soul keeps slipping further into the quick sand of darkness and degeneracy.

The following verses articulate Krishna's displeasure and fury, clearly spelling out the nemesis in store for the wrong-doers.

These cruel and envious persons, the basest of all humankind, I repeatedly hurl into the wombs of those with similar demoniac natures in the cycle of rebirth in the material world. These ignorant souls take birth again and again in demoniac wombs. Failing to reach the Supreme Soul, O Arjuna, they slowly sink to the lowest kind of existence.

–Verses 16.19–20

chapter 16

Daivasura Sampad Vibhaga Yoga
Yoga as Two Paths—the Divine and the Demoniac

16.01–03

श्रीभगवानुवाच |

अभयं सत्त्वसंशुद्धिर्ज्ञानयोगव्यवस्थिति: |
दानं दमश्च यज्ञश्च स्वाध्यायस्तप आर्जवम् || 1||
अहिंसा सत्यमक्रोधस्त्याग: शान्तिरपैशुनम् |
दया भूतेष्वलोलुप्त्वं मार्दवं ह्रीरचापलम् || 2||
तेज: क्षमा धृति: शौचमद्रोहोनातिमानिता |
भवन्ति सम्पदं दैवीमभिजातस्य भारत || 3||

16.01–03: The Supreme Lord said: Fearlessness, purity of mind, unwavering pursuit of spiritual knowledge, charity, control of the senses, performance of sacrifice, study of the sacred books, austerity, and simplicity; non-violence, truthfulness, absence of anger, renunciation, being peaceful, restraint from undue criticism, compassion towards all living beings, absence of greed, being gentle, modesty, and determination; vigour, forgiveness, fortitude, cleanliness, bearing enmity towards none, and absence of vanity, O scion of Bharata, these are the transcendental virtues of those endowed with a divine nature.

The sixteenth chapter starts with Krishna explaining both the transcendental nature and its attending qualities, and the demoniac nature and its identifying qualities. He also talks of the advantages, disadvantages and the outcomes of both.

In these three verses Krishna describes twenty-six virtues of those who are of divine nature. These should be cultivated as part of our spiritual endeavours for elevating ourselves to the supreme goal:

- absence of anger, enmity, greed and vanity
- austerity and modesty
- being fearless and gentle
- charity, cleanliness and compassion
- forgiveness and fortitude
- love for peace and nonviolence
- renunciation and performance of sacrifice
- self-control and restraint from undue criticism of others
- simplicity and purity of thought
- spiritual pursuit and study of sacred texts
- truthfulness, vigour and unwavering in one's devotion.

16.04

दम्भो दर्पोऽभिमानश्च क्रोध: पारुष्यमेव च |
अज्ञानं चाभिजातस्य पार्थ सम्पदमासुरीम् || 4||

16.04: O Partha, the qualities of those who are born with a demoniac nature are hypocrisy, arrogance, conceit, anger, harshness, and ignorance.

After explaining the twenty-six transcendental virtues of those endowed with a divine nature, Krishna now talks of the six traits of those who possess a demoniac nature. Such individuals are identified by their

- hypocrisy
- arrogance
- conceit
- harsh speech
- anger
- ignorance

Such individuals lead double lives, and pretend to be what they are not. By their very nature, hypocrites are not sincere or truthful, and cannot be trusted. They might make a great show of their propensity for spirituality and good work but in reality their devotion is only a pretence, and related activities are carried out more for the sake of form rather than for an actual desire to perform selfless service. This is quite reminiscent of those hankering for political power indulging in social work, when time for the elections draws close.

Addressing Arjuna as Partha, son of Pritha, Krishna says arrogance, conceit and harsh speech go hand in hand, and most arrogant people suffer from a chronic misplaced sense of superiority. Apart from their actions, their manner of speaking to others, specially to the underprivileged and downtrodden, is harsh and unfeeling. Empathy is an emotion they are not familiar with, and self-aggrandisement coupled with an elevated self-image is the driving force of their lives. It is often said that if you want to know more about people you might be eating out with, notice the manner in which they speak to the waiter in a restaurant.

Anger, of course, is one of the most debilitating traits of character. On the face of it this might seem empowering—and may also result in short-term gains—but in the long run a person who cannot be in control of his temper is unpopular, avoided by most, untrustworthy and not dependable in times of crises. Responsible leadership positions can be given only to those who can maintain their composure in traumatic situations, and act in a balanced manner. A person not in control of his own self, can hardly be expected to be a good manager of people, or a trouble shooter. At present any number of life-skills training are held on anger management issues. Containment strategies have been defined by qualified psychologists and trained counsellors who make fortunes helping people control their anger.

16.05

दैवी सम्पद्विमोक्षाय निबन्धायासुरी मता |
मा शुच: सम्पदं दैवीमभिजातोऽसि पाण्डव || 5||

16.05: Transcendental qualities lead to liberation, while the demoniac qualities bring about a continuing destiny of bondage. Do not worry, O Arjuna, as you were born with divine qualities.

Having described different characteristics of divine and demoniac individuals Krishna now declares the consequences of both kinds of life. He talks of liberation and the word here means the soul's release, or liberation, from the cycle of birth and rebirth.

Demoniac qualities keep one chained to the sensual pleasures of life, thus resulting in a continuous circle of life and death. Nurturing one's divine qualities on the other hand, helps one break out of this vicious circle, and reach the doorstep of the Ultimate Abode.

However, since change is the only constant, in this context too it is important to work on change, i.e., self-improvement. Being blessed with saintly attributes of character should not make us complacent—for two reasons. Firstly, because there is always room for improvement, no matter at what level we may be. And secondly, because complacence itself is a vice. The minute we assume that we have now reached the optimum level of moral rectitude, arrogance and conceit set in.

Similarly, if one is governed by predominantly demoniac characteristics, it is not to be seen as a point of no return. If a person decides to work on himself, to leave behind ignorance and move towards acquiring knowledge, to learn to control one's anger and rise above sensual gratification, to try to be humble, truthful and courteous, it is possible to move closer to the recommended spiritual path. To understand that it is never too late to rectify, reform and rehabilitation are the first steps towards an improved life.

So as not to allow Arjuna to indulge in self-doubt, Krishna asks him not to worry about his own spiritual journey, as Arjuna was born with divine qualities and is walking on the right path.

16.10

कामनाश्रित्य दुष्पूरं दम्भमानमदान्विता: |
मोहाद्गृहीत्वासद्ग्राहान्प्रवर्तन्तेऽशुचिव्रता: || 10||

16.10: Nurturing insatiable lust, filled with hypocrisy, pride and arrogance, the demoniac cling to their false qualities. Driven by illusion, they are attracted to that which is not permanent, and thus work with impure conviction.

Having reassured Arjuna of his divine qualities Krishna goes on to speak of the individuals in whom demoniac qualities dominate. Such people pander to lust which is insatiable. Eventually both their minds and hearts become impure and contaminated, as they lead hypocritical lives. Driven by arrogance and pride, they fail to overcome their desire for earthly pleasures, and are constantly attracted to a shallow life which is transactional and transitory. Unable to see the lack of permanence in these pursuits they remain engrossed in the world, wallowing in an existence driven by illusion and impurity.

16.11–12

चिन्तामपरिमेयां च प्रलयान्तामुपाश्रिता: |
कामोपभोगपरमा एतावदिति निश्चिता: || 11||
आशापाशशतैर्बद्धा: कामक्रोधपरायणा: |
ईहन्ते कामभोगार्थमन्यायेनार्थसञ्चयान् || 12||

16.11: They are caught up with fears and anxieties that end only with death. They continue to believe with conviction that gratification of desires and accumulation of wealth is the ultimate purpose of life.

16.12: Seeking gratification from innumerable desires, and driven by lust and anger, they strive to accumulate wealth by unjust means, all for the satisfaction of their senses.

Continuing further, Krishna says that earthly desires and the apprehension of not accumulating enough or of losing one's possessions amounts to a life of uncertainty, fear and constant anxiety. It is impossible for such people to concentrate or meditate. Tormented by thoughts of acquisition they completely lose sight of the larger picture.

As the desire for worldly pleasures grows, the lines between right and wrong, fair and unfair, just and unjust begin to blur. Soon sensual gratification and accumulation of wealth becomes the sole purpose of life, and such individuals are prepared to go to any length to get these.

Of course, the desire to earn money and to live a comfortable life is natural. As a matter of fact, money can be a major motivator in making people work and prove themselves. Money, position, status, power are all driving forces that push us to do our best. In the absence of these, the world would become a static place as no one would feel the need to wake up each morning and work to make their lives better.

What is debatable is the means we adopt to earn money and fame. Are we doing it at the cost of relationships, friendships? Are we grabbing what is rightfully not ours? Are we being unethical in our work? And most importantly, are we forgetting that money is a means and not the end. Wealth is simply a tool with which we can make ourselves comfortable.

When money becomes the purpose of living, it is time to stop and take stock. Time to self-introspect, and analyse whether our financial profits are resulting in moral and ethical losses. And if it is so, then these so-called gains are hollow and are merely figures ending with a certain number of zeroes on paper.

16.19–20

तानहं द्विषतः क्रूरान्संसारेषु नराधमान् |
क्षिपाम्यजस्रमशुभानासुरीष्वेव योनिषु || 19||
आसुरीं योनिमापन्ना मूढा जन्मनि जन्मनि |
मामप्राप्यैव कौन्तेय ततो यान्त्यधमां गतिम् || 20||

16.19-20: These cruel and envious persons, the basest of all humankind, I repeatedly hurl into the wombs of those with similar demoniac natures in the cycle of rebirth in the material world. These ignorant souls take birth again and again in demoniac wombs. Failing to reach the Supreme Soul, O Arjuna, they slowly sink to the lowest kind of existence.

Reinforcing the theory of karma, Krishna once again describes the outcomes of living a life driven by demoniac qualities. He emphasises that such people are heartless and devoid of morals, and are therefore the lowest kind of human beings. They fail to walk on the path of goodness and so, as an of act retributive justice, the Lord condemns them to the cycle of birth and rebirth.

Not stopping at this Krishna adds that as a mark of his displeasure he ensures that each time they take birth from a demoniac womb, and thus repeatedly go through the agony, angst, anxiety and apprehension that are essential aspects of a life on earth.

Many of these demoniac souls are unable to reform, and thus fail to reach anywhere close to the Lord, even after successive births. They continue to live their lives in the same undesirable manner frittering away the opportunities available to them. Forgetting that they are blessed with intelligence, and the ability and freedom to make choices, they continue living in an undesirable manner. Eventually they lose the advantage of being granted life as a human being, and may be condemned to be born as some other species or life form.

16.21

त्रिविधं नरकस्येदं द्वारं नाशनमात्मनः |
कामः क्रोधस्तथा लोभस्तस्मादेतत्त्रयं त्यजेत् || 21||
एतैर्विमुक्तः कौन्तेय तमोद्वारैस्त्रिभिर्नरः |
आचरत्यात्मनः श्रेयस्ततो याति परां गतिम् || 22||

16.21: There are three gates leading to the hell of self-destruction of the soul—lust, anger and greed. Therefore, all should abandon these three.

16.22: Those who are freed from the three gates to darkness work towards self-realisation, and thereby attain the Supreme goal.

Having described in detail about those who have a divine disposition and those who are of demoniac nature, Krishna now defines the qualities that lead to ultimate self-destruction. These are

- lust
- anger
- greed

These three attributes of character are found condemnable in all societies and cultures. Almost every crime committed anywhere in the world is likely to have been propelled by one of these. Sexual offences, crimes committed in the heat of the moment, and of course the desire for money and power, are known to drive people to indulge in heinous behaviour.

These three traits are not only deplorable on their own but also feed on one another. Those who cannot reign these in, are likely to find themselves caught in a vicious cycle of lust, anger and greed. If they fail to condition their minds to not give in to these forces, their souls are bound to find themselves consigned to hell, and rot there for eternity.

On the other hand, those who can distance themselves from these deadly attributes devote themselves to a life of purity and self-realisation. Having lead a pristine, immaculate life, such devotees are bound to attain the Supreme goal, and find themselves at one with the Lord.

17

Faith and Kinds of Faith

In Chapter Fourteen, Krishna had explained the three *gunas*, or the modes of material nature, and how these determine our personalities and behaviour. In the seventeenth chapter he delves deeper into these three categorisations of human nature, and how these determine our temperament, actions and behaviour.

...no one can be said to be devoid of faith—each one of us has faith in something or the other, however, the focus of faith may differ for every individual.

Arjuna raises the question of faith, and wants to know which kind is superior—that which follows traditional instructions, or the one that defines its own protocols or a real life guru.

Krishna discloses that no one can be said to be devoid of faith—each one of us has faith in something or the other, however, the focus of faith may differ for every individual. Where faith is concerned, one size does not fit all.

During the discourse, some interesting aspects emerge about our likes and dislikes, and the manner in which we react to situations and handle them, based on the predominant *guna*. We are told of how the following are determined by our dominant trait.

- faith—*nishtha*
- food—*ahara*
- sacrifice—*yajna*

- austerity -*tapah*
- charity- *danam*

The list of foods recommended for a good and healthy life in the *Gita* is sure to make any present-day dietician sit up. It is truly amazing how some nuggets of wisdom have remained alive and relevant over thousands of years. It is equally disappointing to realise that humankind has still not paid heed to these timeless and invaluable prescriptions.

Krishna reveals that foods that are

- juicy, succulent, wholesome, naturally delicious—increase life span, bring health, happiness, and satisfaction,
- bitter, sour, pungent, dry, hot and spicy—cause distress, pain, misery and disease
- overcooked, stale, putrefied, decomposed, impure—can only be the choice of the ignorant (we can safely add frozen foods and those containing preservatives and artificial sweeteners to this list as a later development)

This list does make one wonder how different, if at all, can a twenty-first century doctor's guide to healthy eating be from this?

It is well known that the syllable *om* is considered to be the sound of the universe. *Om* chanting tunes us into that sound, and acknowledges our connection to everything in the world and the universe. It is believed that rhythmic chanting and the resulting vibrations have a calming effect on the body and the nervous system, similar to the effects of meditation.

The words '*om*', '*tat*', '*sat*' chanted in this order add more potency and meaning to the syllable *om*. Each of the three sounds is a symbolic representation of God and invokes the following:

- *Om*—the entire universe
- *Tat*—ultimate reality, and all that is
- *Sat*—pure and Absolute Truth

Drawing attention to this significant combination of meaningful words and their sounds, Krishna elaborates on them in the following verse.

From the beginning of creation the three words om tat sat have been used as symbolic representations of the Supreme Absolute Truth. These have been used by priests while chanting of Vedic scriptures and sacrifices performed for the satisfaction of the Supreme.

–Verse 17.23

chapter 17

Shraddhatrya Vibhaga Yoga
Yoga as Faith

17.01

अर्जुन उवाच |
ये शास्त्रविधिमुत्सृज्य यजन्ते श्रद्धयान्विता: |
तेषां निष्ठा तु का कृष्ण सत्त्वमाहो रजस्तम: || 1||

17.01: Arjuna said: O Krishna, where do they stand who ignore the principles advised in the scriptures, but still worship with complete faith? Is their faith in the mode of goodness, passion, or ignorance?

Earlier, in Chapter Four it is said that a person committed to a particular kind of worship gradually evolves and attains the highest stage of perfection after living a life of peace and prosperity. In Chapter Sixteen it is concluded that the one who does not follow the principles laid down in Vedic scriptures is one with demoniac personality traits, while the one who does is closest to the gods.

Arjuna now wonders what is the fate of those who are devoted and committed to goodness, but do not strictly follow Vedic scriptures. Some people may have charted their own path and might be following their own rules. There are others who choose a real life guru and follow his or her teachings and dedicate their lives to the path shown by the guru. Arjuna has several questions in his mind. He wants to know:

What happens to those who do not follow the rules and regulations prescribed in the scriptures, but who have faith in something or someone, and worship gods and demigods sincerely and regularly?

Are they rewarded for their efforts? If so, then how? Are these rewards at par with those that are bestowed on devotees who strictly adhere to Vedic teachings?

How will these devotees be identified? Will they be considered to be in the mode of goodness, passion or ignorance?

Can such people attain perfection in life? Is it possible for them to imbibe Ultimate Knowledge and live by it? Are they then rewarded for the perfection attained during their time on earth?

17.04

यजन्ते सात्त्विका देवान्यक्षरक्षांसि राजसा: |
प्रेतान्भूतगणांश्चान्ये यजन्ते तामसा जना: || 4||

17.04: Those in the mode of goodness worship celestial gods; those in the mode of passion worship demons; and those in the mode of ignorance worship ghosts and spirits.

As the old adage goes, like attracts like. This remains as true even today as it may have been at the time of the *Mahabharata*. We attract people like ourselves and get attracted to those who are like us.

Similarly, different people find different things in the same place. For instance, if you enter a grocery store with a child, chances are that within minutes she will find where the chocolates are displayed. You as an adult may immediately spot the cooking oil or spices, or whatever else is in your shopping list. Consciously or subconsciously we are drawn to what interests us and eventually we find it.

Thus Krishna rightly says those who are predominantly good-natured and have goodness at the core of their being, will worship gods and goddesses and feel one with them. They aspire to be like them and try to live their lives along the path shown by the gods.

Those who are driven by passion are naturally attracted to demons, who manifest themselves in sensual pleasures, avarice, anger and envy. Such passion is insatiable and is a whirlpool of gratification that is difficult to get out of.

Others who live a life of ignorance and incomprehension vis-à-vis the ultimate destination, are drawn towards ghosts and spirits, and are not repelled by their immoral characteristics, and propensity for everything negative. Voluntarily they indulge in evil practices and thrive on pettiness, stoking ill-feeling towards all.

17.07

आहारस्त्वपि सर्वस्य त्रिविधो भवति प्रियः |
यज्ञस्तपस्तथा दानं तेषां भेदमिमं शृणु || 7||

17.07: The food each person prefers is according to one's temperament. The same is true for the sacrifice, austerity, and charity they are inclined towards. Now hear of the distinctions between them.

We are not merely the living cells our physical bodies are made up of. If that were to be so, we would be no different from animals. What differentiates and sets us apart from other life forms is our intelligence, and our individual character traits.

Human beings are more than mere life forms, they are persons, and the choices they make and the paths they walk on determine who and what they are in life. Needless to say, this also determines where they reach in this life, and beyond. Our thought processes, actions and reactions, personal convictions, individual experiences, education and upbringing, social status, financial situation etc. contribute to making us unique.

As individual persons we react differently in, and to, different situations. Our food preferences, acts of charity or absence of generosity, living in austerity or extravagance, being engaged in selfless service and sacrifice, or pre-occupation with self-aggrandisement—all of these decisions are outcomes of the kind of person one is.

Krishna goes on to explain what these distinctions are, and how, who we are affects our choices, as it's our choices that make us who we are.

17.08–10

आयुःसत्त्वबलारोग्यसुखप्रीतिविवर्धनाः |
रस्याः स्निग्धाः स्थिरा हृद्या आहाराः सात्त्विकप्रियाः || 8||
कट्वम्ललवणात्युष्णतीक्ष्णरूक्षविदाहिनः |
आहारा राजसस्येष्टा दुःखशोकामयप्रदाः || 9||
यातयामं गतरसं पूति पर्युषितं च यत् |
उच्छिष्टमपि चामेध्यं भोजनं तामसप्रियम् || 10||

17.08: Persons in the mode of goodness prefer foods that increase lifespan, instil virtue providing strength, health, happiness, and satisfaction. Such foods are juicy, succulent, wholesome and naturally delicious.

17.09: Food that is too bitter, or too sour, salty, pungent, dry, burning hot and full of chillies, is preferred by persons dominated by the mode of passion. Such foods cause distress pain, misery and disease.

17.10: Food that is overcooked, or stale, putrified, decomposed, or impure pleases persons in the mode of ignorance.

Eat to live and don't live to eat is what the wise say. The purpose of food consumption is to nourish the body, keep it healthy and active, and prolong life. Even a child understands hunger, and instinctively reaches out for food. Eating is a survival mechanism inbuilt in our psyche.

Depending on our personal traits and preferences, we relish different kinds of foods. Those who are in the mode of goodness and have risen above attractions of worldly life eat for good health, happiness and overall well-being. These people choose to have a *sattvik* diet, i.e., natural products that are juicy, succulent and wholesome. These include grains, pulses, milk, fruits, vegetables, natural juices, and any other source of nutrition that is easy on the digestive system and does not traumatise it.

Foods that are excessively bitter, sour, salty, hot, pungent, dry, and full of chillies can result in health issues including heart burn, poor sleep and an overworked digestive machinery. This can, in turn, lead to internal abrasions, ulcers, etc. But, foolishly ignoring these possible outcomes those who are driven by passion and are in the *rajas* mode recklessly pander to their taste buds. Poor health may lead to agitation and despair, but since, for these people food is higher in priority than good health, they remain obsessed with such food at any cost. Most people in their midlife have to impose dietary restrictions on themselves to neutralise the over consumption of the past years.

Present day lifestyles have made the refrigerator an essential part of our lives. Frozen, semi-cooked and dried foods, jams and jellies with preservatives, canned foods, artificial drinks, etc., help us stay ahead in our work schedules, as these minimise the time spent in cooking. While consumption of these may be an occupational hazard, one should remember that these foods are also a serious health hazard.

Now let us see what Krishna had to say about this thousands of years ago. Almost as though foreseeing the future, he tells Arjuna that food that is not fresh, or freshly cooked, in other words stale, is to be condemned. Decomposed, putrid, and contaminated food can only be the choice of those who live in ignorance.

Those persons who are uninformed and not willing to improve fall in the *tamas* category, and could well be the only humans who would be willing to eat such repugnant food. Such individuals are the lowest kind of humans.

17.11–13

अफलाकाङ्क्षिभिर्यज्ञो विधिदृष्टो य इज्यते |
यष्टव्यमेवेति मनः समाधाय स सात्त्विकः || 11||
अभिसन्धाय तु फलं दम्भार्थमपि चैव यत् |
इज्यते भरतश्रेष्ठ तं यज्ञं विद्धि राजसम् || 12||
विधिहीनमसृष्टान्नं मन्त्रहीनमदक्षिणम् |
श्रद्धाविरहितं यज्ञं तामसं परिचक्षते || 13||

17.11: Sacrifice that is performed in accordance with scriptural prescriptions and without expectation of rewards, with firm resolve of the mind that it is a matter of duty, and with no desire of reward, is in the nature of goodness.

17.12: Sacrifice performed for material benefit, or for ego, O best of the Bharatas, you should see as being in the mode of passion.

17.13: Sacrifice performed without adhering to scriptural directions, in which no food is distributed, no mantras chanted, and no act of charity, is to be considered as in the mode of ignorance.

Talking of performing sacrifices and the spirit behind the actions, Krishna says that the nature of these is in consonance with the three *gunas*. It is important here to interpret the word sacrifice in a larger context, and not limit its ambit to *yagyas*, *havans*, or any other rituals.

When a caregiver stays awake through the night to ensure the comfort of her ward, it is a sacrifice. When a parent cuts down on his expenses so as to meet the needs of his children, it is a sacrifice. When a young person lets go of a professional opportunity to take care of ageing parents, it is a sacrifice. As a matter of fact, these sacrifices, whether big or small, that we make in our daily lives are far more important than, and certainly more challenging, than an elaborate one-time activity which might be a socially-accepted norm or expectation.

The usual tendency is to visit a temple or any religious place when we are in trouble or are looking for some returns. For instance, promising God that if a wish is fulfilled one will fast for a certain number of days, etc. Or giving up something as a sacrifice in the hope of some gain. This is transactional and conditional, and nothing but an attempt to strike a bargain with the Almighty.

A sacrifice by a person steeped in the nature of goodness is performed without expectation of any reward. It is carried out in accordance with scriptural prescriptions, in a broader sense this simply means the path of righteousness. Most important, the sacrifice is both the means as well as the end. There is no ulterior motive or a hidden agenda behind the act.

Those in whom the mode of passion dominates are likely to make a great show of their actions. The sacrifice may be performed more as a display of power amongst peers or as an indication of one's prosperity, and thus be carried out with a lot of pomp and show. Those of *rajas* nature will also ensure that all and sundry are duly informed of the so-called noble act. This is reminiscent of the present-day pseudo-philanthropists distributing alms to the poor, but first ensuring that the cameras are strategically positioned and the people who matter have been invited to witness the act.

Those in the mode of ignorance are either unaware or do not have faith in the scriptures. They may carry out religious ceremonies but show no regard to form and procedure. The sacrifices are carried out in a random manner, possibly for personal gain or out of sheer indolence and indifference. Such sacrifices are of the lowest kind, and do not find favour with the Supreme Power, and thus a waste of time and resources in terms of spiritual gains.

17.14

देवद्विजगुरुप्राज्ञपूजनं शौचमार्जवम् |
ब्रह्मचर्यमहिंसा च शारीरं तप उच्यते || 14||

17.14: Austerity of the body comprises worship of the Supreme Lord, the Brahmins, the spiritual master, the wise, and the elders. This is to be done along with observing cleanliness, simplicity, celibacy, and non-violence.

The term austerity, which frequently occurs in this discourse can also be defined as self-discipline, self-containment, self-denial or adoption of an overall frugality as a way of life. By practising genuine austerity with sincerity, human beings can transform themselves from ordinary mortals to exalted souls.

Krishna elaborates on three kinds of austerity. These are austerity of the body, speech and mind. All the three complement each other and make the act of austerity complete. In this verse, he talks of austerity of the body. It must be pointed out here that the reference to Brahmins here is not to do with birth or caste. It simply means anyone who is pure, saintly, learned and endowed with goodness.

When self-control is effectively exercised over the body and one is dedicated to the service of the good and the learned, it is a mark of austerity. Austerity of the body also includes restraint from sexual indulgence and recommends celibacy. When self-control is effectively exercised over the body and one is dedicated to the service of the good and the learned, it is a mark of austerity. Austerity of the body also includes restraint from sexual indulgence – celibacy is recommended. Taking care of the elderly, according them due respect, living a simple, peaceful, non-violent life, where cleanliness and simplicity are the basis of daily existence, are desirable qualities. When all these are accomplished, austerity of the body can be said to be complete.

17.15

अनुद्वेगकरं वाक्यं सत्यं प्रियहितं च यत् |
स्वाध्यायाभ्यसनं चैव वाङ्मयं तप उच्यते || 15||

17.15: Austerity of speech lies in speaking words that do not cause distress, are truthful, inoffensive, and beneficial to all, and also in regular recitation of the Vedic scriptures.

According to Plato, wise men speak because they have something to say; fools because they have to say something.

Nothing could be closer to the truth. Where speech is concerned it is wise to follow the maxim, less is more. A careful choice of words, time, tone, purpose and occasion, add value to what one has to say. Someone who is speaking all the time is less likely to find a receptive audience as compared to a person who speaks sparingly, and only when required.

Austerity of speech lies in speaking words that are truthful, soothing, and useful. Also the words we speak must not cause any distress or pain to anyone. Even when saying what is true, but could be painful to some, it is advisable to initially sugar-coat the bitter pill. Words are like an arrow; once the archer has pulled the string and let go, there is no way of retrieving it. Words once spoken can never be taken back.

Krishna also includes Vedic mantra recitation as an austerity of speech. This is important as regular chanting reinforces the words and helps internalise the meaning and purpose.

17.16

मन: प्रसाद: सौम्यत्वं मौनमात्मविनिग्रह: |
भावसंशुद्धिरित्येतत्तपो मानसमुच्यते || 16||

17.16: Austerity of the mind is mastered when there is simplicity, gravity, self-control, purity of purpose, and overall mental satisfaction.

What you think, you become. What you feel, you attract. What you imagine, you create.—Buddha

Our thoughts, imagination, feelings and emotions make us who we are. The thoughts we entertain and encourage play a critical role in character building. As the saying goes, if you can think it, you can do it. Whatever can be thought of or imagined can also be achieved. This may sound evolutionary and motivational if we are naïve enough to assume that thoughts in the human mind are always progressive and positive.

So what happens when a person's thoughts are negative? Or depressive? Or violent? Clearly the outcome is likely to be negative. Negativity can lead to anti-social activities, self-harm or violence. Mental hygiene is as critical as physical hygiene, perhaps even more.

As a matter of fact, austerity of the mind is more important than austerity of body and speech. If we can control our minds, learn to channelise our thoughts in a positive manner, and determine the direction our train of thoughts will take, then the body and speech are naturally in our control.

In a manner of speaking, austerity of the body and mind are subsets of austerity of the mind. The former two are not possible unless we become masters of our mind.

An old proverb says, all wealth begins in the mind. What it does not say is that so does impoverishment. Of all kinds.

17.17–19

श्रद्धया परया तप्तं तपस्तत्त्रिविधं नरैः |
अफलाकाङ्क्षिभिर्युक्तैः सात्त्विकं परिचक्षते || 17||
सत्कारमानपूजार्थं तपो दम्भेन चैव यत् |
क्रियते तदिह प्रोक्तं राजसं चलमध्रुवम् || 18||
मूढग्राहेणात्मनो यत्पीडया क्रियते तपः |
परस्योत्सादनार्थं वा तत्तामसमुदाहृतम् || 19||

17.17: This three-fold austerity when performed with genuine faith and without yearning for material rewards, is said to be austerity in the mode of goodness.

17.18: Austerity that is performed for the sake of gaining honour, respect and adoration is in the mode of passion. It is driven by false ego and is transitory and temporary.

17.19: Austerity performed for ambivalent reasons, which involves torturing oneself, or causing harm to others, is said to be in the mode of ignorance.

The dictionary meaning of austerity is severity of manners or life; extreme rigour or strictness; and harsh discipline. It also stands for freedom from adornment, plainness or severe simplicity. When people live their lives adhering to these qualities, they are said to be austere.

At another level, there are times when governments adopt austerity measures. This means adopting a policy of lower spending, higher taxes, or both. Clearly, austerity is a known phenomenon, both at the personal and national levels.

Having described in detail austerities of body, speech and mind, Krishna now explains the characteristics of austerity when it is performed in the mode of goodness. When austerity or penance is performed with complete, unwavering devotion, with no desire for any material returns, then it is an act of the most superior kind, and is usually driven by undiluted goodness in the person.

When social workers or politicians dress in simple clothes, not because they believe in simplicity but because they are either looking for donations or votes, it is not quite the best form of austerity. The same applies to those who are supposedly spiritual, dress in saffron for effect, and pretend to be pious, in the hope of gaining a large following and having hundreds and thousands of people beholden to them. Such kinds of fake lifestyles are temporary and transactional, and this kind of austerity is driven by love for power and money, adopted by those in whom the mode of passion dominates.

There is a third category of people who, in their ignorance and simple-mindedness, adopt wrong means of following austerity. This is a consequence of their lack of knowledge, misplaced beliefs and a confused thought process. Sadism, masochism, perversion, causing pain and humiliation are all outcomes of so-called austerity performed by those who live in the mode of ignorance.

17.20–22

दातव्यमिति यद्दानं दीयतेऽनुपकारिणे |
देशे काले च पात्रे च तद्दानं सात्त्विकं स्मृतम् || 20||
यत्तु प्रत्युपकारार्थं फलमुद्दिश्य वा पुनः |
दीयते च परिक्लिष्टं तद्दानं राजसं स्मृतम् || 21||
अदेशकाले यद्दानमपात्रेभ्यश्च दीयते |
असत्कृतमवज्ञातं तत्तामसमुदाहृतम् || 22||

17.20: Charity given to a deserving person as a sense of duty, without consideration of anything in return, at the proper time and place, is said to be in the mode of goodness.

17.21: Charity given grudgingly, in the hope of a return or a reward, is said to be in the mode of passion.

17.22: Charity, given at the wrong place and time to undeserving persons, without showing respect, or with contempt, is held to be of the nature of ignorance.

For a person who truly believes that to give is to get, that is, the satisfaction one gets by the sheer act of giving is in itself the reward, is one who performs acts of charity in the mode of sincere goodness. This kind of charity is unconditional, ensuring that the most deserving are the beneficiaries, and is carried out at an appropriate time and place. This could mean helping people when they need it the most, for example, people affected by a natural calamity. Or reaching out to those who are surviving in the remotest of areas, having no access to a decent life.

There are times when people are under pressure to donate, or might do so to create a favourable impression in their peer group. For instance, while visiting a holy place there is an expectation to give something to the priest, it can be in cash or kind, or both. One may not be doing so out of conviction or a desire to help, but simply to go along with social norms. Similarly, donating to a public fund with the objective of seeing one's name in the list of donors is driven by the mode of passion and hidden agendas, and is more of a bargain of sorts.

Giving at an inappropriate time or place, and to an undeserving person is a waste. Determining the suitability of the receiver is critical, and can only be done by people who have clarity of thought and purpose. Those who are confused, ambivalent, vulnerable and gullible might not be in a position to make the right choices. For instance, donating to a flood relief fund much after the calamity; or donating to a person who already has enough.

In a nutshell, charity must emanate from a sense of duty and sincere conviction, and must be done in a manner to help those who are the most in need. It should not be accompanied by a hope of getting something in return, or any other personal gain in the form of position, designation or recognition.

17.23–27

ॐ तत्सदिति निर्देशो ब्रह्मणस्त्रिविधः स्मृतः |
ब्राह्मणास्तेन वेदाश्च यज्ञाश्च विहिताः पुरा || 23||
तस्माद् ॐ इत्युदाहृत्य यज्ञदानतपःक्रियाः |
प्रवर्तन्ते विधानोक्ताः सततं ब्रह्मवादिनाम् || 24||
तदित्यनभिसन्धाय फलं यज्ञतपःक्रियाः |
दानक्रियाश्च विविधाः क्रियन्ते मोक्षकाङ्क्षिभिः || 25||
सद्भावे साधुभावे च सदित्येतत्प्रयुज्यते |
प्रशस्ते कर्मणि तथा सच्छब्दः पार्थ युज्यते || 26||
यज्ञे तपसि दाने च स्थितिः सदिति चोच्यते |
कर्म चैव तदर्थीयं सदित्येवाभिधीयते || 27||

17.23: From the beginning of creation the three words *om tat sat* have been used as symbolic representations of the Supreme Absolute Truth. These have been used by priests while chanting Vedic scriptures, and sacrifices performed for the satisfaction of the Supreme.

17.24: Therefore, when performing acts of sacrifice, charity, or penance, those knowledgeable of the *Vedas* always begin by chanting *om* according to the scriptural regulations of Vedic texts.

17.25: Persons who actually desire liberation and do not desire rewards, chant the word *tat* along with acts of austerity, sacrifice and charity.

17.26-27: The word *sat* means that which is in the nature of the Absolute Truth. O Arjuna, son of Pritha, it is used to describe devotional sacrifice and also used to describe the performer of the sacrifice. Penance and charity too are described by the word *sat*. And so any act for such purposes is named *sat*.

In these verses Krishna mentions the mantra *Om Tat Sat* and its significance. These three words symbolise different aspects of the Divine.

Each of the three sounds is a symbolic representation of God.

Om is the sound indicative of the entire universe
Tat is the ultimate reality, and all that is
Sat is the pure and Absolute Truth

Priests and those who are well versed in Vedic scriptures initiate every activity, be it an act of sacrifice, charity or penance, with the chanting of *Om*, invoking and addressing the entire universe, in other words all of God's creation.

The word *tat* means everything belongs to the Supreme Lord, and by repeating it one is seeking liberation from the material world, while selflessly performing acts of charity, sacrifice and penance.

Sat represents all the actions and duties that are performed with honesty, sincerity and truthfulness. Such actions are solely meant for the satisfaction of the Supreme Power, and are performed in honour of, and to please the Lord.

According to some beliefs

- *Om* represents Brahma as he is the Creator of the Universe

- *Tat* represents Shiva as the Ultimate Reality, and the sum total of all that comprises the Universe
- *Sat* represents Vishnu as the Absolute and Ultimate Truth.

Thus when chanted in consonance *Om Tat Sat* can be understood as the entire creation, its supreme reality, Absolute Truth or all that is there in universe.

This mantra may sometimes include the prefix *Hari*, referring to God in the physical, even earthly, form. Believers frequently chant the four words together, *Hari Om Tat Sat*. It thus becomes a holistic mantra used to offer respect to the Lord and also to remind oneself of what lies beyond the physical body, and be awakened to the true or higher self.

Chanting *Om Tat Sat* is believed to successfully awaken and encourage higher consciousness as a means of connecting with the inner self. It is one of the most frequently used mantras, often recited during Hindu religious practices and rituals.

When used with the prefix *Hari* as in *Hari Om Tat Sat* it acknowledges and pays respects to God in all forms, that which has *akaar*, i.e., is visible and has form, and also that which is *nirakaar*, i.e., invisible and has no form but is present in everything. Thus all forms of God are addressed, the Ominpotent, the Ominiscient and the Omnipresent. The greeting *Hari Om Tat Sat* is a reminder that like God we too must strive for an existence which is more than the body and earthly, material life.

The repetitive chanting of this mantra encourages the mind to enter into a transcendental state, so that the practitioner may begin to connect with the higher self or the divine within.

17.28

अश्रद्धया हुतं दत्तं तपस्तप्तं कृतं च यत् |
असदित्युच्यते पार्थ न च तत्प्रेत्य नो इह || 28||

17.28: Anything done as sacrifice, charity or penance without faith in the Supreme, O son of Pritha, is said to be *asat*. These are useless, both in this world and the next.

Any act performed without faith and sincerity is of no use. Krishna tells Arjuna, in the last verse of this chapter, that be it sacrifice, charity or penance, if driven by some material intent or purpose, it does not please the Lord. As a contrast to all that is pure or *sat*, these insincere activities amount to *asat*, i.e., untrue or impure.

Devoting time and resources to such impure activities may bring about some short-term gains, but in the eyes of the divine these have no value. Those who are over-confident and egotistical often forget that hypocritical acts may fool ordinary mortals, but to imagine that the Supreme Lord can also be taken in by these is only a proof of their own naivety and ignorance.

Not only do lack of faith, integrity and ethics encourage one to indulge in wrongdoing in this life and take one away from the Absolute Truth, such character traits have to be accounted for in the next life too. If it is true that acts of goodness add to one's good karma, then the reverse of it is true as well.

18

Renunciation, Deliverance and Liberation

The last chapter of the *Bhagavad Gita* is also the longest. It largely reiterates all that has been said in the previous chapters. On Arjuna's request Krishna elaborates on the difference between renunciation of actions (*sanyas*), and renunciation of desires (*tyag*).

Of the two Krishna recommends renunciation of desires. Talking of actions he advises that the following should never be renounced.

- sacrifice
- charity
- penance
- and other essential acts of duty

Right through the *Gita* Krishna not only comes across as a patient and knowledgeable teacher, we also see him as being extremely empathetic and pragmatic. Here he says that it is impossible for human beings to give up all activities or withdraw completely from actions, no matter how detached from the world one might feel.

Human beings can never stop communicating. If not interpersonal then it is intrapersonal, but communication is a continuous activity.

This is similar to what is said of communication. Human beings can never stop communicating. If not interpersonal then it is intrapersonal, but communication is a continuous activity.

For instance, when we are silent we are conveying to others that we are not speaking, or that we have nothing to say. When we are asleep we are conveying to those who are awake that we are sleeping. Also, in both instances communication with ourselves is ongoing. When not speaking we are thinking, and while asleep we might be dreaming.

Besides, our organs are always at work, and no matter how detached we may be from the world, it is impossible to stop eating, sleeping or walking. Therefore, any definition of renunciation must include these basic activities.

The conversation in the last chapter also dwells significantly on professional occupation and dharma, or duty. It is important here to contextualise the two. In the present-day scenario what we are good at becomes, or should become, our occupation. A creative mind must engage itself in creative activities. Someone interested in animal lives in all probability will take up biology or zoology as an area of study. A person with a good voice must sing and put the talent to good use.

This brings us to the next part of this thought process. Is not refining our talents our dharma, our duty? Should a person who likes to take care of people not become a nurse, and thus contribute to society? Is that not their duty? Should not someone good at acting make it his professional choice, and perform on stage or screen to the best of his ability? If everyone were to, by and large, , follow this, will it not bring out the best in people, and as a result make the world a richer and happier place?

Is not refining our talents our dharma, our duty? Should a person who likes to take care of people not become a nurse and thus contribute to society? Is that not her duty? Should not someone good at acting make it his professional choice, and perform on stage or screen to the best of his ability? If everyone were to, by and large, follow this, will it not bring out the best in people, and as a result make the world a richer and happier place?

When we are blessed with a distinctive talent, could it be God's way of telling us what to do with our lives? Would ignoring this unique gift from the Almighty not amount to shirking from one's duty? Living in a world full of choices, first identifying our distinguishing capability, and then transforming it into our work, could well be a contemporary definition of dharma or duty.

Going forward Krishna recommends to Arjuna to focus on the Supreme Power, and not get deflected by alternatives. Krishna says that those who study this conversation between him and Arjuna in the form of the *Gita*, or even listen to its recitation, and follow the teachings encapsulated in it, are bound to make great progress on the coveted path to liberation.

Krishna pointedly asks Arjuna if he is now free of his despair and despondency, making sure that his distressed cousin has listened carefully to the discourse and internalised it. Purged of his confusion and agitation, we see Arjuna regaining his composure and clarity of thought, and set to perform his duty as a warrior, ready to fight.

Far away in the palace with his king Dhritarashtra, Sanjaya also concludes his narration of the events currently taking place on the battlefield. Blessed with clairvoyance Sanjaya could see and hear the exchange between Krishna and Arjuna. Sanjaya is amazed at what he saw with his eyes, the cosmic form of Krishna, and feels truly blessed to have had this opportunity of hearing words of wisdom from the Lord himself.

Sanjaya here is a via media for taking this conversation to a larger audience, and not restricting it to Arjuna alone. Perhaps as part of the grand plan to annihilate evil, this was Krishna's way of ensuring that Dhritarashtra gets to hear what is being spoken by him. This is important, as in a manner of speaking, by not being in control of his own sons, the blind king himself was responsible for the blood bath that was to follow on the battlefield of Kurukshetra.

Ironically, those present on the battlefield, and in all likelihood within earshot of the two speakers, are unable to hear the conversation as Krishna has cast a spell, and time stands still for the two armies for as long as the discourse lasts.

Coming back to the issue of profession and duty, or shall we say professional duty, Krishna says that it is better to face some initial setbacks while pursuing one's own passion rather than trying to engage in something else and meet with temporary success. What we are cut out to do and are naturally capable of doing, can eventually only lead to positive outcomes.

The following verse is virtually the last word in this regard.

It is better to engage in one's own assigned occupation even though one may perform it imperfectly, than to accept someone else's occupation and fulfil it perfectly.

Duties prescribed in accordance with one's nature never result in sinful outcomes.

–Verse 18.47

chapter 18

Moksha Sanyasa Yoga
Yoga as Liberation and Renunciation

18.01

अर्जुन उवाच |
सन्न्यासस्य महाबाहो तत्त्वमिच्छामि वेदितुम् |
त्यागस्य च हृषीकेश पृथक्केशिनिषूदन || 1||

18.01: Arjuna said: O mighty-armed Krishna, I wish to understand the nature of renunciation from material pursuits, and renunciation from material returns. O Hrishikesha, I also wish to know the distinction between the two, O Keshinisudana.

Having seen Krishna in his overwhelming Divine form, Arjuna now addresses him as the mighty-armed one. Arjuna is now keen to know the meaning of *sanyasa* and *tyagasysa,* and the difference between the two.

It is significant here that Arjuna addresses Krishna by three different names. Being aware of Krishna's infinite strength, he first calls him the mighty-armed one. Arjuna then goes on to addressing him as Hrishikesha or the master of the senses, followed by Keshnisudana, or the killer of the demon Keshni.

This choice of address has a direct bearing on Arjuna's troubled state of mind. Disoriented, confused and disheartened, he realises that he needs to be in control of his senses and emotions, and for this Krishna as Hrishikesha, master of the senses is the best guide. Arjuna is expected to slay his villainous cousins on the battlefield and all those who are on the side of evil, and this makes him look up to Krishna as the slayer of demons and someone to look up to and emulate, especially during a battle.

The reference to demons can also be seen as an euphemism here. When our thoughts are troubled, and we are perturbed and agitated, that state of mind is also akin to being possessed. There are times when our inner demons can be far more threatening and intimidating than the ones that may exist outside our mind.

18.02

श्रीभगवानुवाच |
काम्यानां कर्मणां न्यासं सन्न्यासं कवयो विदुः |
सर्वकर्मफलत्यागं प्राहुस्त्यागं विचक्षणाः || 2||

18.02: The Supreme Lord said: Giving up of actions based on material desire is what the wise understand as *sanyas*. And giving up the desire for material returns is what the learned declare to be *tyagam*.

On Arjuna's request, Krishna begins to explain the distinction between the different kinds of renunciation.

We all make sacrifices, whether small or big, sometime in our lives. Giving up sugar, not taking a vacation to take care of a loved one, supporting someone financially, or even waking up early to drop one's child to school, each of these activities may be looked upon as sacrifice.

But do these qualify as *sanyasa* or *tyaga*, or both, or neither? That is the question at hand.

It might not be easy to define in one's spiritual journey what comes first, *sanyasa* or *tyaga*? It might play out differently for different people, and in different situations.

Krishna explains that when one loses interest in, or fails to find any joy or satisfaction in activities that may be profitable, financially or socially, it is the first step towards renunciation.

Let us look at a real life scenario. At some point in life even the most ambitious of people may slow down, the same top job that one may be working towards all one's life may no longer seem attractive. One may not experience the same thrill looking at one's pay cheque as one did earlier on. This lack of desire for material returns can be looked upon as *tyaga*.

However, professional, social, financial, and familial responsibilities cannot (and should not) be abandoned abruptly, as this may cause a major disruption in the lives of many around us. And so one may continue performing the same activities, but as a duty, and no longer for material gains.

Subsequently, a stage may come when it is possible to even give up the said activities, and enter a stage of complete renunciation. Living a life where there is no desire for material returns of any kind can be said to be a state of *sanyasa*.

However, not everyone who looks like a *sanyasi* may really be one from within, as also not everyone who says that power and money mean nothing to them might actually have experienced *tyaga*.

18.04–06

निश्चयं शृणु मे तत्र त्यागे भरतसत्तम |
त्यागो हि पुरुषव्याघ्र त्रिविध: सम्प्रकीर्तित: || 4||
यज्ञदानतप:कर्म न त्याज्यं कार्यमेव तत् |
यज्ञो दानं तपश्चैव पावनानि मनीषिणाम् || 5||
एतान्यपि तु कर्माणि सङ्गं त्यक्त्वा फलानि च |
कर्तव्यानीति मे पार्थ निश्चितं मतमुत्तमम् || 6||

18.04: O best of Bharatas, on the subject of renunciation now listen to my final words; renunciation has been declared to be of three kinds.

18.05: Acts of sacrifice, charity and penance should never be given up; they must certainly be performed. Indeed, acts of sacrifice, charity and penance purify even those who are wise.

18.06: All these activities must be performed as a duty, and without any attachment or expectation of reward. This is my definite firm opinion, O Arjuna, son of Pritha.

Continuing the discourse on renunciation, Krishna says these are of three kinds, and now shares his final view on each. The word renunciation means to give up, and renunciation as a way of life is recommended. However, it does not in any way imply giving up all activity. For instance, acts of sacrifice, charity and penance must never be discontinued. As a matter of fact, these further the resolve of renunciation as one moves closer to one's ultimate destination by continuing to engage in these activities.

Addressing Arjuna as the bravest of men, Krishna reminds him that it is important to bear in mind that all acts of sacrifice, charity and penance, must be performed as a sense of duty, and as duty alone. These should be completely devoid of even an iota of desire for self-aggrandisement. Any expectation or hope of material reward or returns dilutes the sanctity of the act.

For instance, someone may have risen above materialistic desires and be in a state of renunciation, but must continue to take care of one's elderly parents. A personal choice to renounce the world cannot justify abandoning old and dependent parents. As such activities are performed selflessly, these are viewed as pure and sacred. Those who are wise perform utilitarian and propitious acts in a selfless manner.

Renouncing the world both in body and mind is a slow, gradual process. Initially it may be a combination of withdrawal from material pursuits while performing worldly duties, as these may be essential to deliver. Eventually this should lead to a gradual and convincing withdrawal from all material desires and rewards.

In the following verses Krishna now explains the three kinds of renunciation.

18.07–09

नियतस्य तु सन्न्यास: कर्मणो नोपपद्यते |
मोहात्तस्य परित्यागस्तामस: परिकीर्तित: || 7||
दु:खमित्येव यत्कर्म कायक्लेशभयात्यजेत् |
स कृत्वा राजसं त्यागं नैव त्यागफलं लभेत् || 8||
कार्यमित्येव यत्कर्म नियतं क्रियतेऽर्जुन |
सङ्गं त्यक्त्वा फलं चैव स त्याग: सात्त्विको मत: || 9||

18.07: Prescribed duties should never be renounced. If one gives up prescribed duties based on some misconceptions, such renunciation is said to be in the mode of ignorance.

18.08: Anyone who gives up prescribed duties because they are inconvenient or cause physical discomfort, the renunciation is considered to be in the mode of passion. Such renunciation is never spiritually gainful or elevating.

18.09: Arjuna, when actions are performed as a response to duty, and there is no attachment to any reward, it is considered renunciation in the nature of goodness.

Talking further Krishna says abandoning prescribed duties in the name of renunciation is in the mode of ignorance which only demeans the soul. For as long as we are alive, as part of family and society, we have obligations which must be fulfilled. We are not self-sufficient islands that can live in isolation. Performing obligatory duties rounds off our personality, teaches empathy, tolerance, the joy of sharing and the pain of suffering. Prescribed duties purify the mind and elevate the soul to the next higher level.

Having come into this world, we all have obligatory duties, and escaping from them shows our ignorance. On the other hand, fulfilling them helps develop many qualities in an individual, such as responsibility, discipline of the mind and senses, tolerance of pain and hardships, etc.

These duties vary according to one's quality of life. Duties and social expectation also evolve with age, time and station in life. For someone from an under-privileged background, cooking for the family is an essential duty and food is a luxury. Whereas for a family living in luxury there are chefs and house maids to do the work, and the food is taken for granted.

Abandoning one's duty for selfish reasons, or because it is not convenient is despicable. This amounts to escapism, and is not true renunciation. Driven by the mode of passion, bypassing one's responsibilities does not elevate the soul, nor does it help one progress on the spiritual path.

Those who belong to the mode of goodness, understand and fully accept their duties and obligations and perform every one of them dutifully and selflessly. They do not entertain any desire for a reward or recognition for their acts. This is the true spirit of renunciation.

Most people have a superficial understanding of renunciation, and often mistake it for a change of postal address, appearance and clothing. Ochre robes do not make anyone a saint, just as wearing khadi does not make one a Gandhian. This is facetious renunciation, is hollow, and has no meaning.

It is also important to understand the sequencing to be followed when starting out on the path of renunciation. Instead of changing the outwardly appearance, the first step must be to train oneself to be detached in the mind. Once detachment has been achieved in spirit, to follow it in body will not be a challenge. This is also the most superior and genuine kind of renunciation.

18.11

न हि देहभृता शक्यं त्यक्तुं कर्माण्यशेषतः |
यस्तु कर्मफलत्यागी स त्यागीत्यभिधीयते || 11||

18.11: It is impossible for an embodied being to give up all activities entirely. But the one who renounces the fruits of actions is the one who has truly renounced.

As the old saying goes, we are alive until we die. And if we are alive in the true sense of the word we cannot be static. Even if we are prosperous enough to not having to work for a living, the basic functions have to still be performed. As a matter fact even the old and incapacitated must have a routine. Basic acts of eating, sleeping, thinking, walking, talking have to be performed. An ascetic might renounce the world, but he too needs food, shelter and clothing, however minimalistic these might be.

In other words, it is not possible to be entirely free of responsibilities till one is alive. One may withdraw from responsibilities vis-à-vis the rest of the world, but one still has responsibilities towards one's own mind and body. And to keep these healthy and active, certain activities will have to always be performed.

Thus Krishna says that it is impossible for an embodied being to give up all activities entirely. But this is not to say that renunciation too is impossible. The truth is that when one renounces both the desire for material possessions and the reward for any selfless activity, it is considered perfect renunciation.

18.46

यत: प्रवृत्तिर्भूतानां येन सर्वमिदं ततम् |
स्वकर्मणा तमभ्यर्च्य सिद्धिं विन्दति मानव: || 46||

18.46: By performing one's own work, one worships the Supreme Soul who is all-pervading and has created all living entities. A person can easily attain perfection by working.

In the fifteenth chapter we are told that life has been infused into each and every living being for a reason. No one is here by accident, nor is one's existence superfluous. However redundant some individuals may seem to be, the fact is all living entities are part of a grand design. This includes those who are debilitated, incapacitated, or even comatose, because till there is life there is a purpose. It is a different matter that we as ordinary mortals might not be able to see the purpose, with our limited capacity as visionaries.

When ants build an anthill, each member of the swarm has a role to play, and none is small or insignificant. As each ant performs the assigned role it eventually attains perfection. This assigned role is *swadharma*, or one's own duty which is in accordance with our nature, aptitude and position in life. By performing to the best of our capabilities we participate in the divine plan for our own deliverance, as our work itself becomes a form of worship.

In a nutshell, the old adage 'work is worship', is what Krishna is endorsing. The message gains contextual relevance here as Arjuna displays reluctance in performing his duty as a warrior. In this verse, Krishna is reinforcing that by going ahead and slaying the enemy, Arjuna will only be performing his duty, paving the way for his own deliverance.

18.47

श्रेयान्स्वधर्मो विगुण: परधर्मात्स्वनुष्ठितात् ।
स्वभावनियतं कर्म कुर्वन्नाप्रोति किल्बिषम् ॥ 47॥

18.47: It is better to engage in one's own assigned occupation even though one may perform it imperfectly, than to accept someone else's occupation and fulfil it perfectly. Duties prescribed in accordance with one's nature never result in sinful outcomes.

What would be the outcome of a cricket match if the batsman were to start bowling, and the bowler were to start batting? Other than being initially entertaining, it is ultimately bound to be disastrous. It is also possible that by some stroke of luck the batsmen may clean bowl a wicket, or the bowler may swing a hat trick of sixes. But in all likelihood this swapping of roles will not be sustainable through the match.

In other words, abandoning our *swadharma*, i.e., what we are assigned to do or what we are inherently good at doing, is not advisable. An accountant might find it difficult to paint, while a pilot may not turn out to be the best chef. A data entry operator may not be a good dancer, while a dancer may not quite make the cut as a tailor.

In this context dharma can also be interpreted as talent. By and large, all of us are good at performing certain tasks or we are trained to pursue particular professions. But no single individual, no matter how gifted—can do everything equally and efficiently.

Most of us are either born into professional families and tend to follow the same work, or we learn something new and enter a profession of choice. A majority of people eventually find their niche, some sooner than others, and remain engaged with it. This is most fulfilling and will, over a period of time, lead to success, expertise and professional perfection.

18.48

सहजं कर्म कौन्तेय सदोषमपि न त्यजेत् ।
सर्वारम्भा हि दोषेण धूमेनाग्निरिवावृताः ॥ 48॥

18.48: Just as fire is covered with smoke, every endeavour has its negative aspect. O son of Kunti, one should not abandon duties borne of one's nature, even if one sees defects in them.

Every profession requires specific skillsets and there is no line of work that has no downside to it. Not even the most highly-paid or the most glamorous of jobs, every job has its occupational hazards. A singer cannot afford to have a sore throat, and a newspaper boy cannot oversleep a single morning. No matter how diligently a professor may have prepared a lecture, she cannot be late for class because students are not likely to wait indefinitely, and a millionaire cannot enjoy his money without stressing about taxes.

Despite these realities, singers continue to sing and millionaires continue to multiply their money. Doctors routinely wake up at odd hours to attend to emergencies, and sportspersons never compromise on their exercise schedule.

Krishna says that just as fire is covered by smoke that gets into the eyes of those around it, and burning coals are covered by ash that take away the warmth and brilliance of the coal, similarly, every endeavour has its pitfalls. But this should not make us withdraw and withhold our efforts. One must continue to apply oneself wholeheartedly to the assigned duty, and strive for perfection.

Life is a mixed bag and so are all activities. We have to take the good with the bad, and learn to accept disappointments along with success. A batsmen who hit a century in the first innings may be run out on the first ball in the second innings. But this must not stop him from playing the next match.

18.66

सर्वधर्मान्परित्यज्य मामेकं शरणं व्रज |
अहं त्वां सर्वपापेभ्यो मोक्षयिष्यामि मा शुच: || 66||

18.66: Abandon all varieties of beliefs and duties and simply surrender unto me alone. I shall liberate you from all sinful reactions; do not fear.

This is an extremely interesting verse which has multiple messaging. On a cursory reading it may appear that Arjuna is being told to abandon his duties, neglect his faith and surrender to Krishna, to be liberated from the cycle of birth and rebirth. But then all this while, wasn't he being told to perform his duty to the best of his ability! So is this a contradiction in terms? Is Arjuna being asked to follow the path of adharma instead of dharma, and from being faithful now expected to be devoid of any faith?

Not quite. What Krishna is suggesting here is much more sublime and all-encompassing. At this point it is important to remember why this entire discourse started in the first place. On the battlefield Arjuna is perturbed and agitated at the thought of having to decimate his own flesh and blood. He is unable to distinguish between his roles as a warrior, cousin, nephew, student, etc., and is unsure of the action to take. Krishna then counsels a distraught Arjuna reminding him of his duty as a warrior.

Having choices in life is no doubt a luxury, but at times having to make a choice is in itself a challenge. For instance, from a well-stocked library it may be difficult to pick only two books, or while shopping, it may be mind boggling to decide which dress to buy out of the available options. Similarly, at times life throws up several options, and if we are in a vulnerable state of mind, we may feel completely confused and disconcerted. This can result in an inability to make a choice or settling for the wrong option.

In the last seventeen chapters Krishna has spoken of various aspects of duty, sacrifice, charity, penance, etc. Having shared a storehouse of knowledge with Arjuna he has to now bring him back to the reality of the battlefield, and the path of action. The discourse must end and the battle must be fought, as the words spoken by Krishna are a means to the end, i.e., to annihilate evil.

Conscious of Arjuna's delicate state of mind, Krishna continues to hand hold him till he is ready to fight. Thus, when he asks Arjuna to abandon all dharma he is asking him to focus on the task at hand, and temporarily set aside all other roles that he may be playing in life. Krishna now wants Arjuna to closely follow his advice as his strategist and charioteer, and do what he says—surrender unto me. He promises Arjuna that if he does so, Krishna will assure victory for him.

While working in an office, professionals utilise their subject expertise to get work done. Reacting as a parent, friend, cousin or tenant is not going to resolve issues at work. Thus, while at work all other roles have to be put aside and professionalism is expected. Similarly, an engineer trying to make a baby sleep will not find the right techniques in his books of engineering. Some other means will have to be adopted.

Thus, first we need to understand our roles and duties, and then prioritise them, according to the situation. Depending on the need of the hour all energies must be focussed on the requirement.

It is also important to remember that this list of priorities must be adaptable and dynamic, while we need to be discerning and single-minded to achieve the goals.

18.70–71

अध्येष्यते च य इमं धर्म्यं संवादमावयोः |
ज्ञानयज्ञेन तेनाहमिष्टः स्यामिति मे मतिः || 70||
श्रद्धावाननसूयश्च शृणुयादपि यो नरः |
सोऽपि मुक्तः शुभाँल्लोकान्प्राप्नुयात्पुण्यकर्मणाम् || 71||

18.70: It is my opinion that those who study this sacred dialogue of ours will worship me with their intelligence, by offering the sacrifice of knowledge.

18.71: Even those who only listen to this knowledge with faith and without envy, will be liberated from sins and attain the auspicious planets where the pious dwell.

Commenting on all that he has shared with Arjuna, Krishna discloses that all those who read this dialogue will greatly benefit from it. Reading and understanding the *Gita* is an effective way of acquiring Ultimate Knowledge, and a dedicated study is in itself a form of worship of the Lord.

Aware of the layered meanings of what he has spoken, Krishna says that to truly interpret and comprehend the deep meaning of each verse will require high intellect. When those who are blessed with it apply themselves to a sincere study of the text they optimise on their skills of comprehension, and will be duly enlightened.

Reading the *Gita* is the perfect way of utilising one's intellect, and in a manner of speaking offering it to the Lord, who in turn will help us understand his will. Those who study this sacred dialogue, worship God with their intellect.

As not everyone is blessed with an exalted level of intelligence that can help them unravel the multiple meanings hidden in this sacred dialogue, Krishna reassures Arjuna that if ordinary people with honest faith merely listen to it being read out aloud, they will also benefit. There must also be an absence of malice, envy or any other negative thoughts while focussing on the *Gita*. Those who can listen to it earnestly, and with sincerity, will be rewarded for their effort. Over a period of time, they too shall be purified and can hope to eventually reach the portals of celestial planets where the Gods reside.

18.72–73

कच्चिदेतच्छुतं पार्थ त्वयैकाग्रेण चेतसा |
कच्चिदज्ञानसम्मोहः प्रनष्टस्ते धनञ्जय || 72||

अर्जुन उवाच |
नष्टो मोहः स्मृतिर्लब्धा त्वत्प्रसादान्मयाच्युत |
स्थितोऽस्मि गतसन्देहः करिष्ये वचनं तव || 73||

18.72: O Arjuna, have you heard this with an attentive mind? And are your ignorance and delusion now dispelled ?

18.73: Arjuna said: O infallible one, by your grace my illusion has been dispelled, and I am situated in knowledge. I am now free from doubts, and I shall act according to your instructions.

Having reached the end of his discourse, like a good teacher Krishna now asks Arjuna if he had been listening attentively. He is also keen to know if his words have helped resolve Arjuna's uncertainties and dilemmas. And whether his misconceptions about his duty have been duly corrected.

If Krishna is a good teacher then Arjuna is an equally good learner. On hearing his mentor's question, Arjuna addresses him as the invincible and the infallible one, and reassures him that he is now free from doubt and dilemma. He promises to abide by Krishna's instructions and follow his advice in its entirety.

Not only is Arjuna feeling relieved of the torment he was experiencing earlier, he is also thankful to Krishna for the graciousness and patience with which he has thrown light on the lesser-known paths to salvation. Clearly, it is not merely the words and their meaning, but also the tone and manner in which something is shared and taught, that is important for putting the learner at ease, and in helping him absorb the teachings.

At the end of the discourse, Arjuna is once again composed and confident, and ready to take on the enemy, irrespective of how he may be related to them, either by blood or association. His confusion has turned to conviction of duty, and his agitation has been transformed to strong belief. Finally, Arjuna, the greatest archer of all, is ready to pick up his bow and arrow, and with his proverbial concentration and focus, pierce through the evil hearts of the enemies of the Pandavas.

18.74–75

सञ्जय उवाच |

इत्यहं वासुदेवस्य पार्थस्य च महात्मनः |
संवादमिममश्रौषमद्भुतं रोमहर्षणम् || 74||
व्यासप्रसादाच्छुतवानेतद्गुह्यमहं परम् |
योगं योगेश्वरात्कृष्णात्साक्षात्कथयतः स्वयम् || 75||

18.74: Sanjaya said: Thus, have I heard this dialogue between Krishna, the son of Vasudev, and Arjuna, the noble-hearted son of Pritha. So illuminating is the message that my hair is standing on end.

18.75: By the grace of Veda Vyas, I have heard this most confidential discourse about yoga from the master of yoga, Krishna himself.

The eighteenth chapter sees Krishna coming to the end of his discourse. Miles away, Sanjaya's narration of the divine discourse of the *Bhagavad Gita* that he has been hearing, also draws to a close.

Sanjaya refers to Krishna as the son of Vasudev, and Arjuna as the son of Pritha—perhaps a reminder of the basis of their relationship as cousins and childhood friends. What Sanjaya leaves unsaid is how the relationship has since evolved to that of a mentor and protégé, strategist and warrior, spiritual guide and learner, and guru and shishya.

Sanjaya is now feeling enlightened and so invigorated that he says his hair is standing on end, a clear sign of his excitement and exhilaration on listening to this unique conversation. Other than the knowledge shared with Arjuna, what also makes this discourse invaluable is that here the master of yoga, Krishna himself, talks about yoga.

We hear Krishna not only explaining the Absolute Truth to Arjuna but also talking about himself. Repeatedly, Krishna mentions his omnipresence, omnipotence and omniscience. To hear this from the Lord himself is indeed reason to feel specially fortunate. Thus Sanjaya now remarks how amazed and astounded he is on being privy to this divine dialogue.

Sage Ved Vyas the spiritual master of Sanjaya, had blessed him with a unique power of clairvoyance. This special power makes it possible for Sanjaya to see all that was transpiring on the battleground of Kurukshetra, while he himself sat in the palace of Hastinapur. Here, Sanjaya acknowledges that it was by his Guru's grace and generosity that he had the ability to hear this discourse.

While Krishna blesses Arjuna with divine sight to see his *viraatroop*, the magnificent divine form, Sanjaya is able to see it on his own. Interestingly, Sanjaya's exceptional abilities do not end here. Clearly blessed with more than a remarkable second sight he is also able to comprehend the philosophy that lay beneath what he sees and hears. As we know seeing is believing, but for most people seeing is not always understanding. Here not only is Sanjaya able to see from afar, he is intelligent enough to understand the deeper meaning of what he sees and hears.

This is in sharp contrast to Dhritarashtra who is blind not just physically, but is also nowhere close to being a visionary or philosopher. The Absolute Truth shared by Krishna reaches the blind king through Sanjaya but fails to change his short-sighted view of the situation. Sanjaya on the other hand, feels blessed and enlightened when the discourse ends. Sadly, his efforts at making his king see the truth fall on deaf ears and blind eyes.

Sage Ved Vyas, was the author of the *Brahma Sutras*, the *Puranas*, the *Mahabharata*, and several other scriptures, and himself possessed several clairvoyant powers. Thus, he not only heard the conversation between Krishna and Arjuna, but also the one between Sanjaya and Dhritarashtra. Subsequently, he included both conversations in his compilation of the *Bhagavad Gita*.

Epilogue

The Bhagavad Gita—A Way of Life

I. THE LIFE-CHANGING CONVERSATION

a. The Journey

As we find ourselves at the end of the eighteenth chapter of the *Bhagavad Gita*, a quick look at what has emerged from the text would be interesting. It may not be inaccurate to say that the *Gita* is a detailed flowchart illustrating 'how to live an exemplary life'.

But unlike most flowcharts that start at the top of the page and end somewhere below, the arrows of this one seem to go around the back of the page, disappearing for a while from view, and then emerge right back, once again on the top of the page…flowing downwards all over again. And so it goes on…page after page, life after life. Till the arrows reach home.

Ordinary mortals, blessed with 20/20 vision even at the best of times, are unable to see what goes on at the back of the page. It is that journey that the *Gita* tells us about, gently assisting us in joining the dots. Or was it the arrows?

Which box in the flowchart will lead to ultimate joy and satisfaction, and which one spells doom? Which actions of ours will lead to glory and salvation, and which will bring about misery and damnation? The *Gita* is a cautionary tale that clearly lays out the options before us, and spells out the prognosis for each.

b. The Spirit of Inclusivity, Equality and Affirmative Action

Is the *Gita* a product of its times, or are there layers of interpretation and underlying subtexts that ensure its timelessness?

Or like its principle speaker, Krishna, are the messages, revelations and teachings of the *Gita* omnipresent, omnipotent and omniscient, outliving everything and everyone?

While the focus of the teachings is on the self, which includes self-control, self-reliance and overall self-improvement, all along it is well-appreciated that the self operates within a social or political system. Indeed, it is from the lure of these that one must learn to detach oneself.

So what does the *Gita* say about social structures? Without harping too much on society and its norms, it does clearly give a message of impartiality and inclusivity, where the attainment of moksha is concerned.

In a refreshing bunching together of groups—highly unusual in those days of strict social and hierarchical compartmentalisation—Krishna declares that everyone, irrespective of their birth, class, gender and caste, can merge with the divine provided their devotion is genuine and sincere. This also takes into its purview the under-privileged who have been scorned by society on the basis of questionable and discriminatory societal norms.

This is interesting.

One the one hand, we have Krishna prodding Arjuna to perform his duty as a warrior. As Arjuna is born into a kshatriya family, the warrior class it is his duty to fight. The messaging therefore is clear that under no circumstances can anyone shirk from their professional duty, in this case determined by birth, irrespective of the circumstances.

On the other hand, Krishna is also telling Arjuna that anyone and everyone is entitled to moksha, irrespective of birth, social position or gender. Clearly, the pre-requisites for both, duty and success, on earth are quite redundant and superfluous when it comes to qualifying for attainment of moksha. A unique example of man proposes but God disposes!

In verse 9.32, Krishna declares—'All those who take refuge in me, also those of low birth, women, business people and traders, and those who do manual labour, even they will attain the supreme destination.'

Here the use of the word *api*, meaning even or also, continues to be a topic of discussion and debate.

Is it derogatory to say 'even women', or while speaking to a stressed high-born kshatriya, does it simply amount to doing a course correction of his expected patriarchal mindset?

Is saying 'even' or 'also' an indication of inclusion or contempt? Is it an attempt at laying down new ground-breaking rules, or is it an admission of one's own underlying disdain of the group/s in question?

When politicians and guardians of law repeatedly reassure the general public that women are safe in their area, is it a declaration of safety or an admission of lack of it? When we say we respect women and that they are synonymous with goddesses, are we being truthful, condescending or odious? Why do we never have to reaffirm that we respect men and justify the gender of God?

In any case it is unclear if we, in the twenty-first century, living in and feeding into a harshly xenophobic and misogynistic world, have any moral right to pick on the use of a single word thousands of years ago. A self-introspection here might be in order. That being said, this is an issue on which each one will have to take a call herself...or 'even' himself!

If affirmative action continues to be viewed as patronising or platitudinal, then what other routes are there to be taken to arrive at even ground? One wonders.

So semantics apart, while society may play a damaging role, sometimes even wrecking lives, by putting people into boxes on the basis of perceived differences, when it comes to attaining salvation, the doors of paradise are open to all. In short, social and gender discrimination is a man-made phenomenon, and in no way affects success in the ultimate journey that every soul must undertake.

In another instance, in verse 10.34, Krishna underscores sterling qualities in women that have his blessings—'Fame, prosperity, fine speech, memory, intelligence, courage, and forgiveness'. Nowhere does he mention beauty, grace, fair complexion, height, medium of education, servility, compliance etc., qualities that came to be associated with women thousands of years later in so-called 'modern' societies.

This is indeed refreshing. Each and every quality mentioned above in a text compiled during ancient times is clearly gender- agnostic and is as desirable in men as in women, anywhere in the world, and at any point of time.

Thus the *Gita* celebrates the spirit of inclusivity and impartiality. These form the basis of statements made about humankind, while manmade social structures are clearly ignored and disregarded. In what must be viewed as unique affirmative action, the follies of the privileged are set right by a declaration that when it comes to the final journey, the one that really matters, everyone is equal.

A wonderful example of equal opportunities, gender and social equality.

c. Introspect and Identify, Accept and Apply

All discourses, motivational or inspirational, have a common purpose, i.e., to help us do better in life, to make something of our time in this world. This largely depends on what we actually do each day, how we keep ourselves engaged during our productive years.

This naturally brings us to the question of occupation or profession. The significance of choice of profession can be best described by the fact that right from the time we learn to speak our name we also learn to be in a state of readiness to answer the next inevitable question 'what will you be when you grow up?' Some thoughtful grown-ups might be gracious enough to phrase the evergreen query differently, 'what do you want to be when....'.

How will this be decided then? What is the process, if any, behind this decision? Who suggests options and who takes the final call? Family, friends, peer group, current trends? Could it be, or rather, should it be, something else?

Krishna seems to suggest so. Talent, capability, interest and aptitude must be the deciding factors while making a choice of profession.

In verse 4.13 he tells Arjuna, that 'according to people's qualities and activities the four categories of occupations were created by me.'

Krishna then goes on to, in verse 18.47 encourage remaining engaged *'in one's own assigned occupation even though one may perform it imperfectly'* rather than try to do what someone else might be doing well.

Initial challenges and less-than-perfect early outcomes have been factored in here while taking up an occupation of choice. Krishna adds with conviction, that—*'duties prescribed in accordance with one's nature'* can never have undesirable results.

This might appear paradoxical taking into account the four categories of occupations created by Krishna himself. These four categories (which alas remain alive to this day) were presumably created to establish a social structure in early societies. These were

- The Brahmins—men of letters and a spiritual bent of mind tasked with performing religious ceremonies and related duties
- The Kshatriyas—physically strong warriors who owned land, and whose brief was to protect people from the enemy
- The Vaishyas—traders and businessmen who propelled the economy, and created wealth

- The Shudras—who performed menial tasks, and worked with their hands

One assumes, in olden times when job descriptions had fewer variables, that these four options by and large covered the entire population. Any attempt at trying to keep this categorisation relevant today would clearly bring out the obvious limitations of this brief list.

Be that as it may, nowhere in these verses is it laid down that professional choices are to be made on the basis of birth. Individual qualities and activities were meant to be of essence. The intent of bringing out the best in each one based on natural talent and aptitude unfortunately appears to have got distorted along the way, as caste became a matter of birth, and ultimately of right. Right to proprietorship for those from the pampered upper classes, and a lifetime of doom, exclusion and oppression for the others.

This diverted focus is reminiscent of the confusion that often occurs in the understanding, and subsequent implementation of curriculum vs. syllabus in teaching situations. More often than not, the acquired significance of the syllabus throws the well-intended and painstakingly developed curriculum into the dustbin of the classroom. The syllabus of course is duly 'completed' by a zealous teacher.

One can perhaps conclude this ever-debatable issue building on the words of the bard, some are born into a profession, some choose to learn and willfully take up one, while others have a profession thrust upon them.

As always the middle option seems the most sensible. Introspect and identify your talent and aptitude, work on your interests, and choose an appropriate profession to bring out the best in yourself.

II. LESSONS IN LIFE SKILLS

a. What are life skills?

Life skills are essentially those abilities that help promote mental well-being and competence in people, especially the young, as they face the realities of life. It refers to the skills one needs to optimise on opportunities, and handle critical situations that arise from time to time.

The term gained currency in the last few decades, and is now frequently recognised as the key to professional success and personal wellbeing, as also for preparing professionals for striking the right work–life balance.

A description of life skills here may seem like a peculiar digression, but only till the reader gets started making connections with underlying messaging of the *Gita*. A look at the content below will lay the ground for establishing this connect.

*The World Health Organization (WHO) has defined life skills as, 'the abilities for adaptive and positive behaviour that enable individuals to deal effectively with the demands and challenges of everyday life'.

The United Nations Children's Fund (UNICEF) defines life skills as 'a behaviour change or behaviour development approach designed to address a balance of three areas: knowledge, attitude and skills'.

WHO categorises life skills into the following three components:

1. Critical-thinking skills/Decision-making skills, including problem-solving skills and information-gathering skills.
    - The individual must also be skilled at evaluating the consequences of their present actions, and the actions of others.
    - They need to be able to determine alternative solutions, and to analyse the influence of their own values, and the values of those around them.

1. Interpersonal/Communication skills which include verbal and non-verbal communication, active listening, and the ability to express feelings and give feedback.

    - Also in this category, are negotiation/refusal skills and assertiveness skills that directly affect one's ability to manage conflict.
    - Empathy, which is the ability to listen to and understand others' needs, is also a key interpersonal skill.
    - Teamwork and the ability to cooperate include expressing respect for those around us.

1. Coping and self-management skills refers to skills to increase self-control, to prepare to make a difference in the world, and affect change.

    - Self-esteem, self-awareness, self-evaluation skills and the ability to set goals are also part of self-management skills.
    - Anger, grief and anxiety must all be dealt with, and the individual should learn to cope with loss or trauma.
    - Stress and time management are key, as are positive thinking and relaxation techniques.

b. Life Skills and the Gita

At this juncture obvious connections between internationally- recognised life skills laid down in the twenty-first century, and an ancient text compiled thousands of years ago, could well be spelt out point by point.

But this will deprive readers of drawing their own conclusions, arriving at individual interpretations. And as said earlier, the *Gita* strongly advocates exercising of personal choices so this may best be left open to discussion and analysis.

- Suffice it is to say that the *Gita* starts with a breakdown of Arjuna's decision-making skills and lowered self–esteem. As an anxious Arjuna articulates his inner conflict, Krishna deals with the situation with utmost empathy, negotiating his discourse into the realm of problem-solving.

- Seeing Arjuna unable to lead with his current work-life balance issues, Krishna makes ample use of verbal communication. We see Arjuna listening actively as the moment of self-awareness arrives with the help of information gathering skills. Arjuna eventually learns to manage his battered emotions as conflict resolution gradually appears in sight.

- As Krishna offers life-changing solutions, he also details both the short-term and the long-term consequences of present action or inaction, as the case may be. With his self-esteem restored and now in control of himself, Arjuna is finally ready to perform his duty, with newly acquired coping skills standing him in good stead.

- Making good use of self-evaluation skills Arjuna is prepared to deal with loss and trauma, making a difference in the world and being an instrument of change.

- Armed with tips on positive thinking and stress management techniques Arjuna's assertive skills come into play. Providing Krishna with positive feedback, Arjuna is back in action, ready to face the challenges.

Readers are humbly requested to mull over this and add their observations to this rather cursory list of instances of life skills lessons deduced from the *Gita*.

III. THE CONCEPT OF THE AERIAL—A MAGICAL PANACEA

The dictionary defines the word aerial as something 'existing, happening, or operating in the air'. We come across this word in varied contexts. An aerial view of a flood-hit terrain, use of an aerial in a radio or transistor for better reception, or aerial roots of very old trees, specially banyan and peepul where, the trees sprout branches that extend downwards and grow back into the ground, for greater stability and nourishment.

a. The spiritual

The *Gita* makes interesting use of the idea of 'something operating in air'. Krishna talks of the upside-down banyan tree, a fascinating analogy of the soul's journey to the material world. The journey of the soul originates from above and fructifies on earth, where it lives ensconced in a human body. When its time here is up, it returns where it came from, completing the loop.

In the analogy cited
- the roots of the upside-down tree are the beginning of the soul's journey
- the trunk is the journey itself
- the leaves and fruits symbolise the soul's time on earth

The aerial roots that a banyan tree grows with time reach out to the ground of the main roots. This connects the soul back to where it came from. All along its journey to earth, the tree draws sustenance from its source through its basic roots and aerial roots.

Ordinary mortals fail to see this circular journey in its entirety, and being able to view it only partially, most people believe the time on earth to be the be-all and end-all of the soul's odyssey. A classic case of a round trip being mistaken for a linear point-to-point sojourn.

Herein, lies the ineptitude and inadequacy of the human mind, says the *Gita*.

b.   The physical

To the above exalted and enchanting analogy allow me to take the liberty, of sharing a mantra that goes a long way in putting things in perspective in troubled times.

And that is, taking an aerial view of the situation at hand.

- When situations get complicated beyond control, when objectivity loses out to subjectivity, when the micro overtakes the macro, when casual concealing of information results in a lifetime of deception, it is time to take an aerial view of the situation at hand.

- When one is expected to withdraw, recalibrate, take stock, detach, impersonalise; when emotions overcome logic, when there is too much advice coming from too many sources, when it is tough to differentiate between well-wishers and detractors, it is time to take an aerial view of the situation at hand.

To be a fly on the wall in your own room, to be a tall tree and watch the garden from a vantage point, to rise above physical reality and make a quick assessment from above, is a magical way of gaining fresh unbiased perspective.

An aerial view can, not only make calm detachment a possibility, and lend exceptional equanimity to an individual, it is also an extremely humbling experience as one sees oneself as a mere speck in the larger scheme of things. When the reality of this hits home, a lot of 'issues' seem to get resolved.

Two thought-provoking takeaways from the concept of the aerial, one for the immortal soul, and another for the troubled mortal mind.

- The aerial roots growing back from the branches and serving as the connect between the origin and the destination, provide sustenance for the soul in transit.
- The aerial view facilitates a detached visual from above, as a leveller for a troubled mind.

IV. GUIDE TO UNDERSTANDING ONESELF

One can try, but it is near impossible to draw out a 'complete' list of the takeaways from the *Gita*. This is a challenge for three reasons.

One, the *Gita* is so multi-layered and multi-dimensional that even the most immodest might find it beyond their league to confidently declare that they have a grip on it all.

Two, the *Gita* says different things to different people. Or rather, gives the same message differently to different people. Much like a mixed group of tourists on a sight-seeing trip, where the same commentary is being narrated to each one in their own language. It is all about the headphones you opt for!

Three, each reading of the *Gita* makes one sit up and think, 'how did I miss this out last time?' Subject to one's state of mind, passage of time, changed circumstances, altered worldview, personal experiences—setback or success—as the case may be, new meanings and interpretations emerge from this multivalent text.

That being said, an attempt might be made at broadly encapsulating what the *Gita* teaches. Here are some takeaways one is not likely to miss even on a first reading. Keeping in mind the impossibility of prioritising, these have been arranged in alphabetical order.

- Action, devotion and pursuit of knowledge are the recommended paths leading to deliverance.
- Analyse your state of mind and reach out for help when in distress. Choose your guru carefully.
- Be in quest for long-lasting rewards, not short-term gains.
- Be mindful of the fact that the soul's time on earth is temporary and part of a longer journey.
- Be true to your nature, and concentrate on what you can do best. Optimise on your talent and aptitude.
- The body is mortal, the soul is immortal. The soul never dies.
- Contentment is a virtue.
- Control over the five senses is critical.
- Duty is supreme. Emotion, sentiment, attachment must not come in the way.
- Everyone is entitled to moksha—irrespective of social class, caste, gender etc.
- Focus must be on work, not its outcome.
- Food choices reflect temperament, and vice versa.
- Human beings are driven either by goodness, passion or ignorance. With discipline and self-realisation, one of these can override another.
- Identify the enemy within and gain control over it.
- In friendship, as in any relationship, compassion and understanding are of utmost importance.
- Multiplicity of faith, beliefs and practices is natural, and must be accepted.
- No effort, major or minor, successful or unsuccessful ever goes waste. Each and every action is eventually accounted for.
- Qualities of a good teacher are patience and empathy.
- Renunciation of worldly desires is the first step towards detachment.
- Right action is important. Intent behind any action is equally important.

- See the Creator in every work of creation.
- Self-introspection and self-realisation are the key to success.
- Some of the most important battles are those that we fight within ourselves.
- The mind can be one's best friend but also one's worst enemy.
- There are several routes to liberation—none is superior to the other.

There is hardly any aspect of human existence that has not been touched upon in the *Gita*. It is the remarkable understanding of human nature, its strength and weakness, simplicity and complexity, clarity and confusion, depression and exhilaration, that make it possible to delve into each of these and suggest solutions that cater to every individual. The intricate detailing is nothing short of a report compiled by a modern-day psychoanalyst.

a. Human Body and Mind—a linear journey on *terra firma*

While the continued relevance of the *Gita* speaks volumes for what it has to say, it also drives home a reality which is not so encouraging. And that is that human nature and the human mind have remained unchanged over thousands of years. Our battles, both within and without, are still the same. We may have become more mobile, accessible and connected, but that's about it.

Money, power and lust are the drivers behind most pursuits even today. Human beings continue to be emotionally fragile, gullible and vulnerable, as also violent, xenophobic, misogynistic and oppressive. We are a peculiar species that traverses planets in body, but keeps going back to the drawing board when it comes to evolution of the mind.

Sadly, therein lies the secret of the contemporary relevance of the *Gita*—our own lack of evolution.

b. The Journey of the Soul—a cyclical sojourn

Much has been said about the transient nature of our time in this world, and focus on detachment from worldly desires has been intense. It is important to understand this in the spirit in which it is intended. One's life in this world may be finite, but it is not to be confused with the futile.

We have been given this time as an opportunity to improve our prospects and enrich our souls for its journey beyond. Life on earth as a human is a sensitive assignment, where we must deliver to the best of our capability. This is not time to be frittered away because it is temporary. This is time to be optimally utilised because it can facilitate eternal peace for the soul.

It is also of essence to be ever cognisant of the pattern of the soul's journey. It is not concurrent with that of the body in its totality. Unlike the living body, the soul's journey is not linear, i.e., it does not start at point A and end at point B.

The journey of the soul is cyclical, i.e., it starts at A, and merges back in A itself. Perhaps there is no such thing as 'point' A as the soul has no beginning, middle or end. It is eternal and infinite.

Soul—the everlasting, untiring traveller who resides in a life form from time to time, and moves on.

Once this concept of the cyclical is clear and internalised, and when fortified with lessons on life skills we live our lives as advised, we can feel reasonably certain that the message of the *Bhagavad Gita* has impacted us.

Acknowledgments

First and foremost, I wish to record my deepest gratitude to Dr Savitri Singh, a scholar of Sanskrit & Ayurvigyan, who unravelled the *Gita* for me and helped me join the dots…life-changing conversations indeed!

I'm grateful to Sukrita Paul Kumar, author, academic and poet, who has held my hand right through this work's journey—suggesting, advising and supporting with suggestions and ideas.

Many thanks to Shweta Rao, creative graphic and web designer, and to Shveta Uppal, editor par excellence—both long-time friends—for the initial ideation of the concept and for meticulously reading my writing in the very initial stages and encouraging me to go on. Warm thanks to my very dear friends, Neelkamal Puri and Vandana Chandra, for providing succour to my soul by always being there—literally a phone call away.

Over the years, I remain constantly amazed by my sons, Karan and Arjun, for having seamlessly graduated from being young receptive minds to discerning and insightful sounding boards—my new pillars of strength!

Special thanks to Mr Jairam Ramesh, prolific author and eminent public intellectual, for encouraging research and enquiry as a way of life. This work is partially a fruit of one such pursuit.

I'm grateful to Mr Bibek Debroy, distinguished economist, highly regarded writer and translator, for always gently enquiring about my next writing! The prodding finally worked…

I'm grateful to Mr Nirmal Kanti Bhattacharjee of Niyogi Books for making my manuscript see the light of day, and to Niyogi Books for making the book a palpable reality. My gratitude to Mr Arkaprabha Biswas for painstakingly editing the book and the art team for accommodating my suggestions.